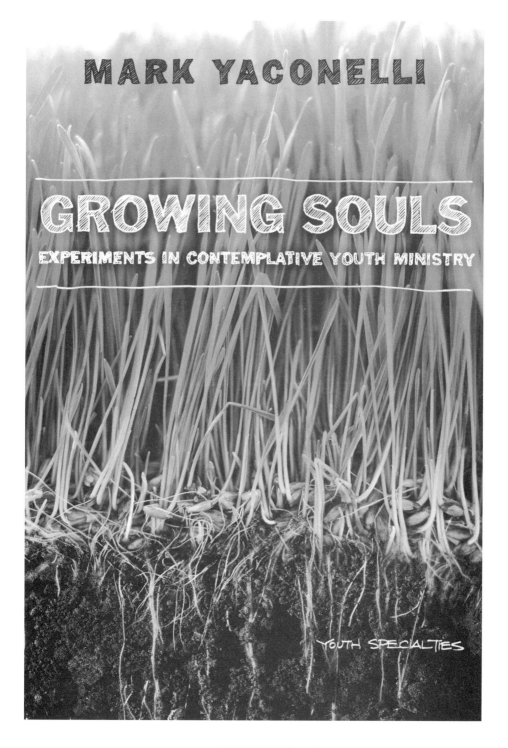

MARK YACONELLI

GROWING SOULS

EXPERIMENTS IN CONTEMPLATIVE YOUTH MINISTRY

YOUTH SPECIALTIES

ZONDERVAN®

ZONDERVAN.com/
AUTHORTRACKER
follow your favorite authors

Youth Specialties
.com

Youth Specialties

Growing Souls: Experiments in Contemplative Youth Ministry
Copyright © 2007 by Mark Yaconelli

Youth Specialties products, 300 South Pierce Street, El Cajon, CA 92020 are published by Zondervan, 5300 Patterson Avenue Southeast, Grand Rapids, MI 49530.

Library of Congress Cataloging-in-Publication Data

Yaconelli, Mark.
  Growing souls : experiments in contemplative youth ministry / by Mark Yaconelli.
    p. cm.
  ISBN-10: 0-310-27328-5 (hardcover)
  ISBN-13: 978-0-310-27328-8 (hardcover)
  1. Church work with teenagers. 2. Church work with youth. 3. Contemplation. I. Title.
  BV4447.Y325 2007
  259'.23--dc22

                                                                    2006032524

Web site addresses listed in this book were current at the time of publication. Please contact Youth Specialties via e-mail (YS@YouthSpecialties.com) to report URLs that are no longer operational and replacement URLs if available.

Portions of this book were previously published in *Contemplative Youth Ministry* by Mark Yaconelli (Copyright © 2005 by Youth Specialties) and are reprinted with permission.

The article "Spirituality and Youth Ministry: What Are We Doing?" by Mark Yaconelli is reprinted with permission from the November-December 2004 issue of *Youthworker Journal.*

*Creative Team: Doug Davidson, Rich Cairnes, Heather Haggerty, Mark Novelli, IMAGO MEDIA
Cover design by Toolbox Studios*

Printed in the United States

07 08 09 10 11 12 • 15 14 13 12 11 10 9 8 7 6 5 4 3

Dedication

To the participants and staff of the Youth Ministry and Spirituality Project 1997-2004.

If Christianity cannot recover its mystical tradition, and teach it,
it should simply fold up and go out of business.

—BEDE GRIFFITHS

Contents

Introduction: Ministry as Unceasing Prayer   9

Section 1: The Project   15

Chapter 1   Listening for Crickets   17

Chapter 2   Becoming a Spiritual Guide: Formation in Contemplative Youth Ministry   38

Chapter 3   The Journey of the Beloved: A Theology of Youth Ministry   60
by Michael Hryniuk

Chapter 4   The Youth Ministry and Spirituality Project Charter: 83
A Summary of the Principles of Contemplative Youth Ministry

Section 2: Images of Prayer and Presence   91

Chapter 5   The Upper Room: Sabbath in Youth Ministry *by Mark Yaconelli*   93

Chapter 6   The Beloved Community: Covenant Community in Youth Ministry   116
by Doug Frank

Chapter 7   Creating Space to Listen for God's Call: Discernment in Youth Ministry   148
by Kathleen A. Cahalan

Chapter 8   Mission Projects, Prayer Retreats, or Bowling Nights: 170
Practicing Authentic Action with Young People *by Frank Rogers Jr.*

Section 3: Testimonies   191

Chapter 9   Learning to Listen to God: A Conversation with YMSP Youth Workers   193

Chapter 10   Seeking a Life of Love: A Conversation with YMSP Youth   232

Conclusion: Just Show Up   248

Appendixes   259

Acknowledgments

This book and the work it represents would not have been possible without the support of the Lilly Endowment Inc., a private family foundation in Indianapolis. I'm particularly grateful for the encouragement of Chris Coble, who serves as program director within the endowment's religion department.

I owe a debt of gratitude to my friend and colleague Michael Hryniuk, who served as the Youth Ministry and Spirituality Project codirector from 2001-2004. Michael was instrumental in the development of this book. In addition to writing the chapter on the theology of the project, Michael cowrote the charter of the project, helped oversee the development of the case studies in section 2, and offered comments on the first draft of the book.

Special thanks to Andy Dreitcer, cofounder and director of the Youth Ministry and Spirituality Project from 1997 through 2000. My appreciation to Don McCullough, Ron White, and Scott Schaefer, who worked to establish the project at San Francisco Theological Seminary.

Thanks to my friend Deborah Arca Mooney, who served as the project's program manager and was instrumental in compiling and fact-checking the interviews and transcripts used in chapters 9 and 10.

The seeds of this book were planted within a small group of scholars who met regularly from 2001 to 2004 for prayer, sharing, and discernment on behalf of the Youth Ministry and Spirituality Project. It was in response to the conversation with project scholars Carol Lakey-Hess, Luther Smith, Frank Rogers, Kathleen Cahalan, and Doug Frank that the section 2 case studies and the chapter 9 interviews came into being.

Gratitude to my oldest friend, Kirk Wulf, for his careful comments and suggestions on the first version of this book.

Thanks to Jay Howver, Roni Meek, David Welch, Holly Sharp, and the folks at Youth Specialties, as well as to Jamie Hinojosa and John Topliff at Zondervan for their care and support in making this book a reality.

I'm grateful to word surgeon Doug Davidson for his compassionate and thoughtful editing. This book is a more cohesive work because of his efforts.

Thanks to the wise and patient spiritual directors, advisors, and staff who served within the Youth Ministry and Spirituality Project. I'm forever grateful to the youth, youth directors, pastors, parents, and congregations who gave their time and energy to participate in the Youth Ministry and Spirituality Project. This book is another of the fruits from our time together. It is to these spiritual explorers that I dedicate this book.

My deepest love and gratitude to my wife, Jill, for the generous attention she has given to this book, to the Youth Ministry and Spirituality Project, and most importantly, to me. The book and my life are more grounded because of her care.

Finally, my love to Noah, Joseph, and Grace, because you are beautiful and amazing and you're my kids.

Introduction: Ministry as Unceasing Prayer

In 1994, I left my job as a youth minister and enrolled in seminary, hungering to learn a way of ministry grounded in continual attentiveness to God. I wanted to find a way of ministering that addressed the human soul. Like the seeker in the 19th-century spiritual classic, *The Way of the Pilgrim*, I was searching for a life and ministry grounded in unceasing prayer, rather than the unceasing activity that so often characterizes modern approaches to youth ministry. I knew if I were going to continue to serve the church, I needed to cultivate a way of ministry in which communion with God could be the central desire and practice.

Sadly, most seminaries are not prepared to help students develop a prayer life. I had to sort through many professors, academic classes, pastoral counselors, and theological texts. But eventually I encountered wise and prayerful guides who knew how to address my longing for communion with God. Through my own study and research I began to design a way of practicing youth ministry that placed contemplative prayer and awareness at the foundation of the ministry.

I soon discovered I wasn't alone in my desire to find a more transforming way to practice ministry. As I shared my studies at youth ministry conferences and gatherings, I found there were many other youth workers who were similarly seeking to deepen their ministry. At conferences in Chicago, San Francisco, Portland, and Philadelphia, I met hundreds of other youth workers who expressed a growing restlessness with prevailing models of ministry that relied on fun and easy-access lessons, but neglected the deeper yearnings of the human soul. Through e-mails, phone calls, discussion groups, and late-night conversations I swapped ideas with many of these youth workers as together we sought to discern a more prayerful, soulful way to open kids to the heart of God. Over time many of us began to feel that the problem with youth ministry was a problem of depth. Youth ministry had become shrill and clanging, often mimicking the bells and whistles of the consumer culture. We needed to drop down an octave. We needed to stop piggybacking on the cultural images and trends that shaped adolescence and begin speaking to the deeper longings of the adolescent soul. The question was, "How?"

In 1996, I partnered with Andy Dreitcer, the founding director of the spiritual direction certification programs at San Francisco Theological Seminary, to create the Youth Ministry and Spirituality Project. (Andy served as the project's codirector through 2000; Michael Hryniuk followed Andy and served as codirector from 2001 to 2004). The initial hope of the project was to address the spiritual yearning of youth and youth ministers. Aware of the high burnout within the field of youth ministry, we initially provided retreats and events where youth directors would be encouraged to practice "unceasing" awareness of God within their lives and ministries.[1] We wanted to offer nourishment for the souls of youth workers, trusting they in turn would be better able to address the longings of the adolescent soul. We began by holding retreats for youth workers, providing spiritual directors at youth ministry conferences, and writing articles describing the need for ministry models that were more intentional in seeking the presence of God.[2] We trusted that if youth leaders could make prayer the central activity within their ministries they would find greater solace and guidance. We hoped that if more youth workers were taught to "practice the presence of God," then youth ministry, with all its chaos and activity, might become more transparent to God's love.

Beginning in 1997, the Youth Ministry and Spirituality Project received a series of grants from the Lilly Endowment to test and develop what we called a "contemplative approach" to youth ministry. With funds from the endowment, we gathered together a diverse group of churches that embodied a wide variety of youth ministry programs. We brought pastors, youth leaders, youth, and adult volunteers from

[2] "Youth Ministry as a Spiritual Discipline." *Youthworker Journal*, 8:3, 1997, 52-55; "Youth Ministry: A Contemplative Approach." *The Christian Century*, April 1999, 450-454; "Ancient-Future Youth Ministry." *Group Magazine*, July 1999, 32-39.

[1] This included weeklong *Sabbath* retreats sponsored by Youth Specialties and Upper Room Publishing as well as the spiritual care track developed within the Youth Specialties National Youth Workers Conventions.

each of these churches to San Francisco Theological Seminary for a series of formation retreats in this newly formed, contemplative approach to youth ministry.

There is a strange mix of expectations when a grant-funded project, set within an academic institution, sets out to explore the integration of contemplative prayer and youth ministry. There are budgets to create, reports to file, evaluations to undertake, results to be measured, scholarly advisors to be consulted, and growing expectations that something is being discovered and progress is being made. But how do you measure prayer? How do you track the effectiveness of silence and contemplation? And to further complicate matters, how do you measure the effect of contemplative prayer within the stretching and changing lives of young people? Trappist monk and author Thomas Merton captured the problem we faced in trying to measure our effectiveness: "Contemplation cannot be taught. It cannot even be clearly explained. It can only be hinted at, suggested, pointed to, symbolized."[3]

Unfortunately, we weren't as wise as Thomas Merton. Too often we tried to explain, teach, measure, and systematize. And if I'm completely honest, a part of me hoped this book would provide statistics and graphs and other "hard data" that proved, inarguably, that prayer and the desire for God are the foundations of Christian life and effective ministry with youth. But that's not how Christianity works. When the project research ended in 2004, all we had was a collection of experiences, stories, and testimonies. And like the Bible, these testimonies and stories come in a variety of voices and written forms.

Growing Souls: Experiments in Contemplative Youth Ministry is an attempt to say to all who long to address the adolescent soul, "You're not alone." This text brings together scholars, youth directors, pastors, and youth who speak about their struggle in exploring contemplative prayer and presence in youth ministry. It is a collection

---

[3] Thomas Merton, *New Seeds of Contemplation* (New Directions Books, 1972), 6.

of stories, experiences, conversations, and insights from a group of Christians seeking to reform youth ministry and speak to the deeper cry of the adolescent soul. It is a chronicle of our experiences in working to move Christian spirituality out of the retreat center and into the youth room. All the ideas and visions within this book are grounded in experience: real churches with real youth ministers struggling to integrate prayer and presence with real kids.

My hope is that this book will encourage churches and youth workers to let go of approaches to youth ministry that seek simply to keep young people distracted and entertained. Most youth workers want to address the deeper, spiritual longings of young people. Most youth workers know their real calling isn't to keep kids amused. Most youth workers long to work beside Jesus in addressing the great need within the human heart for love and truth and meaning. We desire basic, more authentic forms of adolescent discipleship. Yet we know that to address young people at this level is to create discomfort and resistance. Our efforts to minister to the souls of kids can result in anxious church boards, bewildered parents, and sometimes even restless youth. For most of us in North America, the soul is a dark and mysterious country. Even within churches the soul is a well-kept secret, hidden within the shadows of our lives. As ministers we find ourselves well trained to address the intellectual, emotional, and physical desires of human beings, but tragically unprepared to understand and address the needs and desires of the human soul.

The soul prospers in silence and prayer and ritual. The soul seeks to befriend suffering and pain. The soul is bored by material goods, security, results, and accomplishments. The soul prefers poverty, emptiness, and simplicity. The soul trusts life in its rawest form. The soul seeks to realize our interconnectedness with others. The soul enjoys great risks in the service of love and eagerly goads us to abandon our hopes and plans to God. Most importantly, the soul trusts Jesus.

It's no wonder youth ministry avoids the soul. Could anything be more counter to North American life than silence, prayer, surrender, poverty, suffering, trust, and befriending strangers? And yet, the longing to minister to the souls of youth persists. Contemplative prayer and presence was the way I became more sensitive to and aware of the needs of the adolescent soul, as well as more aware of and responsive to the movement of the Holy Spirit. It was in my willingness to wait and trust that I became aware of God's longing to grow peace within the human heart.

This book presents the testimony of many of us who have persisted in seeking to address the deeper longings of youth and youth ministers through a contemplative approach to ministry. But my hope isn't to convince you to practice "contemplative youth ministry." My deepest hope is that by reading this book you might be encouraged and inspired to create ministries with youth that address the great spiritual hunger that exists within our culture. My hope is that you will discover that addressing the spiritual longings of kids is possible, and that there are others who are engaged in this work.

In *Contemplative Youth Ministry: Practicing the Presence of Jesus* (Zondervan 2006), I tried to present my own understanding and experience of an approach to youth ministry that addresses the spiritual longings of youth and youth ministers. Much of that book was developed through my teaching and work with the Youth Ministry and Spirituality Project. *Growing Souls* is an attempt to deepen and expand the conversation regarding contemplative youth ministry by presenting the work of the project and giving voice to the scholars, youth workers, pastors, and youth who shared in its work.

This book is divided into three sections. Section 1 outlines the rationale, design, and theology of the Youth Ministry and Spirituality Project. I wanted to make transparent the way in which the project sought to reorient churches from anxious, results-oriented youth programs to ministries that were more patient and transparent to the life of God. Section 2 presents the stories of four different youth ministries, focusing on how each of them embodied a particular principle of contemplative youth ministry. These chapters present the struggles of ordinary congregations as they sought to practice a more contemplative approach to youth ministry. The third section contains interviews with youth directors and youth from the churches that participated in the project. These interviews allow the people involved in the program to speak directly about their own experiences in engaging contemplative youth ministry. These interviews are followed by my own summary of the struggles and difficulties of a contemplative approach to youth ministry. The book also includes seven appendixes that collect many of the practices and processes used within the Youth Ministry and Spirituality Project.

In many ways, through many voices, this book seeks to hint at, suggest, and point to a new awareness in life and ministry—an awareness that we are not alone. An awareness, as Merton further claims, that "somewhere near the centre of what you are...at the very root of your existence, you are in constant and immediate and inescapable contact with the infinite power of God."[4] In this awareness is comfort and guidance for the minister's soul. In this awareness is empowerment to respond to the spiritual longings and suffering of young people. In this awareness is the joy and hope of all seekers who trust that our longing for God is all that is needed.

---

[4] As quoted in Dorothy Soelle, *The Silent Cry* (Augsburg Fortress, 2001).

section one

THE PROJECT

The Youth Ministry and Spirituality Project was an experimental venture created to explore the integration of contemplative prayer and awareness within youth ministry. Its mission was to *foster Christian communities that are attentive to God's presence, discerning of the Spirit, and that accompany young people on the way of Jesus.* This first section presents the basic rationale, design, theology, and charter of the project.

Chapter 1 asserts that listening to God is central to the practice of youth ministry and reveals some of the breakthroughs that occurred within youth ministries that began to explore contemplative awareness within ministry. Chapter 2 outlines the way in which the project sought to transform youth leaders and churches from conventional youth ministry models to ministries that intentionally sought a regular attentiveness to the presence of God. Chapter 3, written by Michael Hryniuk, lays out the basic theological principles behind contemplative prayer and ministry. This "theology of the beloved" became the grounding theology of the project. Finally, chapter 4 presents the YMSP "charter," a summary of the principles we discovered within churches that practiced contemplative youth ministry.

Listening for Crickets

"The central pastoral office is to make people aware."
—WALTER BRUEGGEMANN

A friend of mine attended a Christian pastors' conference in downtown Atlanta, Georgia. The participants, gathered from across North America, included one Native American pastor who was on his first trip to a major metropolitan city. During a lunch break the Native American pastor took a walk outside with one of his colleagues. As they stretched their legs along the busy sidewalk, the pastor suddenly stopped, turned to his companion and said, "Do you hear that?" The friend paused and considered the bustling noise of the city. "Hear what?" he replied.

Planted along the downtown sidewalk was a small row of trees. At the base of each tree was a circle of flowers. The pastor walked over to one of the trees, knelt down, reached beneath one of the floral clusters, then stood and opened his hand, revealing a small black bug. "It's a cricket."

Dumbfounded, his friend replied, "How could you possibly hear that?" The Native American pastor reached into his pants pocket, took out a handful of coins, and threw them into the air. As the coins hit the cement, people from all directions stopped and looked down. The pastor turned to his companion and said, "It depends on what you're listening for."

In the New Testament Jesus identifies his followers not as those who hold orthodox beliefs or embody moral purity. Jesus says his followers are those who have "ears to hear" (Mark 4:23)—those who walk with heads tilted, straining to hear the voice of the "good shepherd" (John 10:14). Jesus claims that those who know how to listen will one day hear the voice of the Beloved and will overcome death (John 5:25).

Sadly, the Christian church is losing its capacity to listen. We forget what it means to sit still, to be silent, and to wait until we hear the voice of the One who calls us by name. We're losing our capacity to be surprised and amazed by what we hear. We've become a church more responsive to the predictable clinking sounds of the marketplace than the surprisingly still, small voice of God. Instead of heeding the call to "be still before the Lord, and wait patiently," we "fret" and worry and "plot" (Psalm 37). Driven by our own fearful voices we run ahead of grace, frantically seeking a plan, a strategy, a formula for securing a Christian life. A culture that no longer listens to God becomes increasingly noisy. Every idea must be exploited, every insight publicized, every sermon downloaded, every passing thought blogged and posted. We live in a time when everyone is talking at once—a time when the truth isn't hidden, but drowned in a sea of irrelevance.

Christianity is relationship; and any counselor worth her salt will tell you that every healthy relationship is based in listening. To love someone, to befriend someone, to really know someone, you have to be willing to listen. You have to continually set aside your own agendas, perceptions, and evaluations, and listen in order to avoid misjudging or misunderstanding the other. Listening is difficult. Perhaps that's why most of us continually seek to label, predict, and control our relationships; because once a relationship becomes predictable, you no longer have to listen. When you no longer listen you can sit back, shut down, and shift into automatic pilot.

But when we stop listening, something is truly lost. When we stop listening, the relationship diminishes—until it becomes a chore we attend to rather than a person we are connected to. One of the signs that we've stopped listening within the church is that we're rarely startled, surprised, challenged, or opened to new ways of seeing the world.

It would be so much easier if God invited us to accomplish a mission statement rather than enter into a relationship. It's deeply unsettling to discover a God who seeks a mutual friendship rather than our subservient service (John 15:15). The first disciples knew that it was not always easy to be in relationship with Jesus. When we understand Christianity as relationship, our lives mirror those of the disciples; we misunderstand, we doubt, we feel inadequate, we aren't certain where things are headed, we often feel confused and unsure about the future. If this was the experience of those closest to Jesus, why should we assume our experience of the Christian life would be any less ambiguous? In response to the disciples' misinterpretations and doubts, Jesus continually told them to "listen." Again and again Jesus told his friends and followers to turn their attention away from their own fears and plans in order to focus on what he was saying and doing—even when his parables were difficult to decipher, even when his teachings seemed impossible, even when his actions seemed to ruin the hopes and dreams of his followers.

THE SOUND OF SUCCESS

What does it mean to do youth ministry within a Christian culture in which listening to God is rarely practiced? What does it mean when churches, parents, and youth ministers instead begin to listen to the anxious, predictable voice of society? When we listen and respond to the call of the culture, we want ministries that are practical, rational, efficient, productive, measurable, and hip. We want ministries that strive toward higher and higher levels of "excellence." We want ministries, in a word, that are "successful."

What makes a successful youth ministry? In our consumer culture success means having youth pastors who can get a high return on their churches' investment. It means youth ministers with a plan and proven results. It means ministers who have their finger on the pulse of the culture, know where the trends are headed, and can develop marketing "strategies" to engage the "youth population." It means competence. Below is an ad that was recently posted on the job openings page of a youth ministry Web site:

> We are looking for a highly driven, self-motivated, capital "L" leader to oversee our 9-12th grade program and supervise our 6-8th grade program. This person should have a proven track record of growing student ministry programs (numerically & spiritually), recruiting leaders, and supervising staff. If your philosophy of ministry is to start with a small core group of students and grow into a large crowd... DO NOT APPLY! We are looking for someone who can draw a crowd. First Church [name withheld] is a fast-paced environment that aims to keep stride with the culture. We are highly purpose-driven and committed to providing a top rated student ministries program for the students of our area. Salary will reflect experience and education.

On first read, the ad seems practical and in line with values we prize as industrious Americans: hard work, cultural relevancy, efficiency, and a drive to succeed. Who wouldn't want a capital "L" leader? Doesn't every church seek a youth director who can grow a student ministry both numerically and spiritually? Isn't it important for a youth pastor to "draw a crowd" if a church is to evangelize its youth? Don't all churches that seek to be productive embody a "fast-paced environment?" If a youth ministry is going to be effective, shouldn't it aspire to "keep stride with the culture"?

And yet, if we sit back and reflect further on what this ad communicates, we might have second thoughts: What kind of youth come out of a "highly driven" youth ministry? What kind of youth leader can serve in such a ministry? Who is the God that seeks a "fast-paced environment," capital "L" leaders, and people who "keep stride" with the culture? Within such a ministry, would it even be possible for someone to have ears ready to be surprised by crickets?

The problem with the leadership that this church is seeking, the big glitch in the fast-paced environment that this church celebrates, is that it is in direct contrast to the spirit of Jesus. Somewhere, somehow this church stopped listening to the voice of the One who says, "Come to me, all you that are weary and are carrying heavy burdens, and I will give you rest." Sadly there seems no interest in a leadership that might be "gentle and humble in heart" nor a Jesus whose "yoke is easy" and whose "burden is light" (Matthew 11:28-30). Somehow I don't imagine that Jesus would be considered a "capital 'L' leader." Not when he spends much of his time alone in prayer. Not when he seems more interested in retreating than in drawing crowds. Not when he often asks people who recognize him or experience healing to tell no one. Not when he seems satisfied to leave his teaching and way of life to a small group of followers who frequently misunderstand, abandon, and even betray him.

"Success is not a name for God," Martin Buber once said. And yet as Christians, we long for our churches and youth ministries to be successful. We seek tangible, verifiable results. We wait for the clinking of coins. We search for books, practices, techniques, and strategies that will bring us success. It's easy to point at the ad above and notice the harried, anxious driven-ness to succeed. And yet we know of what they speak. We, too, listen to the voices that sort the losers from the winners. We, too, listen to the voices (within and around us) that trust numbers and concrete results to determine our worth. We, too, lack the courage it takes to wait in patience and trust—uncertain if our ministries will bear long-lasting fruits. We, too, find ourselves too harried to bend down and listen to the ordinary miracle of crickets within an increasingly pressured and jaded culture. We, too, find it difficult and frustrating to attend to a relationship rather than a ministry program. We, too, are compelled to attend to a program instead of the often silent and unseen God who waits to bloom within our relationships with young people.

What does it take to be a listener of God? How do we become people who listen for the still, small voice of peace within the rush of our own lives? What would it mean if our primary practice as Christian ministers was to stop, be still, and listen?

A CONTEMPLATIVE CORRECTIVE

Historically, it is the mystical, contemplative, praying dimension of the Christian tradition that has most concerned itself with listening and attending to the presence of God. It is this arena of Christian life that we call "spirituality" that invites us to seek a deepening awareness of our relationship with God. Spirituality is about listening; about attending to our experience of God. Christian spirituality, in particular, emphasizes the nearness of God, our relatedness to Christ, and the inspiration (in-spiriting) of the Holy Spirit empowering us for acts of mercy, justice, and peace in the world. Spirituality refers to the way we receive and respond to God within our ministries and personal lives. It informs how we eat, play, socialize, consume, and spend our time.

The Youth Ministry and Spirituality Project was formed in response to a youth ministry culture that was becoming increasingly frantic, consumerist, dull, formulaic, and spiritually stunted. The project was an attempt to explore an approach to ministry that would emphasize the heart of Christian discipleship—loving attentiveness to God and neighbor. It was an attempt to combine the wisdom and prayer life of monks and mystics with the creativity and passion of teenagers and youth pastors.

There are many beautiful ways to share the Christian faith with young people—camps and backpack trips that help them experience God in nature; discussion groups that let them discover Christ's witness within the burning issues of the day; game nights that contain a Sabbath sense of play, leisure, and friendship; outings where youth can encounter the diversity of the human family; mission trips that invite youth to join Jesus in responding to the deep brokenness and suffering in the world. The Youth Ministry and Spirituality Project did not seek to undermine the many good practices that exist already within youth ministry. Rather, we hoped that by engaging youth ministry leaders and youth in prayer and discernment, the activities and relationships within the ministry might become more grounded in the life and witness of Jesus. The project was an attempt to hold up the last line of the Gospel of Matthew, in which Jesus says, "Remember, I am with you always." That might serve as a definition of contemplative ministry: *Remembering that God is with us.* Remembering to stop and allow God to love, empower, and guide us before we create programs, before we teach, before we befriend, before we minister.

In the Youth Ministry and Spirituality Project we asked people to stop and pray, and to notice the life of God as the first step in their ministries. We asked them to stop and listen to God before designing programs. We asked them to stop and pray and listen when working with young people. We invited them to gather parents and elders and volunteers and together sit in silence, and listen to Scripture, and trust they would see what God desired of them. We asked youth ministers, youth, and pastors to stop and listen to the whispers too often lost beneath the driven voice of success, the clanking of coins, and the frightened voice of the ego—never satisfied, endlessly insecure, always grasping for validation. We asked churches to listen until they could hear the wonder and miracle of crickets. Until they could hear the Holy Spirit whose song is planted within the heart of each young person. Until they could recognize the voice of the Good Shepherd who journeys before, behind, and alongside our ministries.

We wanted to intentionally draw on the mystical aspect of the Christian life so that wonder, surprise, and spiritual experience would become central to ministry. We wanted to resurrect the forgotten contemplative tradition within the Christian faith, a tradition that emphasizes intimacy with God and encourages communion with God (in prayer as well as activity) as the primary desire within the Christian faith. Our experiment was to see if youth ministry programs might be renewed by integrating contemplative prayer and awareness as the focus of the ministry.

The project started with a handful of questions: Was there a way to help youth pastors deepen their awareness of God within the busyness of youth ministry? Could silence, solitude, and contemplative prayer be integrated into youth curricula? Was it possible to make listening, in prayer and relationships, the central practice of a youth ministry? Could we move beyond youth programs that offered only cognitive information and moral instruction and actually invite youth to attend to their experiences of God? What kind of ministry practices or dispositions would help ministers and youth deepen their awareness of God? What ministry systems and structures would need to be discarded?

Our hope in beginning the project was that contemplative prayer might free youth ministry of illusions: the illusion that we as ministers were the saviors of adolescents; the illusion that if our youth programs weren't full of excitement, then our kids wouldn't know Jesus; the illusion that a ministry's success could be measured. Our hope was that silent, listening forms of prayer might slow us down so we could hear the suffering of youth and their families. Our hope was that prayer and silence might open us to God's imagination and vitality so that our youth programs might find new and refreshing ways of disclosing God's dream for the world. Our hope was that contemplative prayer might help us experience God's love and companionship—in a way that might encourage us to let go of our own agendas and instead allow God's presence to guide and empower us.

INITIAL DISCOVERIES

The first venture of the Youth Ministry and Spirituality Project was a weeklong retreat for youth pastors, titled "Sabbath: A Youth Ministers Retreat." Sixteen youth workers showed up for the first event. The retreat was simple. We opened and closed each day with prayer services that offered Scripture, simple chants, and silence. We kept silence during the morning hours. We taught people classical forms of contemplative prayer like *lectio divina* and the Ignatian awareness examen and gave them an hour each day to discuss their spiritual lives with trained spiritual directors. There were no workshops on leading games with kids, no strategy sessions on peer ministry, no roundtable discussions on working with parents.

That first retreat was strange and new for all of us. I remember two veteran youth workers who couldn't stop giggling during the first silent prayer service. People had questions about whether silence or contemplative forms of prayer could be considered "Christian."[5] Sometimes the silence was painful, revealing repressed doubts, an-

---

[5] Sometimes silent forms of prayer feel alien to traditional understandings of Christian practice. I'm often asked, "Isn't silence Buddhist? Or New Age?" Silence is neutral. Silence is simply a human capacity and experience. Jesus was often alone and silent. The Psalms tell us to "be still and know." What matters is how silence is engaged. What is your intention in the silence? Is it silence that is directed toward listening and communing with God? Where is your attention in the silence? Is it toward the One revealed in Jesus? What matters, as Jesus continually pointed out, is the direction of our hearts. If our hearts are not directed toward God, then any Christian practice (silent or noisy) can be destructive.

ger, or tears. Sometimes the prayer was transformational and healing, disclosing a new awareness of God and self. At the end of the week all of us felt we'd been changed in some way—there was a sense that we had come back to the center of who we hoped to be as ministers and followers of Jesus. We returned to our youth ministry programs revived, more patient, more trusting, and more aware of the real work God was calling us to undertake with young people.

With funding from the Lilly Endowment we began to share our discoveries within a diverse mix of 16 congregations across North America, from Colchester, Connecticut, to Honolulu, Hawaii. From 1997-2000 we sought to cultivate within these congregations an understanding and practice of contemplative prayer and presence. We produced five separate weeks of formation for pastors, youth leaders (professional and volunteer), church members, and student leaders. Later, we refined and repeated the whole process with another 13 teaching congregations from 2001-2004.

We also spent time visiting each of the churches participating in the project. We interviewed the youth. We read the journals of youth ministers. We spoke with church members, parents, and pastors. We sat in youth rooms and watched youth directors from inner-city, rural, Hispanic, Anglo, and African American congregations engage young people in contemplative prayer. Our findings confirmed our own experience and suspicions. We found church members, pastors, and youth longing to make contact with the presence of God. We discovered youth workers eager to move away from ministry practices that often left them feeling isolated and spiritually depleted. We listened as young people told us again and again that adults who embodied a spiritual vitality and passion for life were the most transforming aspect of their youth ministry programs. And we listened as youth from central Los Angeles to central Indiana told us of their desire to encounter God directly and learn how to deepen their experience of God within their own lives.

Below is an expanded summary and description of our initial discoveries:

1. Current approaches to youth ministry neglect the spiritual life of youth ministers, adult volunteers, and youth.

As we began to provide space and tools for churches and youth ministers to slow down and attend to their experience of ministry, people began to identify ways in which their current practices of youth ministry were isolating, burdensome, and destructive to their own spiritual health. Most youth ministers, both volunteer and professional, felt a great desire to nourish the souls of the young people in their community, yet felt completely isolated in their attempts to address the spiritual needs of youth.

Many leaders reported that once they'd assumed responsibility for their congregation's youth ministry program (as either paid or volunteer ministers), they felt abandoned by the rest of the church. Finding other volunteers to participate in the youth ministry was difficult and discouraging. Youth workers complained of an unstated expectation to work long hours, including weekends and evenings, often with little or no compensation or recognition. Youth workers within the project felt they had little or no status among their staff and were marginalized within the congregation. They were continually sent the mixed message that youth ministry was important, but then received little support in terms of volunteers, resources, or acknowledgment of youth within congregational activities. This isolation felt disheartening and alienating to their own spiritual growth.

Current models of youth ministry also neglect the spiritual life of young people. Within the project we often noticed that youth were addressed as activity-consumers and sent to the margins of a congregation's worship life. Youth ministry practices focused mostly on fun activities and moral guidance. Youth were rarely addressed as spiritual pilgrims, seeking healing and transformation. They were given few, if any, opportunities to explore their experience of and longing for God.

As we helped churches develop committed communities of adults who then engaged in contemplative practices within the context of youth ministry, youth ministers and other adult volunteers began to express how lonely and dry their previous youth ministry structures had left them. Youth ministers and congregations involved in the project claimed that contemplative practices of prayer and listening helped them be more discerning of God's activity within their ministries and encouraged them to identify and abandon more anxious and destructive systems of ministry. These adults, in turn, reported that they felt better equipped to meet the spiritual needs of youth and help young people seek out and explore their own relationships with God. As one veteran youth worker from Bayport, Minnesota, expressed, "When you spend time listening to God, you soon discover that what God is really asking of you isn't as hard as you thought. As we began to pray and discern our programs, it was clear that we were trying to do too much. God wanted us to just be a source of love, encouragement, teaching, and guidance to the youth, not just these radical, wild, fun activity directors."

2. People long to experience God within their own lives.

Although the participants in the Youth Ministry and Spirituality Project were from diverse backgrounds, environments, and denominations, they were quite similar in their desire to encounter the God of Jesus Christ. Lay and clergy alike complained of being spiritually dry, burned-out, and overworked. Many had a sense that they were failing in their spiritual life and ministry vocations. We discovered most of the participants had never before been formed in or encountered the contemplative dimension of the Christian faith.

For most youth ministers the Christian life had been reduced to a series of activities. Youth workers tended to measure their worth based on how well they accomplished these activities. My colleague Michael Hryniuk calls this the "unholy trinity of the false self": *I am what I do; I am how much I do; I am how well I do it.* This focus on activity, productivity, and efficiency was strongly embedded within church cultures and youth ministries. Early in the project training events, the majority of participants confessed that they were tired, discouraged, and spiritually hungry.

As we began to invite people to slow down and spend periods of time in silence, biblical meditation, and prayerful reflection, we started to see a new sense of awakening among the youth workers. This transformation was primarily expressed as a new perception or awareness of God in combination with a new (often referred to as "healed") sense of self-identity. Participants expressed a growing empowerment in their vocations as Christian ministers and leaders throughout their involvement in the project. This sense of empowerment came about as participants, through regular contemplative practice, felt free to let go of their anxious self-reliance and overconcern with outside approval, and became increasingly trusting of the power of the Holy Spirit working within and among them.

Youth leaders continually described the project as a place where they were given "permission" to be spiritual leaders instead of program administrators or childcare providers. This invitation to claim themselves as spiritual leaders was often deeply satisfying because of its congruence with their initial calling to enter the ministry—a calling that often felt ignored by the expectations of their congregational or organizational systems.

Most participants also expressed renewal in their marriages, friendships, parent-child relationships, creative endeavors, and overall psychological well-being. They began to use conversion-like language to talk about developments in their faith, images of God, identities, and vocation. As one pastor stated, "Through discovering listening forms of prayer I now see myself and my ministry with new eyes." It was common for evaluations from participants to include comments such as, "I'm not the same person I was before I started this project." During on-site visits, we often heard spouses, parents, workmates, and friends of project participants comment on the transformation they had witnessed.

It was surprising how soon these youth ministers and lay people began to express a desire to share their experiences, insights, language, and training from the project throughout their churches and even within their surrounding communities. In our evaluations we discovered that people had introduced contemplative practices to leadership groups, mission committees, secular work groups, and had used them regularly within their own families. They wrote prayer exercises on bookmarks, in newsletters, and on narthex bulletin boards. They began to add prayer spaces in their living rooms, engage in daily biblical meditations, and keep journals. These unexpected outcomes alerted us to the pervasive hunger that exists within North American churches and culture for authentic spiritual experience.

3. Communities of transformed adults, living lives of prayer and service, attract and transform the lives of young people.

Our bias in the project was that a youth ministry's greatest tool for shaping the lives of young people is adults who have a living faith. Youth, seeking to enter adulthood, are looking for guides or mentors who can show them adult forms of life that radiate with the love of Christ. Youth are not simply looking for information about religion—they're looking for how ideas are embodied, how faith is lived out, how following Jesus impacts an adult's perspective and actions. Youth have no interest in, and simply mistrust, theologies and doctrines that are only prescribed. They're looking for adults who embody and practice their theology with a particular way of life—a way of life that mirrors the freedom and passion of Jesus Christ. Programs and activities cannot produce this way of life, nor can curricula and mission statements. The way people become awake to the Holy Spirit's presence groaning within them (Romans 8:23) is through coming in contact with other Christians who welcome the Spirit's transforming breath. As we focused on helping adults reignite their own spiritual passion, we found that their lives had a powerful impact on the youth in their community.

Youth pastors, parents, and senior pastors who participated in the project reported experiencing new freedom in Christ, a new sense of rest and vitality, a renewed sense of call, and a greater commitment to their faith. Subsequently, when young people were questioned about the impact of contemplative practice within their own congregations, they were most impressed by the faith and love of the adults involved in the youth ministry. They found these adults to be open, authentic, committed, loving, and approachable. They remarked on the diversity of adults (young and old, parents and singles) who seem to be authentically practicing their faith in their midst.

When a group of high school teenagers from Saron United Church of Christ in Linton, Indiana, were asked how the youth ministry had helped their own growth as Christians, one young woman told the story of a youth outing to a water theme park. The youth had asked a 68-year-old woman, Margaret, who occasionally volunteered in the youth ministry, to accompany them on the trip. When they arrived at the park, the kids asked Margaret to join them on the waterslides. Margaret had worn her bathing suit under her clothes and agreed to swim with them. The youth were impressed by the vivacity and joy in this woman, especially when they later learned she had recently lost her husband. The young woman concluded her sharing by saying, "Margaret taught me more about the Christian life just in her joy and friendship with us than all of my Sunday school classes put together."

Later when Margaret was interviewed about her experience of the youth group, she first talked about falling into a deep depression after the death of her husband. She knew she needed some activity to help ward off her loneliness. So upon the invitation of some of the adult leaders she began to attend youth group meetings. In the silent prayer and sharing that preceded youth group gatherings, she had a chance to express her grief and noticed "a new ear for God." She began to attend more and more youth events and was honored when the kids asked her to go to the water park. "I hadn't laughed since my husband died. But being with those kids, I couldn't help but laugh. I discovered I still have something to offer. I ended up going up and down that waterslide until my bottom hurt."

In our interviews with youth it became abundantly clear that young people aren't interested in the words their teachers are speaking as much as the life and soul from which these words arise. As the adults in our project began to experience transformation, they expressed a deepened desire to be authentic and caring toward the youth in their ministries. They sought to share their growing spiritual passion with the youth of their church and to provide settings where the youth could also experience this newfound life. Suddenly, youth ministry became a place of nourishment and creative exploration. Ministry was now about exploring experiences of God and activities of faith alongside young people. These leaders had been freed to become disciples among youth rather than experts transferring religious information.

This sense of new life and transformation led to a desire among the project participants to transform their church cultures. Most participants believed the best way to foster spiritual growth in youth was to begin transforming the culture of the sponsoring church. Many of the lay people and youth ministers participating in the project began to advocate for reform within Sunday morning worship services, committee meetings, and church systems. Youth workers began to provide spiritual growth groups for adults and even lobbied for greater spiritual care of senior pastors. When questioned about these activities, youth workers reported engaging in these broader spiritual renewal activities because they believed that a community of transformed adults would create the best environment to nurture the spiritual lives of young people.

4. Youth desire to recognize God's presence in their lives and to be empowered to live out their calling.

In interviews and events with youth, we discovered that young people were just as tired of youth programs focused on activity and doctrinal memorization as their youth leaders were. We noticed a hunger in youth to be given opportunities to discuss and explore their religious experiences. Contemplative exercises and spiritual disciplines provided such an environment. With regular exposure to spiritual exercises youth began to notice their youth programs felt more centered on God and the spiritual life, and less focused on social and recreational activities. One student commented, "Youth group feels different...Before it was about friends, now it seems to be about God."

In interviews and evaluations with young people, the most frequent comment on the contemplative approach to youth ministry was the transformation in how adults related to them. Young people noticed a new emphasis on hospitality and relationship within their youth ministry programs that invited greater trust in both the congregation and the Christian life. Young people spoke of the adults within their youth ministry as being particularly alive and attentive in a different way than most other adults with whom they came in contact. It was these relationships with "elders" within their faith community that kept young people involved, interested, and even forgiving of their congregations. What seemed most important to young people was feeling welcomed and affirmed by the adults in their churches in a way that allowed a mutual respect and spiritual seeking to emerge.

In evaluating the young people's experience of silence, solitude, and contemplative prayer, we found a majority of students within the project expressed a desire for continual growth in prayer and spiritual practice. Jessica, a 15-year-old from Eugene, Oregon, expressed this sense at the close of a formation retreat: "I'm learning that it's possible to live the way of Jesus and help other people just by listening." Sixteen- year-old Selby from Cleveland Heights, Ohio, commented after a week of regular periods of silent prayer, "Taking moments for silence and meditation can be so powerful."

Young people remarked about the lack of open time and space in their lives and were surprised by the "holy leisure" they encountered in the project's contemplative retreats and in their youth groups. Other young people felt affirmed by the diversity of prayer within the Christian tradition and found the different forms of prayer encouraging to their own spiritual growth. We discovered a widespread desire among youth in our participating churches to integrate spiritual practices into their daily lives. We met kids who started using their workout times (running and swimming) as times for prayer and meditation. Some kids began to journal their prayer life. Others set aside time early in the morning or before bed to practice silent prayer.

Equipped to explore their own connections with God, many young people began to discover a deepened spiritual dimension to their own lives. Sometimes this resulted in the discovery of spiritual gifts. Some of these youth sought to share their newfound gifts with their church communities. In two congregations, students began midweek contemplative worship services; in other churches, youth began to call for more times of silence and contemplative prayer within worship; after participating in a weeklong retreat, one young woman asked her pastor to begin training her for ministry; and in another church, four high school students began volunteering to develop Sunday school classes for younger kids.

Several years ago I was invited to Houston, Texas, to consult with a group of pastors, parents, and youth workers from a struggling mainline denomination. This denomination was and is rapidly losing members, and the regional leaders invited me to speak, hoping I might help them revive their youth ministry programs.

The night before my meeting with the church leadership I spent a couple of hours with a group of 30 teenagers from local churches. I wanted to hear their sense of the denomination's situation before I met with the church pastors and elders. I asked them questions about their spiritual lives and their sense of Jesus, and asked their thoughts on what I should say to the church leadership. The young people were eager to talk and spent most of our time sharing how scheduled and stressful their lives had become. At the close of the evening, in response to their sharing, I asked the kids to find a place outside under the warm, summer stars and spend the remaining 20 minutes in silent prayer. At the end of this time, we gathered again in the church and I asked them to share their experiences. There was a reverence and quiet as the youth spoke of a deep sense of God's presence. A few students became tearful as they shared how grateful they were to be allowed 20 minutes that weren't full of expectation and activity.

At the end of our meeting, a stout senior high boy in a Texas A&M football jersey spoke up: "I found a place between the bushes next to the church wall and just sat there to pray. Then suddenly this cricket starts chirping next to me, and I'm thinking, 'I wish this cricket would shut up.' But the little thing just kept up its song. I got annoyed and started looking through the nearby bushes so I could find the little sucker and crush it, but each time I started to move it got quiet, then as soon as I started to pray again it would start up its 'chirp, chirp, chirp.' I finally just gave up and sat back against the wall and thought, 'Forget it. I'll just sit here.' Then 'chirp, chirp, chirp, chirp, chirp, chirp, chirp, chirp, chirp.' Suddenly I found myself laughing. It was so little and persistent and kind of hilarious that this little bug was going to sit there making its own music. And I realized it was doing its prayers, the way God has made it to pray. It was determined to go on praying whether some big giant tried to squish it or not. For the rest of the time I just sat looking at the night sky, feeling grateful to God, realizing what a miracle that cricket is."

He took a long pause, then leveled his eyes at me. "You're supposed to give our parents and pastors some advice tomorrow?" I nodded my head. Then he said with authority, "Tell them to stop worrying and go outside and start listening to crickets."

Becoming a Spiritual Guide: Formation in Contemplative Youth Ministry

"It is not enough for the priests and ministers of the future to be moral people, well trained, eager to help their fellow humans, and able to respond creatively to the burning issues of their time. All of that is very valuable and important, but it is not the heart of Christian leadership. The central question is, Are the leaders of the future truly men and women of God, people with an ardent desire to dwell in God's presence, to listen to God's voice, to look at God's beauty, to touch God's incarnate Word, and to taste fully God's infinite goodness?"

— HENRI NOUWEN

In the Youth Ministry and Spirituality Project, we wanted to form youth leaders who are spiritual guides, people who know how to tend the life of Jesus within them. Youth ministers have a great capacity for care. But as Henri Nouwen believed, this eagerness to care and to teach, though it is valuable and important, "is not the heart of Christian leadership." To be a spiritual leader one must first and foremost become familiar with the Spirit. A spiritual leader is a person who respects and responds to the longings of the human soul. A spiritual leader's gift to a community is that he or she desires to "dwell in God's presence" and then helps others do the same.

In order to teach people to practice contemplative youth ministry, we worked to design a formation process that would help people notice and respond to their desire for God. We wanted to create a program that would help youth leaders dwell in the transforming presence of God. Working with pastors and youth ministers trained to consume ideas and techniques like fast food, we had to find a different approach from standard academic and vocational training. We couldn't simply present lectures on contemplative prayer; we had to find an approach to teaching that would help youth workers develop a new way of *being* in ministry as well as a new way of *thinking* about ministry.

The question was *how*. How do you help people become not just "religious educators" but "spiritual guides"—people who know how to tend the spiritual hunger within human beings? How could we help youth ministers, pastors, and church members not just increase their knowledge but also expand their experience and awareness of God, self, and neighbor? How do you help people become not only good caregivers, but people who know, in Nouwen's words, how to "listen to God's voice...look at God's beauty...touch God's incarnate word and...taste fully God's infinite goodness"? How do you evoke the kind of mystical passion that Nouwen claims is necessary? How could we help people experience the same journey that the Russian wayfarer in *The Way of the Pilgrim* undertook: the journey from the mind to the heart?

One of the most poignant examples of adolescent spiritual formation is Chaim Potok's *The Chosen*.[6] It is a story of the transformation of Danny Saunders, the bright son of a traditional Hasidic Jewish rabbi, or "*tzaddik*." Danny comes from a long dynasty of tzaddiks and

---

[6] Ballantine Books, 1982.

is raised with the expectation that he will one day replace his father as the reigning rabbi for the community. The adolescent Danny is extremely bright. His teachers and the Jewish community within which he lives are awed by his ability to memorize, categorize, and cite not only the Torah but the many commentaries that contain Hasidic Jewish thought.

Midway through the story the reader discovers that since Danny was a boy, his father has brought him up in silence, speaking to his son only when they study the Talmud together. When Danny's friend Reuven, the narrator of the story, asks him about his relationship with his father, Danny responds, "My father believes in silence. When I was ten or eleven years old, I complained to him about something, and he told me to close my mouth and look into my soul. He told me to stop running to him every time I had a problem. I should look into my own soul for the answer..."

The father's silence isn't explained until the climax of the book. As Danny prepares to tell his father of his decision to break the rabbinical lineage and pursue psychology, the old rabbi invites Danny and Reuven over to his study. Speaking to Danny through Reuven, the rabbi explains his silence:

> The Master of the Universe blessed me with a brilliant son. And he cursed me with all the problems of raising him....there was no soul in my four-year-old Daniel, there was only his mind. He was a mind in a body without a soul....I went away and cried to the Master of the Universe, "What have you done to me? A mind like this I need for a son? A *heart* I need for a son, a *soul* I need for a son, *compassion* I want from my son, righteousness, mercy, strength to suffer and carry pain, *that* I want from my son, not a mind without a soul!"[7]

The father's decision to refrain from speaking to his son is a severe and even cruel parenting strategy. Yet all of us who seek to form

[7] Potok, 264.

young people in the Spirit and life of Jesus know the struggle and pain of the boy's father. We too wring our hands over a world overcrowded with amusing distractions, compelling ideas, and mind-blowing experiences. We, too, worry and suffer over how to grow souls in such a culture. The wise tzaddik recognized that to raise a compassionate soul he had to use the language of the soul. He realized that study, even rigorous theological study, is not enough. He knew that just as the intellect needs stimulating ideas, and the emotions needs passion and inspiration, so the soul has particular necessities for growth and development.[8]

In the Youth Ministry and Spirituality Project, we learned that youth and youth directors were hungry for soul food. We recognized that intellectual stimulation (although many would argue this is also absent in youth ministry programs)[9] and emotional inspiration were not enough. We were convinced that it takes transformed adults to transform young people. We wanted to form youth ministers, pastors, and churches who knew how to help young people cultivate "the soul of a tzaddik."

FORMING CONTEMPLATIVE YOUTH WORKERS

One of the first realizations within the project was that youth workers had to discover a new way of seeing and perceiving their role and ministry if they were to invite youth into the contemplative dimension of the Christian faith. In response, we produced a series of five formation weeks intended to assist youth leaders in embodying the skills and disposition for teaching and practicing contemplative youth ministry. These events were presented in a retreat atmosphere and sought not only to present the principles and practices of contemplative youth ministry but also to model and embody the contemplative disposition upon which the teaching relied.[10] Therefore, although we entered each formation week with a predetermined schedule, the

---

[8] When asked what he most feared, Gandhi once replied, "Educated minds without souls."

[9] Christian Smith with Melinda Lundquist Denton, *Soul Searching: The Religious and Spiritual Lives of American Teenagers* (Oxford University Press, 2005). In Smith's extensive study of more than 3,000 teens, he had trouble finding any teenager who could articulate a coherent understanding of the Christian faith.

[10] A detailed description of the curriculum for each of the YMSP in-services can be found at www.ymsp.org.

staff met daily during each event for prayer and discernment so the schedule could be altered according to the needs of the group and the movement of the Spirit.

While each training offered various contemplative practices, our primary aim was to encourage a different way of "being" with young people and a different set of processes for discerning and implementing youth programs. The progression throughout the various weeks of formation was a movement from prayer to presence, from loving God to loving others. Our desire was to help participants engage in contemplative prayer and then to carry the sensitivity and awareness nurtured by such prayer into mentoring relationships with young people. We took care to see that each formation event was grounded in the following practices and dispositions designed to enlarge the soul of youth ministers, pastors, and churches:

Rest

In a society of busy, tired, and overworked people, rest can be a radical act of liberation. One reason that keeping the Sabbath is included among the Ten Commandments is because the human soul comes alive in holy rest. It's in experiencing God's rest that we sense an invitation to loosen our identification with our roles and tasks and remember our larger identity as daughters and sons of God.

In contemporary society, and even within the church, we've forgotten how to rest. We even sleep two to three hours less per day than people did one hundred years ago. Author and retreat leader Wayne Muller writes, "Illness becomes our Sabbath—pneumonia, our cancer, our heart attack, our accidents create Sabbath for us."[11] Unlike most training events that tend to pack schedules full of meetings and workshops, the schedules for our formation events included regular opportunities for naps, walks in nature, and downtime. We also included a midweek "Sabbath day" in which participants were

11 Wayne Muller, *Sabbath* (Bantam, 2000), 20.

encouraged to sleep, spend time in nature, and enjoy good food and fellowship.

If we were going to form youth ministers as people who had the soul and spirit of Jesus, we needed to provide people with the same sense of holy rest that Jesus embodied. Just as Jesus spent time in solitude and silence, just as Jesus took time to rest (even in the midst of terrible storms of activity), just as Jesus went away to quiet and deserted places, so we sought to provide Sabbath rest and reflection for participants.

Prayer

At the beginning and close of each day, within teaching sessions and small groups, among the larger community and in periods of solitude, participants were invited to turn their hearts to God in prayer. Sadly, within the church and within ministry, prayer is too often a secondary activity, something we tack on to the beginning and end of an activity. We wanted to reverse that practice. We tried to create a formation program in which prayer was always the central habit. We did this because we had faith that the best way to cultivate the souls of youth leaders was by inviting them to turn their attention to God. We believed the more time and space we gave for participants to tend to their life with God, the more receptive they would become to God's healing and guidance.

The primary form of prayer within the project was contemplative prayer, although we also practiced prayers of thanksgiving, petition, and intercession on a daily basis. Contemplative prayer invites a quiet receptivity to the presence of God. It involves an attentive awareness to the activity of God beneath our own plans and agendas. The primary methods of contemplative prayer that were taught within our formation events were centering prayer and *lectio divina* [see appendixes 1 and 2]. However, participants were also exposed to a variety of other contemplative prayer forms including imaginative contemplation ("gazing" and attending imaginatively to the senses within a biblical scene), walking forms of meditation and prayer, the Ignatian awareness examen, body prayer, and prayer exercises that involved creative media such as crayons, clay, and paints.

Prayer is paying attention to the Spirit's transforming work. It is turning our desire and attention to the place where the Holy Spirit tends our inner longings. To practice prayer is to practice welcoming the life of the Spirit. Every act of prayer contains the possibility of our own transformation. By engaging participants in regular periods of prayer, we sought to create formation events that regularly made space and time for God's intervention. We trusted that these times of contemplation helped people slow down and allow their desire for God to grow.

Solitude and Silence

Thomas Merton wrote, "The ears with which one hears the message of the Gospel are hidden in [the] heart, and these ears do not hear anything unless they are favored with a certain interior solitude and silence."[12]

Each formation week included extended times of prayer and silence with one evening dedicated to silence and solitude. These moments of quiet, prayerful reflection invited youth leaders to draw inward and respond to the Holy Spirit. Just as the father in *The Chosen* sought to create a sense of solitude and silence, so we too hoped to encourage youth leaders to "be still and know." We designed each formation event trusting that youth leaders would find that both their own souls and the activity of God would become more apparent in silence and solitude. Rather than an experience of absence, most participants found these experiences of solitude as deep experiences of God's presence.

[12] *Thoughts in Solitude* (Farrar, Straus, and Giroux, 1958), xii-xiii.

Silence and solitude created opportunities for participants to give their full attention to their lives with God. These periods of solitude were also experiences of great honesty. In the silence people found they no longer could distract themselves from hard questions, hurt feelings, disappointments, and longings. In the solitude there was space and time for the realities of people's lives to rise to the surface. Although this could be painful at times, by unearthing hidden experiences, doubts, questions, and feelings, participants were able to become more honest about their ministries, their gifts, their shortcomings, and their relationships with God.

Surprisingly, these moments of silence and solitude often evoked a strong sense of community. People expressed a deeper care and compassion for other participants and a greater awareness of the needs and sufferings of their communities after these periods of prayerful withdrawal. By offering participants regular periods of exterior silence and solitude, we hoped to encourage the "interior solitude and silence" to which Merton referred. We trusted that, just as Jesus withdrew from crowds, youth leaders needed regular times to withdraw in order to have their eyes and ears better attuned to the life of God.

Spiritual Companionship

We provided trained spiritual directors, many of them veteran youth workers, to serve as staff at each event. These spiritual mentors met regularly with youth leaders, aiding them in listening for the movement of God within their own life experience. We tried to find spiritual directors who were "soulful" people, people who had spent time cultivating their own life in God and knew how to help others do the same. These spiritual mentors and directors provided guidance, companionship, and a safe listening space. Through small-group leadership and one-on-one direction sessions, we encouraged participants to follow God's leading and let go of destructive self-images, roles, theologies, and ministry systems while simultaneously embracing a more authentically Christian identity and ministry.

We trusted that a youth leader's greatest skill in ministering to youth was his or her ability to increase young people's awareness of God. To do this, we believed that youth leaders needed spiritual companionship where they could be given the space and time to notice and name the experiences of God within their own lives and ministries. Youth leaders were also asked to commit to regular spiritual direction within their own communities.

Contemplative Reflection on Experience

We often live our lives as if time (and life itself) is a product we produce rather than a gift we receive. Although much of the material we presented on contemplative practice was new to participants, we were not seeking to stimulate people's souls with new and exotic spiritual experiences. Instead, we hoped contemplative prayer might help them slow down and become more attentive and responsive within their lives and ministries. We wanted to form people who had a larger capacity to receive the many experiences of their lives that contained spiritual vitality—experiences of grief and loss, experiences of struggle and chaos, experiences of breakthroughs and insight. Our sense was that youth leaders didn't need lots of new ideas and techniques. What they needed was to pay greater attention to the many ways in which God was reaching out to them within their lives and ministries.

Contemplative awareness trusts that God is already present and working in each and every moment. The challenge in our training events was to help people pay better attention to their own lives and the lives of young people, so they could be more discerning of where life was seeking to break forth.

I once attended a ministry conference where I sat next to a woman who served as an Episcopal priest in Chicago. We began to talk about our work and when I mentioned that I was a youth minister, she told me her first job out of seminary was a position as junior high youth director for a struggling inner-city church, but then quickly added, "I only lasted six months." When I asked her *why*, she told me the following story:

> The church I served was in a very poor area, and the junior high youth ministry was one of the few programs for young teenagers in the neighborhood. Every Sunday night the church would fill with about 50 kids from the surrounding tenement buildings. In those days the junior high ministry consisted of a short worship service designed for junior high students. We'd have upbeat music and a brief, youth-friendly homily, but much of the service was taken from the formal Book of Common Prayer [the worship manual of the Episcopal Church]. This meant there were lots of prayers, readings, and responses the kids were supposed to do. The problem was that most of these kids couldn't read. This fact combined with the young people's excitement at being together made the junior high worship service pure bedlam. The kids would wrestle and giggle in the pews. They'd run and hide in the organ pipes or put on choir robes and chase each other. I was fresh out of seminary and had a very different idea of my life as a priest. I wanted to be this prim and holy priest, but instead I spent most of these youth services chasing, disciplining, and shouting at kids to be quiet.

> In those days the service ended with a blessing. The kids would line up in front of me, then one by one they'd come forward. I'd place my hand on their head and read this little blessing over them. It took a long time to do this because there were so many kids and they had a hard time staying in line. But I was a good Episcopalian, so I pushed ahead and made sure I gave the blessing to each child as instructed.

After six months I couldn't take it anymore. I felt completely inadequate and unprepared for those kids, and the whole thing was just so unruly that I told the rector I was quitting. On my last night with the kids I began the service by announcing my resignation. I guess I hoped that when the kids heard it was my last night, they'd act more respectful. But this was just wishful thinking. The kids were as unruly on my last night as they were on my first. When we came to the end of the service, I lined them up as best I could, then gave them their little blessing and sent them out the door and back to their homes. But halfway through the blessings this young black girl interrupted me and said, "Hey, who gives you a blessing?" I was exasperated and ignored the girl's question, but she just stood holding up the line and again asked, "Who gives you a blessing, Pastor?" I told her to run along with the others, but she wouldn't move. "Who gives you a blessing?"

Exasperated, I told her something quickly about getting blessed by bishops at conferences or something, but then she got this idea and lit up. "Hey, Pastor, can we give you a blessing?" This idea spread through the line of kids like wildfire. Soon the whole gang of them rushed forward, crowded around me, and started clamoring, "I want to give you a blessing! No, let me do it! I'm older—I want to give her a blessing! It was my idea, let me do it!" I shouted at the kids to get back in line, but they wouldn't do it. Finally I acquiesced. I told them if they promised to go quietly from the church and back to their homes, I would let them all give me a blessing.

Well, they became ecstatic. They started crowding around me jumping up and down, climbing on the altar, trying to get their hands on my head. Most of them couldn't reach so they begged me to get on my knees. I walked out to an open space and knelt down and these kids giggled and laughed as they pushed in around me. Then they all stretched out their sweaty young hands and piled over my head, face, shoulders, and back. It got quiet for a moment. They hesitated, not knowing what to do, and then suddenly one of them started to recite this blessing. Immediately, the rest of them joined in. These kids, most of them illiterate, recited from memory the blessing they'd heard me say over each of them...

At this point the woman began to cry. I sat quietly for a while and waited for her to regain her composure. Finally, she spoke again: "You know what? That happened over 30 years ago. And I just realized I never received that blessing."

I looked at her, not fully understanding. She continued, "You know, the whole time those kids were trying to bless me, I was thinking how I was going to get those kids to go home. I was thinking about locking up the church building. I was thinking about how glad I was to be quitting my job. I didn't notice, until just now, what a miracle that was. Fifty or sixty kids had memorized the blessing I gave to them and were eager to return this blessing to me—and I missed it. I missed it. I was too busy worrying about what was going wrong and what I was going to do next."

Youth ministry is often a demanding and thankless job. At the start of our project, many of the youth workers felt drained and depleted. Yet over time, as we invited them to pay more careful, prayerful attention to their lives and ministries, they began to notice many "missed blessings"—moments of grace and mercy that they had overlooked. There were many breakthroughs, insights, and in-breakings of the Holy Spirit within their lives and ministry that had been previously bypassed in order to get on with the next item on the ministry "to do" list.

Contemplative youth ministry is about receiving the ministry you're given. It's about trusting that God is alive and available within the relationships in your church and community. To help youth leaders develop this awareness, we engaged them in exercises that asked them to stop and prayerfully reflect over their ministries. We had them keep journals about their experiences in ministry. We gave time and space for participants to reflect on and pray over questions like, "Where do you notice God in your ministry? Where does God seem absent? What are the longings of the youth you serve? What's the spirit that drives your ministry? Where do you come alive in your ministry? Where do you feel depleted? When do the young people in your ministry come alive? What's God doing in your ministry?"

The spiritual directors at our events listened patiently as participants talked about their lives and ministries, seeking to help the youth leaders and pastors hear and see the ways in which God was present. Each day included small groups led by a spiritual director who invited youth leaders to prayerfully reflect on their lives and ministries: "What happened today? How is God present? What is God's invitation?" In reflecting on and responding to these questions, youth leaders began to listen better to the Spirit and became increasingly attentive to the movement of God within their lives and ministries.

Critical Analysis of Youth Ministry

Our teaching sessions also included a critical analysis of the conventional systems, structures, and practices within North American youth ministry. In formation events we tried to help people broaden their awareness of the prevailing models of youth ministry, the energies that gave rise to these models, and the impact of these various approaches on youth, youth ministers, and churches. We sought to help participants notice the ways in which pragmatism, efficiency, materialism, and a consumer mentality inform most churches and youth ministries. We helped youth workers discern the "spirits" within their own youth ministries, helping them identify those spirits rooted in anxiety and greed versus the Spirit of Jesus. (See the article in appendix 7, "Spirituality and Youth Ministry: What Are We Doing?")

Much of our critique of current youth ministry practices was grounded in the life and ministry of Jesus. We found that most youth ministry models lack the spontaneity, freedom, presence, rest, and reflection that Jesus embodied. Each formation week was grounded in a particular biblical passage that highlighted Jesus' approach to ministry.

The grid on the following page compares the contemplative approach to youth ministry with two of the most common approaches to youth ministry in North America. The "consumer" approach refers to those models of ministry that focus on entertaining youth, thereby reflecting the values and mores of the market culture. The "content" approach describes an educational model directed primarily to the transfer of religious information. Of course, these descriptions are quite general; any youth ministry program will be a complex mixture of all these approaches (and others). Yet the comparison helps to reveal the intention of a contemplative approach and provides a sample of the critical awareness we sought to develop within our teaching.

Three Approaches to Youth Ministry

	CONSUMER	CONTENT	CONTEMPLATION
Rooted in	Anxiety	Complacency	Faith, Hope, Love
Theology	Faith is good fun. God is Judge.	Faith is conformity. God is Truth.	Faith is relationship. God is Love.
Youth Director	Program director. Adolescent "savior."	Instructor. Person with answers.	Spiritual guide. Points to the presence of God.
Volunteers	Chaperones	Classroom aides	Seekers, mentors, elders
Teaching	Civic values	Religious information/ indoctrination	Christian living
Practices	Play, events, programs, activities	Learning, study, memorization, regurgitation	Relationships
Youth	Religious consumers	Potential institutional members	Spiritual seekers, developing a way of life
Constituency	Parents/church board	Religious institutions	Body of Christ/The Living God

Teaching Contemplative Processes

In order to show how prayer and contemplative listening might become central to the practice of youth ministry, we designed and taught various contemplative practices and processes for churches to employ within their ministry. This included a discernment approach to staff meetings known as "the liturgy for discernment" (see appendix 5), a process for calling and recruiting volunteers, and several processes for leading spiritual exercises with youth (see appendix 4). These contemplative processes were designed to alter the systems and structures of conventional ministry. Participants practiced and evaluated many of these processes within formation events. (For a more detailed understanding of these processes, see *Contemplative Youth Ministry: Practicing the Presence of Jesus*.)

Theological Reflection

Through prayer, silence, and solitude, project formation events were rich in spiritual experience. It was also critical, however, to give space and time for participants to put words on this experience—particularly their experience of God. To allow these experiences to go unnamed would be to leave them ambiguous and elusive. Each day participants were given time in small and large groups to speak about their experiences in prayer and contemplative reflection. We invited participants to become "religious interpreters,"[13] finding language to deepen their knowledge and understanding of their life with God. The dialogue that emerged within the project was often encouraged and stimulated by the project's own teaching on the theological and biblical basis of contemplative ministry.

The "theology of the Beloved," developed and taught by Michael Hryniuk, became the primary language and biblical context for understanding the experience and practice of contemplative prayer and ministry. This theology, which is explored more fully in chapter 3,

---

[13] Michael Warren uses this phrase in *Youth, Gospel, Liberation* (HarperCollins, 1987).

is grounded in Jesus' baptismal experience of being named and delighted in as the Beloved of God. Our hope was to help participants deepen their awareness of God's unconditional love as the ground of their identity and ministry with youth. Participants within the project claimed this language of "the Beloved" in articulating their experience of contemplative youth ministry as well as in their own teaching of contemplative ministry within their respective faith communities.

Play

In addition to the intensive periods of silence, prayer, solitude, spiritual direction, and study at each event, we also made room for spontaneous outbreaks of play. Inspired by participants, each week included skits (in which the project staff was regularly lampooned), karaoke nights at a local club, movies, hikes in the surrounding mountains, and afternoons on the seminary green with Frisbees and volleyballs. We found that these moments of play rekindled the soul as much as the more formal "spiritual" times of prayer and worship.

Although each day's schedule included small alterations, the basic daily schedule for our formation events was as follows:

7:15 a.m.   Centering Prayer

Participants were encouraged to ground each day in prayer and silence. Centering prayer invited people to begin the day by drawing their attention to God. (See appendix 2.)

8:00   **Morning Prayer**

The 30-minute contemplative prayer service included simple prayer chants (many composed and led by Stephen Iverson[14]), a reading of the Scripture for the day, 10 minutes of silence, intercessory prayer followed by the Lord's Prayer, and a closing song.

8:45   **Breakfast**

Silence was often kept through breakfast.

9:45   **Morning Plenary**

Each teaching session involved a mix of theology, critical analysis, and contemplative exercises as described above.

12:30   **Lunch**

1:30   **Individual Spiritual Direction Sessions**

Each participant had at least one hour-long session during the week.

2:30   **Afternoon Plenary**

These sessions focused on practicing skills or applying insights from the morning sessions.

4:30   **Reflection Groups**

Each participant was assigned a small group for discussion and reflection on the day's teachings and exercises. These groups were run similar to Quaker clearness committees, in which silence and prayer occurred between speakers in order to deepen the participants' reflection and understanding, and to make room for the Holy Spirit to breathe and move among the participants. Discussions often moved between the practical and the personal. Each group was led by a trained spiritual director.

---

[14] Stephen Iverson has composed a number of contemporary prayer chants for use in Christian worship and meditation. His recordings include *Prayer* and *Songs of Faith and Longing.*

5:30   Evening Prayer
Same format as morning prayer. Once a week the project held a healing service for participants.

6:00   Dinner

7:00   Free Time
We intentionally scheduled nothing after dinner, allowing participants to have downtime in the evenings—a rare occurrence at Christian conferences.

What became profoundly clear to us in leading these formation weeks was the way in which prayer, silence, rest, and spiritual direction not only helped develop an environment of openness and trust but also allowed people to attend fully to theological teaching. Too often theological education, following 19th-century educational models, relies heavily on lecture and cognitive transference of information. Similarly, youth ministry training events also depend primarily on presentation of information either through the spoken word or—in more postmodern events—sound and images. We discovered that, in the work of spiritual growth, less is often more.

Formation in the life of Christ requires space in which people have the opportunity to integrate and participate in what the Holy Spirit is bringing to fruition. We took seriously within each formation week the need for intentional space and time so the Spirit might move and breathe. One of the important learnings from the project was that the lack of spiritual transformation within the Christian church is due not to the lack of good teaching, but to the fact that people have neither space nor the time to integrate the teaching they're given. People are "backed up"—overloaded with words and techniques that are never worked into the soil of the heart.

The teaching content of the formation events progressed from individual teaching and practice of contemplative prayer and awareness to more communal and systemic practices of contemplative prayer and presence. The teaching sought not only to help youth leaders attend to their own lives in God but also to help them develop structures, practices, and processes that make their youth ministry programs and relationships with youth more available to the presence of Jesus.

Below are some comments representative of the kind of feedback we received after these events:

> The return to each training event is a coming home to love and belovedness and renewal and new awareness. It was at these events that I learned the tools for contemplative prayer, real meditation, and spiritual direction, as well as simple tools like candles and music and quiet. I have read so many books from the trainings that have transformed my life and the lives of those around me. These formation weeks have developed in me a new way of relating to youth and adults.
>
> —LAURIE RODNEY, CHURCH OF THE REDEEMER, CLEVELAND HEIGHTS, OHIO

> I came back from the project formation event [in which teaching focused on Sabbath-living] and cancelled my speaking engagements. I turned in my medical volunteering job. Now every time I come to a stoplight, instead of being anxious about when the light is going to change, I notice my breathing and just take three slow breaths, in and out. During this last Christmas shopping season, every time I was in a huge line instead of getting frustrated I stopped and looked around.
>
> I purposely slow down and ask myself, "What can I notice and receive around me? Where is God in this moment?" This slowing down has

transformed how I identify myself, how I operate, and how I think. I've turned into someone who looks for opportunities for reflection, for silence, to stop…before this, slowing down and noticing would've made me anxious…

I'm also much better able to listen to kids when I slow down. When I'm living into Sabbath, I become less stressed and anxious—less like a parent and more like a friend. I can tell I'm clearly an adult acting differently when I'm available, less stressed, and more open around kids. I start hearing conversations I wouldn't have heard in the past. You get past the five-minute "Hi! How are you?" stage of conversation. It's refreshing for kids to see that there are some adults who aren't stressed out.

—JOHN FREY, THE WOODLANDS CHRISTIAN CHURCH, THE WOODLANDS, TEXAS

I was blind and now I see. That sums up my experience after the final formation week. God has been providing all along…and I was trapped in my false, traditional ideas of what a youth leader looks like and what youth ministry "should" look like. Now I don't feel as insecure or as incompetent. I'm proud of what has grown at Immanuel—it's more relational and creative and Spirit-led…

—LEANNA CREEL, IMMANUEL PRESBYTERIAN CHURCH, LOS ANGELES, CALIFORNIA

Through the YMSP formation retreats I have been led into the presence of God and have learned how to be in a new relationship with God. I have felt included and loved and have learned how to be a minister. I have learned how to be a friend, a husband, and a father. I've learned how to follow and how to lead. I have never been so scared in God's presence, and I have never been filled with so much delight.

—ADAM YODER, SEATTLE MENNONITE CHURCH, SEATTLE, WASHINGTON

Youth leaders within the project often reported an experience of "transformation" through their experience of the formation events. What did this "transformation" mean within their personal and ministry lives? It often meant their imaginative capacity, their creativity, and their experience of faith, hope, and love had been expanded. Simply put, their capacity for life had grown.

Similarly, this transformation meant that their propensity for conventional, stifling, anxious, destructive, dull, and defeating forms of ministry was diminished. "Transformed adults" meant adults who felt their lives were more grounded in the life of God. It meant adults who felt they had become increasingly sensitive to the life of the soul. Finally, it meant adult youth leaders who embodied a greater sensitivity to the spiritual yearning within young people and the surrounding world.

Transformation is evident when a volunteer youth director from Kansas writes, "The world has become enchanted." Or when a pastor from Morgantown, West Virginia, states, "I have ears that hear." Or when a single-mom Sunday school volunteer in Abiqui, New Mexico, says, "I'm a different mother."

The emphasis of this project was the resurrection and cultivation of the spiritual, the soulful—the aspect of our faith life that is in communion with God. We did this by encouraging Christian community, prayer and daily reflection in Scripture, worship, and accountability through spiritual direction and pastoral guidance.

Spiritual formation is not the same as learning about a concrete object. It's not the same as trying to retain a theological principle. Christian formation is much more like trying to grow and deepen in a relationship with another person. It takes trust, openness, time, listening, and vulnerability. Information, knowledge, and teaching can help deepen and expand a relationship, but without tending to the actual living relationship, you have nothing. This is what we learned in forming youth leaders as spiritual guides. This is what we hoped would transform stale and distracted approaches to youth discipleship.

The Journey of the Beloved:
A Theology of Youth Ministry
by Michael Hryniuk

Michael Hryniuk, PhD, is a theologian, teacher, speaker, and consultant in the field of Christian spirituality and contemplative formation. He served as codirector of the Youth Ministry and Spirituality Project from 2001-2004. Michael lives in Vancouver, British Columbia, and directs Theosis Ministries, a resource for ministry development and contemplative renewal of church life.

On the surface, the purpose of youth ministry seems fairly simple and straightforward: Bring the kids to Jesus. In fact, the goal of youth ministry often seems so obvious that we jump immediately to the next question: How do we do it? Just get them in the church on Sunday nights, order in the pizza and soda, and open the Bible for a lesson. That's all there is to it, right?

Of course, it is much more complex and confusing than that. There are all kinds of difficult questions surrounding the "how" of successful youth ministry: How do we get kids in the church door when they are so busy with soccer, baseball, exams, family, and social commitments? What do we do with the kids if they do come to our youth events? What programs and activities will both attract youth and nurture them in the Christian faith? What themes do we focus on? How do we open the Bible for them in ways that get them interested and committed to what it says about living the Christian life? What books, videos, practices, and processes do we need to get the job done in a way that satisfies the kids, their parents, the church, and the senior pastor? These "how" questions have spawned a whole industry seeking to provide answers, tools, methods, and resources.

In this chapter, I want to reflect on the deeper theological meaning and purpose of ministry to youth—the "why" behind the "hows." When we attend first to the "why" of youth ministry in light of the loving Spirit of God who names and claims us as beloved sons and daughters and then sends us forth to share that love in ministry to young persons, the "how" question begins to look and feel very different. Rather than focusing solely on how to "fill the space" with pizza or dogma at a Sunday night youth group, we shift our attention to the deeper question of how to "create space for God" in the daily lives of young persons through the disciplines of the spiritual life.

A lot of youth ministry in North America today is driven by fear and anxiety. The fear may be that the church is losing its young people, or that the young people don't know what to believe, or that young people need moral values—but many youth ministries live in what Henri Nouwen has called the "house of fear" and not the house of love. Many youth workers fit Nouwen's description of the compulsive minister—they are very busy people with meetings to attend, visits to make, programs to run, and events to organize. Many are also angry, exhausted, isolated, and confused. They are good and loving people who are driven by an anxious concern to care for their kids, please the parents and church leaders, and stay alive in the midst of the pressures and demands of their ministry.

In light of the gospel's call to radical "rebirth" in the Spirit and abiding intimacy with God through Christ, the Youth Ministry and Spirituality Project sought to teach and promote a *contemplative* approach to youth ministry that places adolescent spiritual formation at the heart of congregational life. Rather than reacting anxiously to the consumer mentality that demands that youth ministries continually offer more and better programming, the mission of the YMSP was to foster Christian communities *that are attentive to God's presence, discerning of the Spirit, and that accompany young people on the way of Jesus.* In doing so, we've focused not only on the spiritual formation of youth but also on the souls of youth ministers—seeking to support them in moving from compulsive ministry to contemplative ministry. In the psalmist's call to "Be still and know that I am God" (Psalm 46:10), we've heard the invitation to deepen our capacity for "being" *in* God so that our doing *for* God in youth ministry flows from a place deeper than our own fears and anxieties.

Contemplative ministry begins with God. It is a whole way of being, seeing, listening, and acting that flows out of an awareness of God's presence in the moment. When Jesus speaks of having "eyes to see" and "ears to hear," he is referring to such an awareness of God's presence within us, around us, and between us. When we learn to live in and minister from such an awareness, the shift in our ministry paradigm can be quite dramatic. When we begin by attending to God's presence, we are gradually freed from the "unclean" spirit of anxiety that so often drives us, and we are opened to the leading of God's love and peace.

The evangelist John reminds his community, "There is no fear in love, but perfect love casts out fear; for fear has to do with punishment, and whoever fears has not reached perfection in love" (1 John 4:18). What happens when youth ministers attend first to *being* in God's presence and *receiving* God's love in their lives and not to anxious questions about *doing* successful youth ministry? How does the image of God's presence and loving activity in the Spirit drive out the fear that binds us and reshape our experience of ourselves? How does it open our potential to become "perfect in love" and joyful witnesses to Christ in the lives of young people?

FRANNY, ZOOEY, AND JESUS: TOWARD A THEOLOGY OF YOUTH MINISTRY

The great writer J. D. Salinger saw it coming. Almost 40 years ago, *New Yorker* magazine published Salinger's now iconic short story "Franny," about a spiritually precocious adolescent girl. Franny has learned the Jesus Prayer at a seminar and is struggling over a lunch date to convey to her frat house boyfriend the meaning and power she finds in practicing it.[15] Her beleaguered but well-meaning boyfriend, Lane Coutell, simply doesn't get it. Like many of us, he wonders why anyone would repeat the name of God incessantly until something *happens*. What is the *result*? he asks. Franny's response: "You get to see God. Something happens in some absolutely nonphysical part of the heart...and you see God, that's all."[16]

Lane is uncomprehending. There is a poignancy and pathos in his spiritual tone-deafness that is itself an image of the blindness of Western enlightenment rationalism:

> He watched the waiter leave, then leaned forward, arms on
> the table, thoroughly relaxed, stomach full, coffee due to arrive
> momentarily, and said, "Well, it's interesting anyway. All that
> stuff...I don't think you leave any margin for the most elementary
> *psychology.* I mean I think all those religious experiences have
> a very obvious psychological background—you know what I
> mean...It's interesting though. I mean you can't deny that."[17]

[15] The Jesus Prayer consists of an interior quiet in which the mind is drawn into the heart while prayerfully repeating "Lord Jesus Christ, have mercy on me." The desert fathers believed that this prayer, repeated constantly, contained all the elements of the Christian gospel. See *Living the Jesus Prayer* by Irma Zaleski (Continuum, 1997).

[16] J. D. Salinger, *Franny and Zooey* (Bantam Books, 1961), 39.

[17] Salinger, 39.

Lane's response triggers a deep reaction in Franny; she literally passes out. It is the beginning of a protracted breakdown and spiritual crisis for the young woman as she tries to cope with the power of the prayer, the religious questions that burn in her, and the soul-killing superficiality she encounters around her.

The ardent desire of Franny Glass to experience God, to see God immediately and directly, is a symbol of the desire that lies deep in the heart of not only every searching adolescent, but every human being. Her instinctive impulse to experiment with a spiritual practice like the Jesus Prayer is emblematic not only of the religious quest of teenagers, but of the perennial human need to turn inward to the taproot of religious experience, especially in periods of doubt, chaos, and cultural upheaval. Franny's quest is that of the youth and youth ministers in our project who long for an experience of God's nearness and power, not just words about that experience from ages past.

The problem is that religious experience has always been held suspect by institutionalized religion. We seem to have lost faith that we too are invited to encounter God directly. Yet every religious tradition, including Christianity, is rooted in such experience. The founders of every spiritual tradition spoke and taught out of their own experience of the divine, and the traditions that developed from their witness uphold the possibility of a direct, immediate encounter with the mystery of the divine presence for *all* of their adherents. The image of Mary sitting at Jesus' feet speaks to every generation of the need to return our attention directly to him, and the church has always taught disciplines to realize this possibility. The Psalms, Gospels, and Pauline letters are replete with references to the search for the "living God" dwelling in the depths of the human heart. Jesus invites his followers to "abide" in him as he abides in them (John 15). Early patristic, medieval, and modern sources, both Catholic and Reformed, have spelled out in great depth the spiritual disciplines necessary for this quest.

While much of this literature has been marginalized within the Christian tradition for centuries, there is today a renaissance of interest in contemplative practices among both Catholics and mainline Protestants. There seems to be a growing desire to explore contemplative consciousness as both the source and goal of Christian life and ministry. The witness of Thomas Merton, Henri Nouwen, Eugene Peterson, and Kathleen Norris points to a gradual reorienting of the practice of faith and ministry in Western churches. The great Catholic theologian Karl Rahner, commenting on this phenomenon, stated bluntly, "The devout Christian of the future will either be a mystic, one who has experienced something, or he will cease to be anything at all."[18] The operative word here is *experience*. Rahner is not referring to mysticism as an ecstatic state reserved for a few exceptional cloistered monks or nuns, but to a spiritual experience accessible to all believers. But what are the theological foundations of this renaissance of interest in contemplative prayer for the practice of youth ministry? What does Franny Glass, a modern day Mary of Bethany, have to say to present generations of youth and their ministers?

Theologically, the starting point of our contemplative approach to youth ministry is found in a fully Trinitarian understanding of God's life, presence, and activity in the world. We discern God moving powerfully in the lives of young persons and their ministers as a creative, redemptive, and sanctifying force, drawing them into an intimate relationship with him and naming, claiming, and sending them forth as his beloved daughters and sons. Like a dancer who is sensitive to the movements of the other, who is leading, ministers to youth are being invited to respond to what the triune God is already doing in the lives of God's young people in calling them to this journey of the Beloved.

[18] Karl Rahner, *The Practice of Faith* (1983), 69-77.

AWAKENING THE DESIRE FOR GOD

In order for ministry to be Christ-centered and Spirit-led, it must be practiced in the context of what the early theological tradition has spoken of as God's "economy of salvation." What is the deeper meaning of this Trinitarian pattern of God's saving grace, and what are its implications for youth ministry?

First, we see the power of the Creator, who continues to fashion the cosmos in love and human beings in God's own image and likeness (Genesis 1:27). We believe the existential and experiential core of God's creative activity is felt in a deep and burning desire within our inmost selves for relatedness to God in love. As Augustine put it so well, "Thou has made us for thyself, and our hearts are restless until they rest in thee." Contemplative ministry to young people starts with a prayerful attentiveness to the mystery of the human person whose innermost self, or "soul," is constituted by this desire for God and God alone. *We see youth ministry oriented first and foremost to cooperating with God's creative love by awakening and responding to this deepest longing of the human heart and soul for union with God.*

In Salinger's story, young Franny Glass expressed that restless desire for God in an acute way that is characteristic of adolescence, and enters into a "spiritual emergency" when she meets the banality and superficiality of her culture. We sense that youth ministers are called to acknowledge the mystery of this desire for God not only in young persons but, even more importantly, in *themselves*. If we adults who minister with youth do not respond to our own longing to know and love God, we will have nothing of value to offer young persons in their quest, as Franny puts it, to "see God." Instead, we will be tempted to respond out of the anxious desires of our own hearts for acceptance, approval, and "results." To paraphrase Augustine, not only our hearts, but our youth ministries, will be restless until they rest in the presence of God.

This deepest human desire to know God is essentially a desire to know God's love. It is ultimately to know ourselves as unconditionally loved by God. To understand and practice ministry that responds to this desire, we have encouraged our partners to focus on Jesus and his redemptive witness to God's unconditional love. Theologically, we look to Jesus as our plumb line in evaluating the integrity and authenticity of our ministry to young people. More specifically, we've focused on three moments in Jesus' life that disclose the core of not only his mission but also the mission of those who minister in his name. These are the moments where Jesus is *named, claimed,* and *sent* by the Spirit. These events make it clear Jesus knew himself as the Beloved of God—and that his desire is that we and the youth we serve would also experience our own deepest identity as beloved.

Being Named as God's Beloved

The first moment, and in many ways the most important one for our theology of youth ministry, is Jesus' experience of being named as Beloved at the time of his baptism in the Jordan. The words of God addressed to Jesus at that moment have become the foundation of our understanding of Christian formation. In Mark's account, we read that Jesus "saw heaven being torn open and the Spirit descending on him like a dove. And a voice came from heaven saying: "You are my Son, my Beloved; with you I am well pleased" (1:11). For us as youth ministers, it is the inner meaning and experience of this event that is absolutely foundational. Jesus is named as the beloved Son of God, in whom God takes delight. It is the awakening of Jesus of Nazareth to his core identity as the Christ, the Anointed One. With this anointing, Jesus knows himself as unconditionally beloved and uniquely valuable in the embrace of his Father, whom he addresses in the most intimate of terms as *Abba,* or "Daddy."

If Christ's baptism is considered the prototype of our own, the invitation to us as youth ministers is to experience for ourselves the redeeming and transforming power of this sacrament that restores us to our deepest and truest identity as the adopted daughters and sons of God. Just as Jesus becomes fully aware of his identity as the Christ, we believe that in our baptism, we followers of Christ are invited to shed the false identity of the "flesh" and to know ourselves as beloved of God. To know oneself in this way is to be anointed with Christ-consciousness, a consciousness of oneself as unconditionally loved and worthy of self-embrace. As Paul says to the Romans, "For you did not receive a spirit of slavery to fall back into fear, but you have received a spirit of adoption. When we cry, 'Abba! Father!' it is that very Spirit bearing witness with our spirit that we are children of God, and if children, then heirs, heirs of God and joint heirs with Christ" (Romans 8:15-17). We believe we are called to receive this inner and hidden *name* and to live in the freedom, joy, and peace that comes through the power of the Spirit: knowing ourselves as children freed from the spirit of fear and embraced by the unconditional love of the Father.

Being Claimed as God's Beloved

The second key moment for us in Jesus' story is his experience of being *claimed* as God's beloved Son. In each of the Synoptic Gospels, Jesus is driven by the Spirit into the desert, where he is tempted for 40 days. Satan attempts to divert Jesus' desire to serve God alone and to obscure the name given to Jesus at his baptism. Satan tempts Jesus to *prove* his identity as the Beloved by miracles and spectacles, and seeks to seduce him with the promise of power.

We youth ministers know well these struggles. Even if we have heard our deepest "baptismal" name spoken as beloved and feel an earnest desire to minister out of that name, we are continually exposed to other powers that seek to distract and divert us from our truest identity in Christ. We hear other "voices" within us, voices of the Deceiver that say we are "nothing" or "failing" if we do not meet certain conditions. Media experts now report that through television, the Internet, and other advertising, persons in this culture are now exposed to as many as 3,000 marketing messages a day. These messages seek to convey to us who we *should* be, what we *should* wear and drive, and how we *should* measure up to cultural images of success. These messages offer us a conditional approval and acceptance that is always contingent upon meeting certain external expectations.

Even within the church, we are tempted to conform to ideal images and standards of the "empowered" or "fully equipped" youth minister who has all the right qualities and tools to bring kids to Christ. Here again, we are in danger of succumbing to the world's false naming, which tempts us to forget that we are already enough—because we are the beloved of Abba. We continually slip into a kind of spiritual amnesia that drives us into desperate attempts to earn the love and acceptance of our youth, our senior pastors, and our churches through well-attended activities, successful programs, and high-voltage events.

Yet in the temptation story, Jesus points the way through our own deserts of distraction and doubt about our true identity. He shows us our continual need to return with him to the Father, to be reclaimed by the presence and power of God's unconditional love, to hear God say, "Do not fear, for I have redeemed you; I have called you by name, you are mine" (Isaiah 43:1). To be claimed as beloved means to allow the Spirit of Christ to meet us in our fears, our desires, our anger, our lust, and our blindness.

The Christian tradition has long referred to our fallen condition in terms of "sin," pointing to the ways we separate ourselves from God and our brothers and sisters. Perhaps the greatest sin, however, is the sin of self-rejection, of refusing to allow oneself to be named and claimed unconditionally as God's beloved. This refusal results in fear, anxiety, and the constant need to prove one's value—instead of trusting that we are worthy because God has first loved us.

No matter how often we forget our identity as beloved, the Spirit is sent to us to reclaim and heal us of the wounds that drive us into sinful separation from God's love. An essential part of being claimed by the Father is opening to the experience of restoration and healing. After his time of temptation, Jesus receives the healing touch of angels sent to minister to him (Mark 1:13). So too, those of us in youth ministry need to open ourselves to the healing touch of the Spirit who seeks to "salve," or "anoint," those places in us that are broken, restless, and resistant to God's love. This is truly what salvation is all about. As Paul says to the Christians in first-century Rome, "Do not be conformed to this world, but be transformed by the renewing of your minds, so that you may discern what is the will of God—what is good and acceptable and perfect" (12:2). Paul calls followers of Christ—then and now—not to be deceived by the world, but to be "re-minded" continually of who we are as God's beloved and "re-membered" back into the community of the Beloved so that we might truly know how to minister in that love. Like the Roman Christians of Paul's era, we need to return and open ourselves again to the love that heals and reminds us of who we truly are. When we allow God's grace to heal and claim us as beloved, we receive the fruits of the Spirit that God promises—the gifts of joy, peace, and freedom that are the birthright of those called children of God (Galatians 5:22).

Being Sent as God's Beloved

The third key moment for us in the life of Christ is that of being *sent*. This is found most dramatically in the fourth chapter of Luke's gospel, where Jesus begins his public ministry by announcing in his own synagogue in Nazareth his mission of healing and liberation: "The Spirit of the Lord is upon me, because he has anointed me to bring good news to the poor. He has sent me to proclaim release to the captives and recovery of sight to the blind…" (Luke 4:18-19; Isaiah 61:1-2). Jesus, in the power of the Spirit, returns to his own people in Galilee to begin teaching and preaching in their synagogues. After his experience of being named and claimed as God's Beloved, after his trial and temptation in the desert, he moves naturally and spontaneously toward sharing this "good news" with others. The Spirit of God is burning in him, sending him to proclaim this good news to his brothers and sisters, to anoint them with the knowledge of their belovedness, and to free them from the spiritual oppression and blindness that is their condition apart from that powerful awareness of God's love. Jesus later speaks of the sanctifying work of the Holy Spirit as leading and guiding the disciples of Christ into "all truth"—not just doctrinal or moral truth, but the truth of their deepest identity in Christ as beloved (John 16:13-15). The Spirit is working continuously to make us whole and "holy" through the progressive revelation of the fullness of our identity as beloved in Christ.

IMPLICATIONS FOR MINISTRY

What are the youth ministry implications of the sanctifying work of the Spirit? There are three. The first concerns the imperative of entering into a disciplined life in the Spirit. It means attending constantly to the ways in which God's love is present in our lives and our ministries. We know as ministers that we can never give what we have not received. To be sent with Christ as ministers of his love means learning the art (as Christ himself did) of continually receiving God's anointing every day in prayer, Scripture, and the fellowship of believers. It means learning to tune in to what Henri Nouwen called the "inner voice of love" that seeks to reveal our beauty and belovedness in God's eyes and that empowers us to reveal that belovedness to others.

The purpose of spiritual disciplines and contemplative practices such as lighting candles, walking labyrinths, and entering into silence and solitude is to help us create space for God in our lives and ministries. These practices help us attend, discern, and respond to that "still small voice" that whispers our hidden name to us and opens us to the peace of Christ that surpasses all understanding. And this peace is the source of true evangelization. As the great Russian monk St. Seraphim of Sarov put it: "If you alone find inner peace, thousands around you will be saved." When we are in touch with God's joy and peace in us, then we become whole and holy persons. Like living torches we radiate the light and heat of God's compassionate love.

The second implication of our being sent into Spirit-led ministry concerns the need for us to be discerning. Just as Jesus was attentive and responsive to the Spirit who named and claimed him as God's beloved Son, so also must be those who minister in his name. In practical terms, this means our continual acknowledgment that God's Spirit is already present and ministering powerfully in every situation. God's Spirit is already working in the minds, hearts, souls, and bodies of young people—to free them, heal them, and guide them into the truth of their deepest identity and vocation as beloved children of God in Christ.

Looking again at the story of Franny Glass, we might discern the ways in which the Spirit is already present and active in her life: signs like her passion for the Jesus Prayer and her deep resistance at the dullness and banality of life around her. The main priority of youth ministry that flows from this quality of discernment is therefore not for us to *do* anything, but to pray and discern what the *Spirit* is doing in awakening Christ-consciousness—and then act in faithful response to that. The effectiveness of youth ministry thus depends not on our capacity to organize activities but rather on our capacity to attune and align ourselves with the activity of the Holy Spirit within us and our young people in order that they all might bear the fruits of that Spirit.

The third implication of Spirit-led ministry concerns a commitment to accompaniment. To accompany young people on the way of Jesus means to speak to them the very words the Father has spoken to Jesus and to us: "You are my Beloved in whom I take delight. You are a child of God in whom God takes delight." Jean Vanier, the founder of L'Arche communities for the intellectually disabled, once defined love as the capacity within each of us to reveal the beauty of others to themselves. To reveal to other people their own beauty and giftedness is to anoint them in the deepest possible way and liberate them to live the lives of grace, peace, and joy. To embrace and accompany the young people in our lives means revealing their beauty to them and holding onto that image of their beauty for them until they can claim and hold it for themselves. It means supporting them as they search, often desperately, for their own true selves in Christ.

There's nothing wrong with all-night lock-ins and high-voltage activities if they serve ultimately to awaken young people to their deepest identity as beloved and lead them into relationships with others who support them in their growth in Christ. Programs, activities, and events all have a place in this journey of ministry with youth. But what is most essential is the quality of *presence* we bring as ministers who know who we are and whose *we* are. When we are full of the knowledge of our own identity as God's beloved children, then we can freely trust that we are enough and that the Spirit of Christ is working in us and through us to name and claim them as God's own. Recognizing the power of the Spirit to "send" us forth to name and claim others is also an invitation for youth ministers to move from prayer to presence, a presence that seeks to free young persons from their false identities and to "anoint" them with a continuing experience of their own deepest identity as beloved children of God.

BECOMING THE BELOVED: TESTIMONIES

In the Youth Ministry and Spirituality Project, we have seen with our own eyes this process of youth ministers and youth "becoming the beloved." We have heard testimonies like that of Will, who confessed to us, "I've been a youth pastor for 20 years, and I've never heard or felt the gospel preached in this way." Or stories like that of Sarah, who grew up as an adopted child and was long filled with loneliness, shame, and anger. Several months after Sarah attended a summer youth event, her mother approached us and said, "I don't know what happened out there this summer, but my daughter is a different person. It's almost scary. She seems to be at peace now and has only kindness and gratitude for me instead of rage and contempt." We believe Sarah heard her deepest name spoken by the Spirit, put her trust in that voice, and was freed to live the risen life of the beloved. Here are some other testimonies we've received from project participants that speak to the power of this anointing:

"I have learned the words of grace: 'You are my Beloved. You are enough.'"

—WALLACE, YOUTH MINISTER AND DENOMINATIONAL LEADER

"I have heard the Spirit say to me: 'I gave you breath. You are mine…take it in, live it out, unafraid.'"

—LAURIE, ADULT VOLUNTEER

"Yes! Yes! Yes! Of course this is how it is! Loved and celebrated—embraced and cherished. What I knew in my head, felt once in a while in my heart, [is] now moving into my bones. I [have] soaked in it, lavished in it without having to fight the 'Yes, but…' temptation that so often in my life I yielded to."

—PAUL, PASTOR

"This changed my life. I can't say that I walked away committing my life to Jesus, but I did feel love that I thought impossible."

—NATHAN, YOUNG PERSON

In summary, the movement from anxiety-driven youth ministry to Spirit-led youth ministry implies a commitment to attending, discerning, and responding to the deepest cry of both our own hearts and the hearts of our young people to know ourselves as the beloved of God. It requires attentiveness to and alignment with the sanctifying work of the Holy Spirit and growth in a contemplative attitude of openness, receptivity, trust, and surrender. It requires discernment of how the Spirit is present and active within us and the young people we serve. Finally it requires a response of offering our accompaniment or presence to the unique beauty and journey of each young person we walk with. This three-fold participation in God's sanctifying grace is the essence of contemplative youth ministry, and it invites youth ministers to serve as spiritual guides to young people and not just program directors.

A wonderful example of this spiritual guidance is given in Salinger's sequel to the story of Franny and her spiritual breakdown. In his story simply titled "Zooey," published two years later, Salinger continues what he calls his "prose home movie" by exploring the attempt by Franny's elder brother to intervene and respond to her crisis. Franny's brother, Zooey, is also something of a spiritual genius. After a protracted and meandering brotherly chat with Franny about her irritations with "phony" professors and academic culture, Zooey passionately confronts her with the goodness but also the serious implications of her confused and misguided attempts to "see God" through the practice of the Jesus Prayer:

I mean it, Franny, I'm being serious. When you don't see Jesus for exactly what he was, you miss the whole point of the Jesus Prayer. If you don't understand Jesus you can't understand his prayer...The Jesus Prayer has one aim, and one aim only. To endow the person who says it with Christ-Consciousness. Not to set up some little cozy, holier-than-thou trysting place with some sticky adorable divine personage who'll take you in his arms and relieve you of all your duties and make all your nasty *Weltschmerzen* and Professor Tuppers go away and never come back. And by God, if you have intelligence enough to see that—and you do—and yet you refuse to see it, then you are misusing it to ask for a world full of dolls and saints and no Professor Tuppers.[19]

Quite beyond the critique Salinger is leveling here against insipid piety and sentimentalism as well as instant mysticism, there is a larger lesson to be learned about the perils of a young person's spiritual quest and the blessing of spiritual guidance. In the characters of Franny and Zooey, Salinger takes for granted the spiritual intelligence and longings of young people and urges us to respond to them seriously. He challenges us to recognize young people's profound need for relationships with adults who are spiritually alive and available to accompany them on a disciplined path, even if that involves confrontation. Zooey perceives (in a way that Franny has not yet understood) that the only purpose of spiritual disciplines like the Jesus Prayer is to open us to Christ-Consciousness. That ultimately implies openness to the power of offering an unconditional love that sees others as beloved, in spite of their oddness, phoniness, or ugliness. Salinger deftly encapsulates the whole meaning of the contemplative life in these two stories, challenging those who minister to youth to pay attention to the "one thing necessary." (See Luke 10:42.)

[19] Salinger, p. 172.

FROM THEOLOGY TO SPIRITUALITY: CREATING SPACE FOR GOD

A final question remains: How is contemplative ministry actually practiced? What practices, processes, and structures are involved? How does it work as a spirituality?

Spirituality is now a much-worn term that simply refers to how human beings, young or old, respond to their desire for relatedness to God. It is about how we channel this desire, the disciplines and habits we choose in our everyday lives to be in conscious or unconscious relationship to this "holy longing."[20] Spirituality is more than spiritual disciplines, prayer practices, and religious rituals. It encompasses how persons eat, sleep, work, and play, as well as how we relate to ourselves, others, and the world in light of our deep and all-pervasive longing for relatedness to the Holy. Seen in this way, spirituality is not an option. It serves the crucial purpose of leading us to greater integration or disintegration within our bodies, minds, and souls and in the way we are related to God, others, and the world around us.

As we've noted, the Youth Ministry and Spirituality Project's mission was to encourage a Spirit-led approach to youth ministry that is *attentive* to God's presence, discerning of the Holy Spirit, and committed to accompanying young persons on the way of Jesus. Over the course of the project, we developed and refined a foundational document that came to be known as the YMSP "charter." This charter specifies seven key disciplines that inform a contemplative approach to youth ministry. Drawn from the ancient tradition of the church's common life, these principles were reclaimed in the project simply as means of grace—ways to open our minds, hearts, souls, and bodies to "create space for God" and free youth ministers and young persons for greater availability and responsiveness to the power of the Spirit naming, claiming, and sending them forth as God's beloved.

[20] Ronald Rolheiser, *The Holy Longing: The Search for a Christian Spirituality* (Doubleday, 1999), 7.

You'll find the seven principles of the YMSP Charter printed in their entirety in the next chapter, and they'll be explored in more detail in section 2 of the book. Here, I simply want to look briefly at how the seven disciplines described in our charter function together to incarnate a spirituality that is *attentive, discerning, and accompanying.*

Disciplines of Attentiveness

A contemplative approach to youth ministry focuses its attention on God's presence. The essential meaning of the term *contemplative* is found in its Latin etymology as a compound of the terms *con* (with) and *templus* (in the temple). The act of contemplation was originally understood to mean marking out or clearing sacred space for careful attention and observation of the mysteries of God. Attention builds awareness; attentiveness to God cultivates an awareness of God's presence within and around us in every moment. This implies a fundamental change in the focus of our attention within the life and ministry of the church. We move away from anxious concern with creating entertaining programming or doctrinally sound instruction and toward a peaceful and prayerful attention to God's presence in the lives of young persons.

We consider two disciplines essential in cultivating attentiveness to God's presence: Sabbath and prayer. A contemplative approach to youth ministry requires that we create space for God through the practice of Sabbath rest. A life that honors **Sabbath** rest keeps us and our youth more in touch with our own hearts and souls, more aware of the Spirit of God, and more available for relationships of love.

Similarly, attentiveness is cultivated through the discipline of **prayer**. We have focused particularly on silence and *contemplative* prayer that invites us to become more open and aware of God's presence at each moment. As Ashley, a 15-year-old in our project put it, "Silence can be so powerful. It's important not to fill it up with noise."

Disciplines of Discernment

As noted earlier, our approach to ministry is grounded in a trust that the Holy Spirit is eager to guide and transform us. Through the practice of **discernment**, we seek to listen and respond to that call in our lives and ministry with youth. Cultivating contemplative awareness is intended to sensitize the ministering community to the gifts, needs, and aspirations of each person, especially the young, and to help them discern their own sense of call.

We also believe it is essential that our efforts to discern God's leading in our ministries be practiced within a **covenant community** of disciples. Discernment has always been practiced in the context of the whole church listening for the common sense of the faithful gathered in Christ's name. No single charismatic leader has all the visions or solutions. Nor do they have all the responsibility for the souls of young people resting on their shoulders alone. The purpose of the group is to name, claim, and discern together how it is called to serve its young people. By sharing in this mission together, there is a possible shift from duty and obligation to wonderment and solidarity. As one youth director told us after forming her community: "I have watched these people change from people who felt obligated to help, to people with conviction and a passion to be part of this spiritual discipline called youth ministry."

One critical way that discernment and covenant community take shape within the ministry is through the "liturgy of discernment" (see appendix 5). This liturgy is a format for group meetings that seeks to create a sacred space and time for sharing and prayer. The liturgy progresses through a sequence of movements in which participants first listen to God's Word (through practices like *lectio divina* or the

Ignatian awareness examen), then respond to the question of how the community is called to minister in the light of their experience and God's Word. Sometimes this may involve the planning of a project or program, or a concrete response to a situation among the youth in their community. The aim is to create a space in which the ministering community is freed to become more fully aware, available, and obedient to God and to how God is calling the ministry to respond at any given moment in the power of the Spirit.

Disciplines of Accompaniment

Finally, a contemplative approach to youth ministry focuses on discipleship through adult **accompaniment** of young people. We encourage adults to support youth in the Christian faith by joining young people in living the way of authentic discipleship. The image of Christ on the road to Emmaus is helpful in understanding the mystery of accompaniment. The story reveals a scene of confusion, disorientation, and even depression that is close in many ways to the inner lives of young persons who are seeking to find their way. It is an image of Christ traveling silently with them, listening patiently but also teaching with authority. Jesus models a ministry of intimate relationship, of walking with them in the same direction, of guidance, and of "sounding out" the personhood and condition of the disciples.

There is a mutuality necessary in the process of accompaniment. Adult companions of youth are invited to allow themselves to be moved by them, to receive their kindness, and ultimately to be transformed by their presence and giftedness. One young man told us during a retreat, "As a young person I am used to feeling helpless, like it doesn't really matter what I do. Laying my hands upon Adam (a youth minister) and praying for him meant so much." We have learned that not only do young people need healing in their lives, but they also have gifts and want to offer them to others, including adults. In order to receive these gifts, adults must seek to allow their hearts to be awakened to this mutuality of presence that is possible in ministry.

To accompany young persons is also to create a space of **hospitality** for youth within the larger faith community. This means attending to and calling forth the gifts of young people within the church community, finding ways to promote their full participation and integration into the community through play, fellowship, worship, and governance. Through their prayer and their own witness, accompaniment also means to model a more whole way of being, seeing, and knowing in faith.

THE FRUIT OF CONTEMPLATIVE MINISTRY: AUTHENTIC ACTION

The ultimate goal of the "contemplative" approach to youth ministry is not contemplation, discernment, accompaniment, or even community. These are not ends in themselves, but means to the larger end of inviting and supporting young persons in following Jesus. Communal practices of Sabbath, prayer, discernment, and accompaniment find their fulfillment in the seventh principle: **authentic action** that makes visible the forgiveness, mercy, and peace of God on earth. It is action that flows, like that of Jesus, out of attentiveness, discernment, and obedient responsiveness to God's love.

The authentic action inspired by a contemplative approach to youth ministry is not a joyless Puritanism that purges all fun, delight, and celebration. Nor is it a pseudomonastic solemnity that experiences the Holy only in silent prayer and candlelight. Joy, laughter, and wonder are also fruits of the Spirit, and any authentic discipleship includes times of playing together, not just praying together. The way of Jesus leads, in his own words, to the joy of the "wedding feast"—an image of gathering in festive celebration.

Contemplative youth ministry has plenty of room for noisy celebration, music, and even silliness. It holds the possibility for any form of action that flows from and expresses an awareness of the fullness of God's life and love. Such love drives out all fear (1 John 4) and makes space for the whole range of human activity and expression. It stands in stark contrast to the anxiety and boredom that can compel youth ministry toward entertainment instead of authentic communion and celebration.

There are formidable challenges to authentic action in youth ministry. Church cultures and ministry systems have been heavily colonized by a business and consumer mentality. Nearly every minister faces a host of pressing demands that seem to leave little time and energy for prayer, sharing, and discernment. The spirit of the dominant culture teaches parents and teachers to be busy and productive to the point of exhaustion, and to expect the same of their children and students. We found that even the most discerning ministers in our project suffered the effects of extreme stress and fatigue.

The influences of individualism, consumerism, and competitiveness in the dominant culture make the intentional spiritual formation of youth more difficult—but also more critical. In the face of the anxiety and pressure young people now contend with, a contemplative approach to youth ministry invites young people and those who accompany them to something radically different. It's an invitation to walk with Jesus on the journey of the Beloved—a journey in which we open ourselves to hearing the still, small voice of God's Spirit, which calls us by name, claims us in God's love, and sends us forth to anoint others in mercy and compassion.

The Youth Ministry and Spirituality Project Charter: A Summary of the Principles of Contemplative Youth Ministry

Over the eight years of the Youth Ministry and Spirituality Project, we developed the following summary of the principles that support a contemplative approach to youth ministry.[21] Within the project this summary came to be known as our "charter," since these seven principles represent a concise articulation of the project's spirituality, pedagogy, and particular approach to contemplative youth ministry.

We believe these principles outline the way in which ministry to youth needs to be undertaken if it is to address the yearnings of the adolescent soul. These principles are not just abstract ideals or hopes, but real struggles that each church within the project faced in seeking to create youth ministries that are more attentive to God and discerning of the Spirit. (See appendix 6 for suggestions for further reading on each of these principles.)

1. **SABBATH.** A contemplative approach to youth ministry is grounded in a Christian community committed to the sacred balance between work and rest. Just as Jesus led a life of simplicity with times for rest, solitude, and silence (Matthew 14:22-23), we also are committed to helping Christian communities find rest and balance in

---

[21] These principles were written by Michael Hryniuk and Mark Yaconelli.

a hyperactive culture. A life that honors Sabbath rest helps us to be more in touch with our heart and soul, more aware of the Spirit of God, and more available for relationships of love. Youth blossom in the midst of adults who know how to savor life through a Sabbath rhythm of rest, work, and play. Companions of the project seek to maintain this simplicity and sacred balance in their own lives and ministry.

2. **PRAYER.** A contemplative approach to youth ministry is rooted in desire for intimacy with God in Christ through a life of prayer. Just as Jesus' life and ministry were grounded in a desire to be in complete union with God (Mark 6:46; John 17:1ff.), we also seek to ground all life and ministry in a prayerful relationship with God in Christ. We practice and teach many forms of prayer but are particularly committed to regular periods of *contemplative* prayer in order to be healed, inspired, and guided by the power of the Holy Spirit. Contemplative prayer invites us to attend to God's mystical presence dwelling silently within the depths of our hearts, opening our whole being to ongoing conversion and freeing us for an ever-deepening awareness of that presence in all persons, things, and events of our lives. Companions of the project seek to practice contemplative prayer with Scripture each day as well as at regular times with their communities.

3. **COVENANT COMMUNITY.** A contemplative approach to youth ministry is practiced within a covenant community of Christian disciples. Just as Jesus called and ministered with others in a community of spiritual companions (Matthew 10:1-4), we also encourage, support, and practice small covenant groups who sense a common call to spiritual growth through Christian living and ministry to young people. These groups offer prophetic witness to a way of life that is creatively resistant to the seductions of the market culture and the

dullness that can inhabit Christian institutions. Companions of the project commit to meeting regularly in covenant communities for sharing, prayer, Scripture study, and discernment in the service of their ministry to young people.

4 **ACCOMPANIMENT.** A contemplative approach to youth ministry is focused on discipleship through the accompaniment of young people. Just as Jesus sought to form disciples through a relationship of love and an invitation to follow him (Matthew 4:18-22), we also seek to initiate young persons into mature Christian faith through relationships with elders who join them in living the way of authentic discipleship. Young people are searching for spiritual guides who are alive in Christ to help reveal to them their deepest identity and beauty as beloved daughters and sons of God and to assist them in discerning their unique gifts and vocations in the service of God's reign. Companions of the project seek to be compassionate elders in the faith who seek out regular accompaniment for themselves and who actively model the disciplines, virtues, and fruits of the spiritual life. They offer youth friendship, guidance, and listening hearts as they make the passage through adolescence into spiritual maturity, "to the measure of the full stature of Christ" (Ephesians 4:13).

5. **DISCERNMENT.** A contemplative approach to youth ministry is guided by discernment. Just as Jesus prayed to know and follow God's desire (Luke 22:39-44), we also seek to discern and respond faithfully to the call of the Holy Spirit in our lives and ministry with youth. We practice and teach the disciplines of individual and group discernment so as to be fully available and responsive to the movement of God's grace in our covenant communities, allowing anxiety-driven youth ministry to become Spirit-led youth ministry. Companions of the project seek to learn and practice the spiritual disciplines of discern-

ment as the basis for opening, listening to, and responding to God's call in youth ministry.

6. **HOSPITALITY.** A contemplative approach to youth ministry seeks to welcome, bless, and joyfully integrate all young people into the whole church community. Just as Jesus exhorted his disciples to "let the children come" (Mark 9:35-37; 10:13-16), we also seek the full inclusion of young people and the many gifts they bring into every dimension of church life: worship, teaching, proclamation, fellowship, and service. Young persons often suffer marginalization in the church and the pain of not feeling accepted and appreciated for who they are. As elders in the covenant community, adult companions of the project seek not only to accompany young people individually on the way of Jesus, but also to advocate for them in finding their place as fellow ministers of the gospel in the larger community of the church and its mission in the world.

7. **AUTHENTIC ACTION.** A contemplative approach to youth ministry seeks to engage youth and adults in authentic actions that reflect God's mercy, justice, and peace. Just as Jesus came out of prayer and solitude to heal the sick, welcome the outcast, and celebrate with friends (Luke 4:18-19, John 12:1ff.), so we also seek to cooperate with the Holy Spirit in a way of life, rooted in the Beatitudes, that witnesses to Christ's love, passion, and joy. Communal practices of Sabbath, prayer, discernment, and accompaniment find their fulfillment in actions with youth that make visible the gifts of the Holy Spirit. Young people desire opportunities to participate in Christ's healing and liberating activity within the world. Companions of the project seek to support youth and adults in becoming instruments of God's grace who creatively reveal the reality of God's love and courageously resist the principalities and powers that oppress life.

We found that these seven principles of contemplative youth ministry build upon one another. It took a sense of Sabbath time and rest before youth ministers and congregations could allow themselves to engage in prayer and community. Prayer and community provided the grounding for developing discerning programs and relationships with youth. These relationships invited a greater sense of hospitality within the larger congregation and encouraged actions within the ministry that were authentic and reflective of the life of Jesus. The flow of these principles is best expressed in the following chart:

Contemplative Ministry Cycle

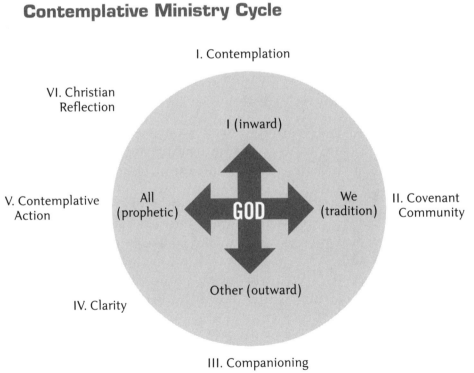

I. **Contemplation.** Sabbath and prayer help us pay attention to the presence of God in our lives and the life of the ministry.

II. **Covenant Community.** We join with others to tend the Spirit, deepen our discernment of God's call, and share the burdens of ministry.

III. **Companioning.** We move out of prayer and community to accompany youth. Youth draw us out of prayer into service and care.

IV. **Clarity.** As we pray and relate to youth, we begin to gain clarity as to how the Holy Spirit is calling us to act. This is the moment for discerning how (programs, relationships, activities?) we are called to minister with youth.

V. **Contemplative Action.** Grounded in God and community, we begin to take action either on behalf of youth or with youth in service to a hurting world. Our programs and ministries are developed at this stage.

VI. **Christian Reflection.** We reflect on our actions in light of Scripture and our Christian tradition. We identify how the Spirit is moving or blocked through our programs and actions.

I. **Contemplation.** We start the cycle again. Returning to the Source—offering the ministry, ourselves, and our actions up to God. We begin again, waiting on God for guidance and renewal.

The Inner Tensions: As we live into this ministry cycle, our prayer, community life, relationships with youth, and ministry activities deepen, growing closer and closer to God's vision for the ministry. Over time, we may notice various tensions that break us open, bringing new life. There is the tension between the "I" and the "Thou"—my individual prayer life and my desire to move out of myself toward young people. We may also notice that as we increase our interactions with youth, we are in greater need of silence and prayer.

There is also the tension between the ministry team, the covenant community that tends the tradition of the congregation, and the prophetic actions that arise in relation to young people. Ministries with youth will inevitably challenge the traditions and practices of the sponsoring congregation.

These are the tensions that make up the Christian life—between silence and service, between the worshipping community and the suffering world. As we live these tensions, our own agendas are broken down. We become more aware of and available to God's vision within our ministries as well as our individual and collective lives.

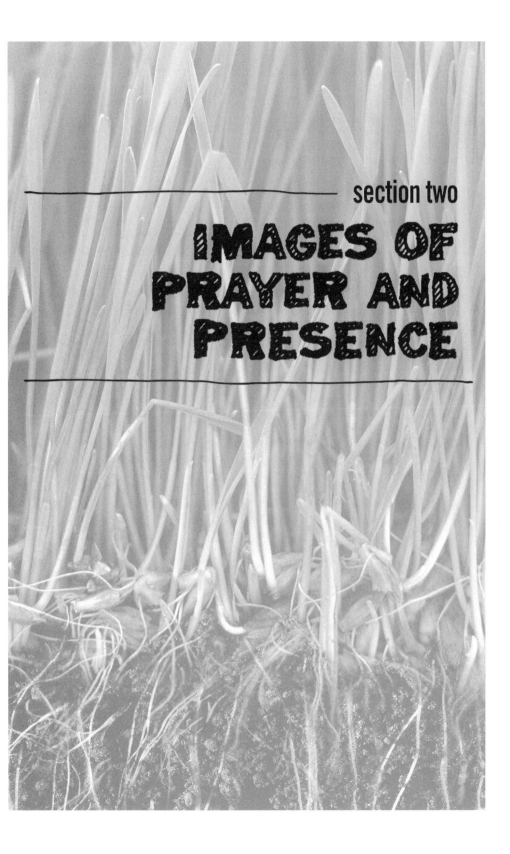

IMAGES OF PRAYER AND PRESENCE

This section presents the stories of four congregations aspiring to practice contemplative youth ministry. In 2001, we invited five scholars to help us investigate and observe the work of the project. Each scholar, as well as the project directors, was asked to explore one element of the project's charter and describe how this particular element of contemplative youth ministry took shape within a particular congregation. Four of those observations are presented here.

Chapter 5 is the story, as I observed it, of The Woodlands Christian Church outside Houston, Texas, as it struggled to integrate a sense of *Sabbath* within its youth ministry. In chapter 6 Doug Frank explores the idea of *covenant community* within a Presbyterian church in Eugene, Oregon. Chapter 7 presents Kathleen Cahalan's reflections on the practice of *discernment* as a foundational element in St. Paul's Episcopal Church in Richmond, Virginia. Finally, Frank Rogers seeks to observe the principle of *authentic action* within the youth ministry of Lake Chelan Lutheran Church in Lake Chelan, Washington.

The Upper Room:
Sabbath in Youth Ministry
by Mark Yaconelli

A contemplative approach to youth ministry is grounded in a Christian commu-
nity committed to the sacred balance between work and rest. Just as Jesus led a
life of simplicity with times for rest, solitude, and silence (Matthew 14:22-23),
we also are committed to helping Christian communities find rest and balance
in a hyperactive culture. A life that honors Sabbath rest helps us to be more in
touch with our heart and soul, more aware of the Spirit of God, and more avail-
able for relationships of love. Youth blossom in the midst of adults who know
how to savor life through a Sabbath rhythm of rest, work, and play. Compan-
ions of the project seek to maintain this simplicity and sacred balance in their
own lives and ministry.

—YMSP Charter, point 1

Mabel warned me this would happen. Now, in the quiet of the darkened room, all I hear is her breathing. I open my eyes and follow the sound of her breath. She sits tucked between a brown vinyl couch and a shabby mustard-yellow love seat. Her head is tilted back against the youth room wall, arms slung loose, hands crumpled on her lap. Mabel's face is relaxed, her mouth slightly agape. But it's the breathing that's the real sign. Mabel is sleeping.

A SIESTA IN THE WOODLANDS

Just outside the George Bush Intercontinental Airport in Houston, Texas, youth pastor Brent Parker pulls up in his cherry red pickup, steps out, and greets me, "Welcome to our A.D.D. community!"

I throw my bags in the truck bed, and we head west toward "The Woodlands," the upscale Houston suburb where Brent lives and ministers. The plan is to meet his wife and 10-month-old son for dinner at a BBQ joint. As we drive I'm a bit surprised by Brent's relaxed and quiet demeanor. He asks about my family and work life, gently nodding and making eye contact to let me know he's listening. He laughs easily and allows space within our conversation.

I can't help but recall the first time I met Brent three years earlier. He had invited himself to accompany a regional staff member of the Disciples of Christ who was picking me up from the airport and driving me to a speaking event. I sat in the backseat; Brent sat shotgun, with his head permanently craned backward, drilling me with question after question. He spoke like a caffeine addict as he grilled me about one youth ministry topic after another, never really hearing (nor appearing interested) in my responses.

Yet now, riding in his truck, he seemed a different person. Present. Calm. Listening. What had happened to Brent over these three years?

A few miles from the exit to The Woodlands we get a call from Brent's wife, Kori. She can't find the restaurant. Brent does his best to guide her, but his instructions are vague ("You know when you pass that one overpass...well it's not right there but a little further...it's like the second turn...") Within five minutes of leaving the interstate we too are lost. Brent chuckles, "I've lived here five years and I still continue to get lost. Every street and shopping center looks the same."

With trees bordering most properties and street signs outlawed, it's easy to see how people get disoriented. The terrain is level with pine, oak, and sweet gum trees four feet deep along the main roads and properties. Homes, businesses, and other landmarks are concealed, so the town feels like a hedged maze of meandering blacktop. County ordinance requires that all roads and streets bend—so trees are always visible, creating a sense of backwoods living rather than a carefully engineered Houston suburb. This would be the first of three times in which local residents would get lost driving me around their community.

Built in 1974 by the Mitchell Energy and Development Corporation as a response to urban growth, The Woodlands is a town of professionals hosting more than 161 companies, 6 "award-winning" golf courses, and a full-scale resort. Manicured parks and community walkways are well kept. Shopping and eating areas, all from major chains, are conveniently located. Homes are grouped in "villages" with names like Grogan's Mill, Panther Creek, and Woodsedge. Just as the chamber of commerce describes, it's a "master-planned community"—and in many ways it is "master-controlled." There is a set palate of colors that owners are permitted to use on their homes. Youth ministry volunteer John Frey once received a citation for putting a yellow, green, red, and blue tarp on his daughter's backyard playhouse—the tarp was not within the range of approved colors for the community. Brent's wife, Kori, told me of a citation they received because they kept their garbage can on the side of the house—homeowners are required to keep garbage cans out of sight.

The trees, walkways, and twisting roads are comforting, tranquil, and appealing. Yet there is something disconcerting about the careful orchestration of homes, parks, businesses, and trees. Brent, who grew up in the racially mixed ("I was the only white kid on my high school basketball team") working-class town of Beaumont, tells me, "The story of this town is the story of the *haves*." Maybe that's what's troubling me—my sense that the *have-nots* are missing.

The Woodlands Christian Church (TWCC) is one of the few upbeat stories in the struggling denomination of the Christian Church (Disciples of Christ). The congregation is made up of mostly white, educated members of the professional class—managers, developers, engineers, and financial administrators. It's been one of the fastest developing churches within the denomination, growing from just 85 members in the early 1990s to more than 600 currently. The expansion was primarily due to the efforts of the church's charismatic senior pastor, David Emery. When I met David three years earlier, he was even more hyperactive than Brent Parker. Working somewhere between 70 and 80 hours a week, David began utilizing revivals, meticulously managed worship services, and hundreds of hours of personal contact to create an energy and excitement that drew the current membership.

According to Associate Pastor and current Interim Pastor Ron Sumter, the church under David's leadership became a highly productive center of activity. "The church was a mirror of Houston culture. Everything was "Go! Go! Go!" David put great pressure on Brent, the church leadership, and especially on himself to produce results. The outcome was that people came in droves."

One year before my visit to the church, David Emery had left TWCC to serve at a megachurch in Louisville, Kentucky. Approximately 150 church members disappeared once he left the congregation. "You could almost feel the energy coming off of David," Pastor Ron explains. "People were drawn to the church because of David, and when he left there was very little allegiance by a significant number of church members to the church or even the faith."

Considering the churchgoing habits of this Bible Belt city, TWCC is considered a small church. One church elder told me it is the smallest church within The Woodlands. After a little investigating I discovered that, within just 10 minutes of the church, there were at least four other congregations that all boasted memberships greater than three thousand.

When Pastor Emery, Brent, and the church leadership expressed an interest in participating in the Youth Ministry and Spirituality Project, it seemed to be a unique challenge. The church was growing and full of activity. The question was whether YMSP's emphasis on Sabbath-living could take root in such a busy place.

RECLAIMING THE SABBATH

Author and former pastor Wayne Muller once said that in the United States, illness has become our Sabbath.[22] When my friend was diagnosed with brain cancer at 46, time suddenly became a precious gift to her. She stopped wearing a watch. She spent mornings lying out in the sun and afternoons napping. She stood in the backyard, remarking on the changing sky and the colors of the trees. She invited friends over for champagne and chocolate. She took slow walks to church, stopping to talk with people and admire flowers. She took pleasure in life.

Muller was right. It seems we give ourselves permission to rest, to receive life, to enjoy creation, to share good food with friends, to be grateful and savor our lives only when we're stricken with a terminal illness. Sabbath, however, is not just for the sick. It is a commandment that all people of God take time to stop our activity, step away from our roles, and enjoy our lives.

[22] Wayne Muller, *Sabbath* (Bantam, 1999).

I have memories of Sunday afternoons in my small town when stores closed and life slowed, but most young people I encounter are growing up without any sense of Sabbath time. They're growing up without Sundays. Instead there's a seamless transition in the pace and quality of life from the marketplace to the worship space. Within most Christian communities, Sabbath has become a well-kept secret or, worse, a blatantly ignored commandment. Sabbath is a retreat from the striving, toiling, and scheming of our active lives. Rabbi Abraham Heschel once called it "a sanctuary in time."[23] Sabbath is a letting go of our need to produce and perform—an opportunity for our spirits, as well as our bodies, to be refreshed and renewed. In Sabbath we're given permission to simply "be." We're invited to trust that we (and those we serve) are loved for who we are, not for what we do. To keep the Sabbath is to be reminded that life, even our spiritual life, is a gift. In a time when people are stressed out, overworked, overstimulated, and pressured to do more, the practice of Sabbath may best communicate the good news of Jesus.

The Youth Ministry and Spirituality Project sought to form youth ministers, pastors, and youth ministry volunteers in a deeper awareness of Sabbath-living. Brent Parker, along with a number of other project participants, attended weeklong formation events that focused on Sabbath-living. Long periods of rest were scheduled throughout each week. Lectures were given on the history and practice of Sabbath-keeping. Participants discussed the busyness of adults in North American culture, and the toll this has taken on children and young people. But after three years of formation, the question still remained: Is it possible to reclaim a sense of Sabbath in our congregations and communities of faith? Is it possible to reclaim a sense of time as an abundant gift from God rather than a scarce commodity? Can Christians who live within such a hyperactive culture make Sabbath a central experience in the spiritual formation of young people?

[23] Abraham Joshua Heschel, *The Sabbath* (Farrar, Straus and Giroux, 1975).

When we finally enter the restaurant, I'm hit with the smell of mesquite and hickory smoke. Brent's wife and son are already seated. Both Brent and Kori encourage me to order a platter with grilled beef, turkey, and pork ribs. The dish includes a choice of two vegetables: "beans" or "coleslaw." Feeling my prostate expand, I politely refuse.

A former bartender and basketball coach, Brent is the first full-time youth minister for The Woodlands Christian Church. In the past, church members often compared him to the church's previous senior pastor, David Emery. Lately, however, people say they've noticed a difference in Brent. I ask him to explain…

"I used to minister out of a fear-and-anxiety model. Everything was win or lose. I was focused on performance: 'How many kids turned out? Did the lesson go over?' There really was no difference between the mode in which I did ministry and the mode in which I did bartending and coaching. Everything was about efficiency and performance. The result was that in my first two years as a youth minister I was never home by 7 p.m.

"I remember one night having this great youth meeting. We had a good turnout of kids. My lesson went over well. Singing was good. I came home after that meeting upbeat and excited to share the good news with my wife. It was after 8:00 when I got home, and as soon as I walked in the door, I started telling her about everything that had happened. Her immediate response was, 'I hate church.' That's when I began to realize I was working too many hours—around 80 a week—and it was hurting my marriage."

Kori nods her head and smiles at me. Brent looks over at his son Caedmon and smiles. Caedmon shoves an impossible handful of mashed potatoes into his mouth. I shift the conversation to Brent's sense of God during this time of overwork. He tells me that before he entered the project, he felt God was a very demanding presence with high expectations—a taskmaster that was never satisfied, always wanting more. Consequently Brent says his focus wasn't "to be close to God, it was to *please* God."

I ask him how his sense of God has changed. "Well, for the first time I'm thinking about grace. My transformation can be embodied by that one word—*grace*. Through the principles and practices of the project I've found this new ability and awareness to give and receive God's grace. I've discovered that spirituality isn't something you work to obtain, but a part of our being that must be found and then appreciated." He pauses to reflect. "It still feels like God has high expectations, and yet at the same time it feels like at any one moment God is satisfied with me, like he's constantly saying, 'If you stopped right now, you've done enough."

When I ask him how this change came about he tells me, "This approach to ministry begins and ends with the realization that each of us is a beloved child of God. When I start from this knowledge or understanding, the anxieties and fears of my call are somewhat eased."

Through the Project's encouragement Brent began a daily practice of contemplative prayer, found a spiritual director to meet with regularly, and started listening more to people and the Spirit of God. But he tells me of the difficulty in making this shift in priorities. He often feels like he's moving against the stream—the busyness that seems ingrained in the community and church culture. "This church is filled with high-powered people who approach church the same way they approach their businesses—they focus on efficiency, productivity. It's easy for me to get caught up in the same thing. I'm ADD, and so I'm tempted to get busy. I need time to slow down and rest. These times of prayer and just stopping my mind and activity have become a great gift to me."

Out of these Sabbath moments Brent's sense of time has shifted. "I've really slowed down. I do less. I delegate more. And really, it's not just that I've slowed down, time itself has begun to slow." As time slows, he tells me, he's begun to develop more gratitude for the little things within his ministry: "I no longer get stressed out about a low turnout at a youth event. Instead, I feel grateful for each kid that does show up—even if it's just a handful."

Brent tries to share this new sense of time with others in his ministry. "Now when people come in to talk with me, I move out from behind my desk and sit on the couch so people know I'm not in a hurry...that I have time for them. I'm slower to answer questions and more ready to listen. I feel like I have this space in me for other people. There's this naked emptiness that I bring when I'm with someone, and I've found people really appreciate this kind of space and presence."

I prod, "But isn't there a drawback to 'slowing down?' Aren't there tasks that get neglected, programs that have to be cut, and dwindling numbers of kids?"

"Yes," Brent replies, looking troubled, "I have to say that sometimes I feel guilty about my priorities around time. I sometimes feel like I need to be doing more, connecting with kids more. Working within the hours the church pays me to work means I see kids less; I harass them to come to church a lot less and so fewer kids come. I worry about that sometimes.

"There's also this new sense of pain, because trying to practice Sabbath is in such direct contrast to the culture—and even the culture of our church. I know life is richer when we slow down. But this creates a lot of conflict. Most of the church community can't be slowed, and it's the same for the kids. Most young people experience time as being scarce. There just isn't enough time—too many activities...I feel compassion for them."

He turns and looks over at his wife and baby. "But now I'm home most nights by dinner time, and with a new baby, I'm really glad I've made this change."

THE UPPER ROOM

The youth room at The Woodlands Christian Church is an anomaly in the recently remodeled church building. The "Upper Room," as it's referred to by youth and youth leaders, is painted a shimmering Mediterranean blue, quite unlike the clean white and barren drywall that covers most of the church's hallways and classrooms. When I ask Brent about the dramatic color, he tells me to look closely at the sole wall hanging. I gaze carefully at a large embroidery of the Last Supper. Jesus and the disciples sit at a low rectangular table that opens to the viewer. Behind the seated figures appear four tan and cream tapestries that seem suspended in air, hinting at a sort of makeshift enclosure. Between these tapestries lies an open iridescent blue. It takes me a moment or two to make the connection between the blue in the artwork and the painted walls of the youth room. "We want this space to feel like a continuation of the Last Supper. We matched the walls of the room with the image from the Last Supper to give us the feeling that we're in the upper room with Jesus."

I'm struck by Brent's sense of youth group as a continuation of the upper room. I turn again to the image on the wall. The upper room is a place of retreat, a place of Sabbath. The disciples sit leisurely with Jesus, eating and conversing. Their bodies are reclined, their gaze turned receptively toward their teacher. Looking at the picture I remember that Jesus will soon kneel and wash the feet of each of his friends. He will offer them comfort and pray for their safety. It is a place of humility, where Peter and Judas are challenged to look truthfully at whom they are becoming. It's also a place of spiritual intimacy in which Jesus invites his friends to share not only bread and wine but also his deepest identity and mission in the world. It is a place of hospitality even to those who will reject or betray him. It's a place for preparation, a place for rest and renewal before engaging the powers that seek to destroy life. The upper room is a place for Sabbath.

The following Sunday morning, I'm sitting in the "Upper Room" surrounded by 28 unnaturally quiet teenagers. Five minutes earlier the group was full of horseplay and lighthearted conversation. Then Brent called them to attention, introduced me, and asked all of the adult volunteers to leave the room. Now the young people sit still, staring and sizing me up.

I feel like an overeager substitute teacher. I'm interested in whether they are being affected by the youth ministry's concentration on Sabbath-living, yet I realize that my zeal to hear from them might make them hesitant to respond. I take an indirect approach and ask them to tell me about life in The Woodlands.

"People have too much money here," a bushy-headed freshman responds. "It's not good for us. We're all C.O.D.—Cash On Demand." Most nod heads, although one young woman disagrees and says that her family is struggling to make ends meet. "There's a lot of 'at-risk behavior,'" says another young man in a schoolmarm voice. Some students giggle. "But it's true," responds a senior dressed in slacks, a button-down shirt, and a worn baseball cap. "Our school is full of drugs. There are lots of parties and lots of drinking."

When I ask them why, they're silent. Then a baby-faced 16-year-old girl with midriff exposed says, "It's because a lot of kids are bitter." The group quiets down. I ask her to say more. "It's because we're, like, totally left on our own." I sense the group energizing around her comment. "Do others feel the same way?"

"Totally," 15-year-old Marcus chimes in. "The more money, the more your parents are gone, which means they're more lenient, which means you're more at risk." He pauses. "I've never even met the dads of my five best friends. The more money they make, the less they see them."

Evan, a wiry freshman, joins in. "Parents are busy and kids are busy. The result is that parents don't get into your life. They don't ask you what you're doing. It kind of makes you mad...like nobody cares, and you start doing crazy things."

"We don't all make bad decisions," Michael counters. "My dad's gone for a week at a time, every other week. I could've started doing bad stuff, but instead I started coming to this youth group—and I mostly just come on my own."

I'm touched by the loneliness that seems to underlie their responses. I'm interested to hear their impressions of the church and whether they are similar to their experiences of the community at large. The group becomes reflective. R. C., a junior lineman on the high school football team, speaks up. "Church isn't like any other thing I do. It's like a siesta every time I come to church." Many in the group nod heads. "Yeah, it's like our Hawaii," asserts another girl who is resting her head on the shoulder of the boy next to her. Sarah, a tall, composed senior adds, "When I come to church it's like time stops. You can be yourself and forget the outside pressures. It's relaxing to be at church." I ask if this is everyone's experience of the church. The response is a boisterous "No!" Amanda explains, "It's not like that for the adults. The rest of the church is still pretty busy. But at youth group it's different. I think for us church is a getaway."

When I ask what the adults are like who serve in the youth ministry, a genuine sense of affection comes across from the group. Evan says, "If Brent, or Ron (the interim pastor), or John (one of the adult volunteers) was preaching a sermon and I raised my hand, they would stop the service and come over and sit by me just to answer my question. That's how much they care about us."

"They're goofy and funny and really easy to talk to," Sarah articulates. "They don't say things to emphasize their greater experience and wisdom, but share their downfalls, struggles, and thoughts with us so we can really see how similar we are to them. They don't have all the answers, and we don't expect them to. They are there to help us out, guide us along so we can learn more about religion in our own way...I think they learn a lot from us, too. The most important thing is that we can talk freely with them and share pretty much anything with them without feeling like they'll look down on us in any way."

She pauses, then adds, "It's not all about the traditional Sunday school stuff. These relationships have formed from random conversations about topics unrelated to religion, time we've spent playing games—basketball, board games—eating together, and things like that."

"The adults treat us different here," a sophomore female contributes. "The youth have a large spot in this congregation. We're treated with respect. There is this understanding that the front row of the church is for young people, and I think it makes us all feel valued. Some Sundays we'll have new people come who don't know the rule and they'll sit in the front row. Someone always comes up to them immediately and tells them, 'That row is for the youth.' If there isn't enough room, we'll like all pile together and sit on each other's laps or on the floor in front of the row. It just makes us feel special."

R. C. adds, "The adults in the youth ministry are my friends." The rest of the group smiles at me, seeming satisfied that nothing more needs be said.

WEDNESDAY NIGHT SABBATH

After an hour with the youth I have even more questions. I look at my watch; it's 15 minutes until the 11 a.m. worship service. I want to hear about their experience of a mid-week program titled "Sabbath" that Brent and some of the youth ministry volunteers have recently created for the high school youth. Parent and volunteer John Frey explains that the youth ministry council created the Wednesday night Sabbath meeting out of a desire to "slow down the youth ministry and be more intentional about just being with youth." The meeting is an attempt to "model Sabbath-living," one of the primary ways both John and Brent feel personally transformed by their involvement in the Youth Ministry and Spirituality Project. When I ask John how the Wednesday night meeting embodies Sabbath, he tells me, "It's an evening that isn't run by the clock. I honestly can't tell you when it starts or when it ends. The message to the kids is really, 'We're here for you and it ends when it ends—when everyone has had a chance to share and pray.' Of course sometimes we get in trouble with parent pickups—but it's freeing to just focus on kids and their life with God instead of the clock."

The format for the Sabbath program is simple: candles, extended personal sharing, and contemplative prayer (usually *lectio divina*). Brent describes it as a night when kids escape their hectic schedules and are allowed to "just be."

I ask the youth to tell me about their experience of the Wednesday night Sabbath meeting. Karli, a sophomore and member of the pastoral search committee responds, "I attend the meeting because it's a complete break from the stress of the school week. It's a time I can relax and listen to God's Word or pray."

Sarah offers, "Sabbath is like a break for me in the middle of a hectic week full of stress from school, friends, family, and softball. It's like a breath of fresh air, a time when I can check in with my friends and enjoy and discuss God's Word. I'm currently trying to get my friends from school to come with me because it is just such a huge stress reliever that totally relaxes you mentally and spiritually, and yet I always leave feeling like I've accomplished so much."

When I ask the group how many of them have attended the Sabbath meeting, about half raise their hands. Then Marcus speaks up, "I'd really like to go...it sounds like just what I need...but I just forget to go." Lauren says, "With choir and schoolwork it's hard to make time to go." Others add similar comments.

I shift the conversation, asking them how they experience God at the Sabbath meeting and other youth ministry gatherings. Almost everyone adds a word or two—I write them down as fast as I can: "Personal. Friendly. Welcoming. Mystical. Peaceful. Gentle. Wise. Active. The opposite of understood. Overwhelming...in a good way." Then Karli says, "To me God is in the silence listening to our prayer. He's just a friend listening to what we are saying to him in the silence."

MEET THE PARENTS

After the worship service I sit down for lunch with a group of adult volunteers who serve in the youth ministry. Most of them are parents of teenagers. I ask them to tell me about their kids' lives. Mabel, Amanda's mom, starts the conversation. "They're too busy. There are only 24 hours in a day, yet every day is a struggle to cram everything into that 24 hours. There's schoolwork, debate team, youth group, and volleyball. It's way too much. Most weeks Amanda can't make youth group. I work at the high school, and I see what all this activity and pressure is doing to kids. It's too many good things, and it's killing our kids."

Lauren's mom, Sarah, adds, "There's this pressure in The Woodlands to be the best—which means each activity demands 100 percent commitment. The choir director makes Lauren feel guilty if she misses practice—even if it's for a legitimate family or church event."

She pauses and then adds, "Parents are just as busy. There are four of us in our family, and it's rare for us to go to church in the same car. Most Sundays we go to church in three separate cars. Our schedules are so full that we never arrive or leave church at the same time."

Another mom shares, "My son is interested in going into the ministry. He thinks he wants to serve elderly people. I told Brent, who offered to set up some times to take him to the local retirement home. I looked at my son's schedule and realized he had no time. I had to tell Brent to wait until next summer before inviting my son to visit the retirement community."

John Frey's wife, Stacey, adds, "And church doesn't make it any easier. John and I are often at church from 7 a.m. until 9 p.m. with praise band, two worship services, youth group, committee meetings, hospital visits...We enjoy what we do, but it's a full day."

I ask them for their reaction to the youth group's new focus on introducing prayer, silence, and a slower pace to youth group and youth council meetings. Mike and Candi, who together lead the high school group, are first to respond: "The silence is refreshing," says Mike. His wife adds, "It helps me relax and let go of all the hard stuff so I can be more available to the kids." Sarah counters, "For me it's still really uncomfortable." Mabel joins in, "I'm used to go, go, goin'—and when Brent has us sit in silence I just fall asleep after two minutes." I wait for other responses. Stacey says, "I think it was really hard for most of us at the start...but now I think it's really good for us to slow down and check in with one another. I really like the silence now. (Her eyes fill with tears.) It slows us down and helps us really look at the issues the kids are facing. It helps us pray, and I think it really has brought us together."

John Frey is a primary youth ministry volunteer, as well as the first elder for Youth Ministries at TWCC. He spends his work hours as the manager of global health and safety for computer company

Hewlett Packard. The father of two teenagers, John has been a volunteer within the youth ministry program for the past eight years. I pull him aside to ask about the emphasis on Sabbath-living within the youth ministry.

"My natural tendency is to be a type A person, always moving from the time I awake to the time my head hits the pillow. The Youth Ministry and Spirituality Project gave me permission to slow down. It's very important to hear that it's good not to work 90 hours a week, that it's okay to slow down. I never heard this in my upbringing. It was always, 'You must hurry! You must work harder! You must make more money!' One of the fundamental shifts that happened for me in this project was a distinct realization that I was doing too many 'good things.' God was saying, 'It's time to slow down and let go of all this good stuff.' I was invited to quit doing things that didn't give me life, or that drained life from me.

"I used to be like everyone else in this community. Time was a countdown clock. Now time is something I can be aware of or not aware of—it's not an oppressive presence. Time has become a gift to be received, and this new sense has shifted my awareness."

I ask him to tell me how this new emphasis on slowing down has affected his time with young people. "First of all I'm much better able to listen to kids when I slow down. When I'm living into Sabbath I become less stressed and anxious—less like a parent and more like a friend. I can tell I'm clearly acting differently when I'm available, less stressed, and more open around kids. I start hearing conversations I wouldn't have heard in the past. I think it's refreshing for kids to see that there are some adults who aren't stressed out and who are available to really listen.

"We used to be activity based, and numbers were the game," John continues. "Now we're relationship based—truthfully we've had a lot of conflict getting there, but I can tell you we're a deeper and better ministry for it." He pauses, and then shares a specific incident. "A few nights ago I saw this picture from Sunday school class maybe four years ago—before we made this intentional shift around Sabbath. I was standing with a group of kids, and we had just built structures out of dried spaghetti and marshmallows. I looked at that picture and thought, 'What was the point of that?' I think it was babysitting or fun. We were trying to keep the kids occupied while the adults were in Bible study. Now, if you were to walk into a Sunday school class you would see long periods of time in which we are having good conversation with kids. You would see us spending time in real prayer with kids. Even the youth room has changed into more of a prayer chapel that is used by both youth and adults.

"Our youth, through the adults that have time for them, have a broader sense of what Christianity is about. Previously religion was a base that you touch every Sunday—mostly so your parents felt safe! Our kids have gone beyond religion toward a deeper spirituality. They know now that this is about a way of life and not just a religious checklist. There is more in-depth opening to God and others and more sharing of faith, and this really comes out of our own shift in time and availability. The spiritual growth that has taken place among the adults demanded growth in the youth ministry. Making this shift has been a struggle, numbers have gone up and down, our own certainty of purpose has gone up and down, but the ultimate result is a stronger, deeper, more committed group of kids."

FAMILY MATTERS

This Sunday night Brent is leading a program called "Family Matters." Family Matters was created after a number of conscious conversations about the use of time among the youth ministry team. "We realized that we were just producing one more activity that kids had to attend away from their families," says John Frey. "So we tried to create

Growing Souls: Experiements in Contemplative Youth Ministry

a program that would combine family time with youth group. It also came out of our realization that others in our congregation (besides the youth) were longing for Sabbath and new ways to deepen their spiritual lives."

I arrive at the church a few minutes before five. Brent, John, and a few other youth ministry volunteers are already setting up tables in the new multipurpose room. By 5 p.m. people begin to arrive. Many place bags from Kentucky Fried Chicken, Pizza Hut, and other take-out restaurants on the buffet table. The most popular meals are the few platters of homemade taquitos, enchiladas, and Tex-Mex casseroles that reflect the flavors of the region. By 5:15 the buffet is assembled, and following a brief prayer the room is filled with the pleasures of food and familiar conversation. A few adults patiently converse around the drink table. Other parents stake out tables for their children and then bustle back and forth to the buffet table assembling plates of cheese, carrots, and cookies for their younger children. An older couple moves from table to table, shaking hands and tapping children for hugs and conversation about school. Some of the kids chase one another under and around the towering trunks of chatting grown-ups. Teenagers with plates piled high amass on rugs and the lone couch in a corner of the room. They're quickly joined by five adults who do their best to look comfortable eating cross-legged on the floor.

After a half hour or so I ask Brent when the meeting portion of the evening will begin. Brent tells me, "Whenever the group seems ready to meet. I want everyone to feel relaxed and just take the time to just enjoy one another."

It's just after 6 p.m. when people clear their tables and seem ready to "move on." Brent directs the younger children to various rooms for activities and then invites the youth and adults to the "Upper Room" on the second level of the education wing of the church. When I finally arrive the thrift store couches that line the perimeter are wedged with bodies like stuffed deli sandwiches. In the room's center the open floor resembles a sixties sit-in with youth and adults sitting jack-knifed, knees pulled to their chests. Someone suggests moving the group to another room, but Brent is reluctant and in a friendly tone tells the group, "I think this is a better space for prayer. Let's try and make this work."

The room is packed and yet people continue to slip in. When Mabel, her husband, and teenage daughter appear the only clear open seat is a folding metal chair inserted between two sofas. Mabel spots the seat and carefully steps across the peopled floor like a heron through the marshes and then sets herself down with a sigh. Left behind, her husband and daughter wiggle into seats across the room.

Sitting on the floor, Brent welcomes the group, lights a candle and asks that the air conditioning and lights be turned off. I feel a sense of relief. There is spaciousness in the darkness and a sense of peace from the single burning flame that keep me from feeling claustrophobic. I look toward the west-facing windows. The setting sun has spread a faint pink afterglow across the glass. Brent tells the group he doesn't have a watch, and asks a volunteer to let him know when he needs to wrap things up.

Youth and adults explore the same subject each week at Family Matters; however, three Sundays a month adults and youth hold their discussions separately. Every fourth Sunday they study together. This is the fourth Sunday in January and the subject is prayer. After a short reading on the nature of prayer, Brent explains the process for *lectio divina*, a form of biblical contemplation that comes out of the Benedictine community. The group enters into silence, waiting for the first Scripture reading. I notice how humid the room has become. I look back at the windows. Night has now completely descended. The youth room has become dark and intimate; the gem-blue walls glitter with the light from the candle. I suddenly remember a warm summer night when my sons and I set candles on driftwood and floated them on the tide.

The Scripture is read once, then twice. A stillness comes over the room. I think of the parents who that very afternoon told me how busy and harried their lives had become. I think how good this time of quiet must be for them. It's then, within the quiet, that I hear Mabel sleeping.

FAITH IS TIME

The one picture the Scriptures give us of Jesus as an adolescent is an image of leisure and reflection in the presence of a community of faith. Slipping away from the procession of pilgrims traveling home from the Passover festival, Jesus stays in Jerusalem. For three days he sits in the temple, his "Father's house," listening and asking questions of the elders. In contrast to the great anxiety of his parents' searching, Jesus seems relaxed and restful. He is among the elders of his faith, who seem to have plenty of time to talk with him, listen to him, and delight in who he is becoming.

The soul of a young person needs open, unprogrammed time to grow. It takes time to fall in love with God; it takes time to notice the gift of each moment; it takes time to feel the beauty and suffering of each person and to meditate on the mystery of faith. In contrast with the concrete, technological, and materialistic spirituality that afflicts American culture, the Christian faith is a faith that lives in time, not space.

The New Testament testifies that neither things nor places, neither techniques nor doctrines, but long, unstructured time in the presence of Jesus forms Christians. Yet for most young people the Christian life is just as stressful as the rest of modern life—harried

Sunday mornings, clock-run worship services, program-packed youth meetings, and somber confirmation exams.

Today's young people are being raised in a time-famine. There are few adults who have the time to sit, listen, talk with, and be amazed by young people. How are young people to mature if they are virtually never given unstructured time among adults? How are young people to hear the call of God if they never have the leisure to pray and listen? How are young people to "taste and see that the Lord is good" if they are not blessed with regular moments to play, feast, and celebrate within a community of faith?

In the current culture of busyness, few people have time for youth ministry. One of the primary characteristics shared by kids from wealthy and poverty-stricken households alike is that neither group is given much time with their parents (or any other adult for that matter). When most churches decide to hire a youth minister, they're really seeking someone who has Sabbath time for their kids. They're looking for a person who has time to listen, play, welcome, pray, study, and reflect with their children. A youth minister, according to conventional wisdom, is supposed to provide the kind of time the rest of us can't afford to enjoy. It turns out, however, that even when a youth minister has time, young people and their parents often have very little time for church and youth ministry activities.

In an attempt to compete with the A.D.D. culture, youth ministries that previously focused on discussion, noncompetitive play, prayer, and singing have been replaced with slick video lessons, rock-show worship services, and theme-park outings. It's what John Frey calls "the activity-and-numbers game." We forget the wisdom that has evolved within Christian formation programs for decades—that young people are most available to the love of God in slow, unstructured, natural times and spaces.

As Brent, John, and the other adults at The Woodlands Christian Church began to incarnate a sense and practice of Sabbath time, not only did the youth ministry programs shift but also the ways in which they related to young people. In a church without Sabbath, young people easily become projects that need managing. Brent talks about feeling the pressure to be the "answer" person—the professional who is in control of the spiritual development of the youth. This is fundamentally different from the listening attitude he and the other leaders now seek to embody with young people.

Can congregations incarnate a different culture of time? Can church leaders seek to create a sense of Sabbath in the formation of their children? How will young people feel about the church and the Christian faith after engaging in a youth program that "isn't run by the clock?" What will their expectations of the Christian life be when they are raised in a community in which adults and youth take long stretches of time to share their lives, pray, and meditate on Scripture? What understandings of God will youth develop when church feels like a "siesta" from the stress of daily life?

The Beloved Community: Covenant Community in Youth Ministry
by Doug Frank

Doug Frank teaches history and religion at the Oregon Extension, a one-semester off-campus study program for college juniors and seniors conducted on the site of a former logging town near Ashland, Oregon. You can read more about it at www. oregonextension.org.

A contemplative approach to youth ministry is practiced within a covenant community of Christian disciples. Just as Jesus called and ministered with others in a community of spiritual companions (Matthew 10:1-4), we also encourage, support, and practice small covenant groups who sense a common call to spiritual growth through Christian living and ministry to young people. These groups offer prophetic witness to a way of life that is creatively resistant to the seductions of the market culture and the dullness that can inhabit Christian institutions. Companions of the project commit to meeting regularly in covenant communities for sharing, prayer, Scripture study, and discernment in the service of their ministry to young people.

—YMSP Charter, point 3

A candle sits on a small, square cloth spread on the floor near the center of the room. As Jen stoops to light it, the hubbub of teen banter gradually subsides. Jen settles into one of the few chairs in a room full of couches. Sprawled on the couches are 13 high school kids—five guys and eight girls—tonight's version of the youth group that gathers every Sunday evening at the Westminster Presbyterian Church of Eugene, Oregon. Jen Butler, pushing 40 and slightly graying, with a broad smile and bright eyes that hint at a mischievous sense of humor, is the associate minister and youth pastor at Westminster Presbyterian. Two other adults join Jen in the mix—Diane and John, the group's adult advisors.

"Okay, let's do it folks," Jen says. "Say your name for our visitors. High, low, and how's your belovedness. Who wants to start?"

"High" and "low"—code for "Tell us about a high point and a low point of your week"—have six years of practice behind them. The question about "belovedness," though, is relatively new. Until a couple of months ago, Jen would have asked: "What's the state of your soul?" But this fall, the high school kids have been exploring how they are God's beloved children. So Jen has suggested that they begin their weekly time together by reporting on how much of this belovedness they are actually feeling.

It only takes a few seconds for the "check-in," as this weekly practice is called, to get rolling.[24]

"I'll start. I'm Hannah. My 'low'? Last week was really, really long, just a lot of homework, it seemed like a lot of things went wrong. I'm just glad the week's over. And my 'high' was the homecoming football game. We rode our horses at the game, which was kind of a disaster. We always have the football players run through this big piece of paper at the goal posts. They wanted us to stand behind the goal posts and there's like these cheerleaders and dancers throwing their pompoms around and I'm like, 'My God, I can't watch,' and all the

[24] The form of the "check-in" at Westminster is drawn from the awareness examen of St. Ignatius. His words for "highs" and "lows" were "consolations" and "desolations." He directed that those on the spiritual path daily name and meditate on their consolations and desolations. A simple, practical exploration of the examen is Dennis Linn, Sheila Fabricant Linn, and Matthew Linn, *Sleeping with Bread: Holding What Gives You Life* (Paulist Press, 1995).

football players come running past and the horses are like, whoa, and I'm like, 'I want to stay alive tonight, guys.' That was my 'high,' and my belovedness is pretty good."

"I'm Andrew and my 'low' is, for the last three days I've kind of had these headaches on and off and on and off and haven't known what to do about them. I suppose my 'high' would be...can't really think of one, maybe that I went to my favorite restaurant in Veneta this morning, kind of a greasy spoon. And my belovedness? I've been more of a human *doing* lately."

"I'm Jessica and my 'high' for the week was on Thursday. I got to see a friend I haven't seen in a while, and she was really doing good, which was nice. And my 'low' was that the rough draft of our senior paper was due on Tuesday, and I got it done by like three in the morning, but then my computer freaked out and I lost everything I'd done that night. So I didn't get to turn it in and I spent all day redoing what I'd done. So that was kind of a bummer, but I think it'll be okay. And my belovedness is kind of in the middle—five, six-ish."

"I'm Mary Beth. My 'low' was like, the whole week I felt like I could never get ahead. It was like I was going down deeper and deeper into a hole and never could get out, and just when I thought I would catch up, something else would come along. And it was just sort of frustrating. It wasn't that it was such a horribly bad week, it just was sort of uneventful and blah and there was a lot of stuff we had to get done, especially for drama, 'cause we're going into required rehearsals and it's overwhelming and scary to know the performance is in less than two weeks and that's just a looming thing in the back of my head constantly. But my 'high'—I went to older girl weekend for Girl Scouts, and it was just tons of fun being back at camp where I hadn't been for a year or two and just having fun and being a goofy kid, not really worrying about stuff. My belovedness is doing better than last Sunday but still is really challenged."

And on around the circle. Elizabeth's "high" is that her history class was cancelled, and Chris's "high" is reading *Sophie's World*. Sonja's "low" is that she was exhausted all week; we all chuckle when she tells us her belovedness is "asleep." Brian's "high" was doing well in districts. Jen's "low" is the soaking rain that promises a long winter of gray skies; her belovedness is only "fair." Diane's "high" is the fall colors on the drive to Klamath Falls. Kasey's is carving pumpkins with her parents, and her belovedness is "way up there." Heather's belovedness is "kind of iffy because I don't feel like I've been able to be myself around some people and it kind of sucks and kind of hurts and it's just not fun to be like that."

The night's "check-in" takes almost 40 minutes of the two-hour meeting. Jen Butler says check-in is "the piece that really holds things together." Whatever else the advisors have planned for that evening—snacks, games, discussions, devotionals, prayer exercises—the check-in always starts things off. It is the only component of the youth program that is never skipped.[25]

I am visiting Westminster on a rainy October weekend, to gain an understanding of three words that, when I first heard them, seemed to qualify as an oxymoron: *contemplative youth ministry*. My own youth group experience in the 1950s was all about fun and games, occasionally relieved by stirring sermons and altar calls. Both components—the games and the sermons—were boisterous events, brimming with adrenaline. But contemplation isn't ordinarily boisterous. It's...well... *quiet*, isn't it? Quiet has been the sworn enemy of every successful youth minister I've ever known. Too much quiet and you lose 'em —if not to "the world," then to the church across town.[26]

But there is a spirit of quiet in the room at Westminster this particular evening. At first, as the kids trickle through the door, there's plenty of noise: small groups tumbling together on the couches, greetings called across the room, bursts of laughter. But all of this fades as

---

[25] In her commitment to this ritual, Jen is in good contemplative company. If you get too busy for your prayer exercises, St. Ignatius told one group of church leaders, you can skip any of them except the examen. See Linn, p. 19.

[26] Support for this phenomenon from within the contemplative tradition itself comes from Wayne Teasdale: "Silence is really an open secret, as older, wiser people seem to prefer it, while young folks often don't yet understand it." *A Monk in the World: Cultivating a Spiritual Life* (New World Library, 2002), 30.

Jen lights the candle. I'm surprised at the intensity of the listening, a posture of attentiveness to each speaker that carries on without interruption through the entire check-in time. No wisecracks, no commentary, nobody offering to fix anybody else. It all seems quite natural, as if each speaker simply assumes he or she will be listened to. As if being truly heard is the normal state of things.

As I learn more about the youth program at Westminster, I come to see that *quiet* is a full-fledged member of this community. Prayer times—a sentence from each person, around the circle, all holding hands—are bathed in an atmosphere of silence. Specific prayer exercises ("nature prayers," "breath prayers," "*lectio divina*") that are taught and practiced from week to week all depend on silence. The prayer labyrinth, which the high school students constructed in the church courtyard and taught to the rest of the congregation, is walked in silence. Many high school students participate with adults in the annual Lenten Retreat, which is mostly silent. And last year, the high school young people talked their advisors into letting them skip the annual denominational youth retreat at a ski resort in the Cascades. Instead, they wanted to go to the coast for a weekend of prayer and conversation.

The freedom these kids seem to have to be quiet and to listen—a freedom not normally associated with American teenagers—accounts for the power and centrality of the check-in ritual. When I ask the kids to name the most important thing that happens on Sunday nights, most of their answers point directly to the check-in: "We get in touch. We share how our lives are going" (Matt); "Just the truth that is here. Everybody is able to be truthful" (Heather); "Everybody's open" (Elizabeth); "Everybody's sharing everything" (Chris); "If you say something, you feel like people actually care and are listening to you" (Kasey).

The night I attend, several kids make oblique reference to painful issues such as depression or family problems, but they give few details. Later, Jen tells me that, with a stranger in the room, the kids used a little more shorthand than usual. In the early years of the program, the kids talked mostly about things they were doing, especially sports and other school activities. She encouraged them to go deeper—"Try to talk about your *being*, not just your *doing*," she would suggest. Now, she says, they often disclose personal difficulties, and she hears them following up with one another in private conversation during the succeeding weeks. Mary Beth, a high school senior, told me: "During check-in we share some really private things sometimes, and it's just understood that you don't take it out of the room. You just trust everybody, and there's something really cool about that, because you know that whatever you share here won't go out of the room. Half of my friends at school, I don't trust them like this. This group is special because of that trust." Ginny, a sophomore, says explicitly what Mary Beth seems to be describing: "There's a sense of community here."

I am thinking about this word *community* because my assignment is to observe how the youth ministry at Westminster is living out the third principle of YMSP's charter: "covenant community." I don't have to look far for the meaning of *covenant*. It's posted in large letters on the youth room wall, six items created by youth group members and their adult advisors:

> We will treat each other with respect, dignity and courtesy. We will treat each other as family members in Christ, using humor, honesty and equality.

> We will help support or be responsible for one another through praying together and for each other, being a supportive community, listening to and caring for every individual.

We expect our adult leaders to be there. We also look to them for guidance through good times and bad times. We expect them to listen to us in confidentiality. We expect them to be fun.

Our leaders can expect us to be involved in a respectful, caring and open way. We can show respect by being cooperative and listening to what everyone has to say. We can show we care by sharing both joys and trials. Being open involves honesty and focusing on courteous communication.

We encourage all members of our group to be involved, support and encourage one another, and grow spiritually.

Our youth group is a place where you can be open, honest and yourself in a caring and fun environment while developing a personal relationship with God.

The quality listening that I observe in the room, steeped in a spirit of waiting and silence, tells me this covenant is working just fine. It has helped these kids become a "community" in what may be the most meaningful sense of a maddeningly imprecise term.

When I ask Jen how she defines *community*, she says: "Community means the commitment and intentionality to be present." She is not speaking merely of physical presence, of course, but of a quality of "here-ness" that embodies a willingness to wait in silence and an alertness for the other to be revealed in his or her mysterious sacredness. If she is right, there is no community where there is no silence. If she is right, then a community that is not in some fashion *contemplative* is perhaps no community at all.

A YOUTH MINISTRY THAT BEGINS WITH ADULTS

When Jen Butler first heard about the Youth Ministry and Spirituality Project, in 1996, she says it "resonated deeply." She knew Westminster belonged in the project. But the churches participating in the project had been chosen already, and Westminster was not one of them. So she and John Pierce, Westminster's senior pastor, started banging on YMSP's door. John had recently invited Jen to go with him to the contemplative retreat he attended yearly in Portland, where he had observed Jen's deep interest in the spiritual practices. He knew YMSP was a perfect fit for both his church and its youth minister. "I told Jen we *will* be included," he says. "We won't take no for an answer."

Jen had become the youth pastor at Westminster a few months after graduating from San Francisco Theological Seminary in 1992. She never thought of herself as the usual "charismatic, rah-rah" youth minister. "I'm an off-the-chart introvert," she says. Quiet times and prayer exercises were part of her youth program from the start. But she also felt pressure to sponsor the kind of entertainment-oriented youth events that most congregations expect from their youth ministers. Nikki, a church member who has known Jen since those days, says Jen was "on the fast track to burnout." YMSP promised a less frenzied spirit to youth ministry that Jen considered "a good fit for my own personal way of living out my faith." But even more importantly, it conceived of youth ministry in an entirely new light: as an outgrowth of adult ministry. It was this wrinkle that most appealed to Jen. It spelled the end to her (mostly) "Lone Ranger" act and the beginning of "covenant community" in Westminster's youth ministry.

When the YMSP charter speaks of "covenant community," it is not actually prescribing a program for young people. It is talking about the adults who work with young people. It suggests that a youth ministry begin by gathering a group of adults, church members who are willing to be interested in young people. These adults meet regularly. They encourage and support the youth minister, making "burnout" less likely. They stay informed about what is happening in the lives of the youth, and they pray for the young people and try to discern their deepest needs. But most importantly, together they pursue the contemplative practices the ministry hopes later to introduce to the young people. The adults don't pursue these practices for the sake of the young people, but for their own sakes. They practice quiet and listening and presence for what it has to offer them as they seek to live out their faith and grow spiritually. That's what it means to practice covenant community.

When I first took this assignment, I assumed I would be observing covenant community among the high school kids. I had no trouble finding it there. But I might not have found it there, in Jen's opinion, if it had not first come to birth among Westminster's adults. Jen is convinced this innovation is YMSP's true genius. "Teenagers are lost in their own world these days. Their parents are often not around, they have little or no contact with adult Christians, the youth ministry is down there all by itself at the end of the hall. So the YMSP said, 'Let's create adult teams and let them do their own spiritual work. Let's grow our own adult Christians, and then bump our kids into them and see what happens.'" That's what makes YMSP unique, and it's what Jen's been working on since she and John banged on the door in 1996, so hard and long that the YMSP staff finally let them in.

At Westminster, there are two different teams of adults that meet together in support of the youth ministry—one focusing on the middle school youth, the other on those in high school.[27] Six years ago, Jen recruited adults from the church for these teams, working from lists that she, John Pierce, and Joanne and Diane, her youth advisors, compiled. Most of those recruits considered themselves unqualified. They seemed a little scared of teenagers. Jen told them this would be a different kind of youth ministry. Their primary job would be to

---

[27] I met with both the middle school and high school youth ministry teams during my visit to Westminster. The high school team meets weekly just before the high school youth group. The middle school team meets on Wednesday evenings, twice a month, just before the middle school youth group. I spoke with about six members of each team. When I quote them in this narrative, I will usually not specify to which group each belongs, since their testimony paints only slightly varying portraits for the two groups.

"meet and pray and grow themselves." They would help Jen "discern what's happening with the kids." They would become "ambassadors to the congregation at large, letting them know what's happening in the youth ministry." Most importantly, Jen says, "I promised them they would not have to have direct contact with the kids."

Jen contacted 18 people. Seventeen said yes. One had to quit because she was relocating. Sixteen are still participating, augmented by three additional volunteers. So these teams have a virtually unbroken membership going back six years. The longevity of the teams was unexpected—"a mystery," Karen says. Jerry, at 80 the oldest member of the middle school team, says: "It's really kind of surprising how we've developed; it's almost magical. I guess we've all been getting so much we just didn't want to drop it." "It's sort of an adult youth group," Katie says. "We're a variety of ages, men and women, a variety of personal temperaments, a variety of spiritual expression and personal experience and emotional types, and it's just been a very incredible situation for me, to come to love these people."

Several team members emphasize that this is not a natural grouping of friends. They don't socialize with one another outside this group. Marcia, also 80 and the oldest member of the high school team, says: "We're not people who would be together otherwise. That's been a very special thing, coming to know people I would not otherwise have met. I think our diversity is part of our strength."

It is impossible to spend time with these adults and remain untouched by the warmth that has formed among them. "It's a group I look forward to all week," Nola says. Many heads nod agreement. Marcia remembers that there was "not much personal sharing" in the beginning, but this has changed dramatically. "It was a quick move toward more openness and transparence," Diane says. "No judgment. No fixing. We listened, and then we prayed." Dawn says: "There's a lot of honesty in this group. What couldn't you say here? Whatever it is, you'll be forgiven." "There's no judgment, no demands," Joanne tells me. Marcia says, "It's wonderful to be part of a community where I'm valued. What I experience here is safety, and trust."

Just as with the kids, the safety and trust to which these adults testify seems rooted in the contemplative spirit: silence, waiting, listening, speaking the truth of their lives—what Jen might call "commitment and intentionality to be present." When I ask the group members what they do together that helps build their sense of community, most of them point first to the check-in, when they share their "highs" and "lows" and the "state of their souls." Anne believes the check-in "rules" have been critical in safeguarding the intimacy she feels in her team meetings. These "rules," suggested by the YMSP staff, function somewhat like the covenant does for the youth group. Anne mentions three: observing a moment of silence after someone speaks; refraining from "cross talk" (commenting on what others have said, or criticizing, or trying to "fix" the problem); and maintaining confidentiality (what is said in the room stays in the room). Because of these rules, Anne says, "It feels safe to come here and talk about things that are often painful or unpleasant. It's very freeing. I've not talked about my life with any other group like I have with this one."

Right behind the check-in in importance, however, are the other spiritual exercises the group practices regularly. *Lectio divina* is a favorite. "I like the way it slows you down," Karen says. The group agrees: "It makes you think"; "You don't take what you're reading at surface value—you're able to steep in it until you hear something new, even in familiar passages"; "For me it's a way not to think and analyze but just to listen and be." Others mention nature prayers, breath prayers, Taizé singing, walking the labyrinth, and guided meditation.

I ask what difference all this has made in their lives. At first, I hear a mixture of themes: "I listen better to God and others"; "I'm more intentional about prayer"; "I'm much more accepting of myself than

I used to be"; "I'm more at peace with myself." Then a central thread begins to emerge. Jerry puts it this way: "God used to be way far away. Now, he's right here." Marcia agrees: "The big change is the closeness I feel to God. I've been a Presbyterian all my life, but I never felt so personally close to God. I don't have to sit down, fold my hands, assume a prayerful position. I can speak with God any time, and feel his presence no matter what I'm doing." Dawn mentions that, despite her faith, God always felt distant. Now, "I've found ways of having a personal relationship with God."

Karen speaks for many of the middle school team members when she says: "This group has made me much more open to living with God all through my day. There's no division anymore between my 'spiritual' life and the rest of my life. It's starting to all blend into one. You come to live the life of the beloved. You start 'being' more than 'doing.' And what you're doing is coming from a different place, from a place of total acceptance. I just feel so much more accepted." In the high school group, Diane says something similar: "Trust—that's the biggest change. I always loved the church, it wasn't a negative experience, but I didn't feel like I had a very personal or trusting relationship with God. I remember Sundays sitting in church feeling like God was very distant. Hearing all those frightful stories about a big, tight God. I don't ever remember feeling God's accessibility to the degree I do when I engage in these prayer practices." She points to the wall of the youth room, where we are sitting. Painted in large blue letters are these words: *You are my Beloved, in whom I take great delight. Matthew 3:17.* "That's really the thing that allows for accessibility," Diane says. "There's no secret handshake, there are no special clothes, there's no correct number of candles. God's always already here. I just need to show up."

After six years of seeking to be present to one another, these adults have become "spiritual companions," as the YMSP charter envisioned. And they have come, in a new way, to experience a God who is present in their daily lives—a God who thinks of each of them as beloved.

"Covenant community" seems to be a reality among the adult members of the youth ministry teams at Westminster. Its purpose— growing Christian adults—is well underway. But are the kids bumping into them?

BECOMING CONNECTED

Jim, a retired public school administrator in his mid-60s, ticks off for me the benefits of his six years on the high school youth ministry team: social interaction, exposure to a variety of spiritual practices, new spiritual energy, a new awareness of a loving God. He says his time with this group is the most meaningful part of his church experience. The group members have learned to share their burdens with one another, a practice that doesn't come naturally to him. As a result, he says, "We're more tied to each other than we are to the youth."

But these are *youth* ministry teams, aren't they? I wonder aloud whether the *youth* part of the experience could be dispensed with. "Couldn't you just meet as adult support groups and forget about the kids?"

Jim doesn't think so. "I'm not interested in just a support group," he says. "Without the kids, we wouldn't be doing this. It's just that the kids come and go over the years, while we've been together the whole time. So naturally we're closer."

When I talk privately with Jim, his eyes fill with tears every time he speaks about the young people. It's evident that he feels emotionally connected to the kids, even though he does not have the same six-year relationship with them that he has with his team members. According to Jim, his ties to the kids have grown much deeper in the last couple of years. The other team members agree that the single most significant change in Westminster's youth program since the first days of its participation with YMSP is the way the adult team members now experience and interact with the youth.

In the early years of the project at Westminster, relationships between the adult teams and the kids were more virtual than real. At their weekly meetings, the adults began with the same "check-in" and learned the same prayer exercises Jen used later with the kids. For Jen, this was helpful practice. But these praying and sharing experiences primarily gave the adults opportunity to listen to their own lives, not the kids' lives. Of course, Jen would let the teams know what was happening with the youth, and the youth would figure in their prayers. But face-to-face contact with the kids was not part of the equation. Face-to-face contact with one another, deepened by the intimacy that grows from regularly sharing joys and sorrows, was the glue that bound them together.

Gradually, however, on the periphery of the team's growing intimacy, the youth of the church began to take on specificity and reality. It started with the prayer cards. Early in the program, Jen put each kid's picture on something that looked like a baseball trading card, to help the adults know and pray for them. On the back of these cards, the young people introduced themselves, sharing important interests and concerns. The adults traded these cards around the group, taking a few of them home for a month or two, praying daily for the youth. Gradually, they realized they were getting to know the youth group members quite well. They would greet them by name at church and ask how the soccer season was going or what was on the docket for this year's high school drama club. The adults began to feel connected to the young people, even though most of the young people did not know them by name.

Muriel, a church elder in her late 70s, remembers one Sunday when she was helping to give out the bread and the wine as the congregation filed to the front for Communion. On this particular Sunday, she happened to be stationed on the side of the church where many of the young people customarily sat. As the young people came and took the bread from her, she recognized them from their prayer cards and began to say their names: "Andrew, this is the body of Christ, broken for you." She felt deeply connected to them, as if she had spent a great deal of time with them—which, in a way, she had, through the medium of picture cards and daily prayer. Later that week, as she told the middle school team about this moment of connection, tears came to her eyes.

Over the next several years, after a few more of these "aha!" moments, the adult teams grew less intimidated by and more interested in these kids. The impression grew among them—particularly after the annual Youth Sunday when the kids gave short talks to the entire congregation—that these kids had something to teach them, something about telling the truth, about vulnerability. "We told Jen we wanted more time with the kids," Jim's wife, Nikki, says. "And the kids seemed to want more time with us."

So Jen and the youth advisors initiated a joint event for each group. At the middle school youth group's next Christmas dinner, the adult team members burst into the room dressed as Santa Clauses and performed a dance they had choreographed, then stayed to eat and talk with the kids. Now it's an annual affair where (according to the kids I talked with) the adults let down their hair and the kids get to know them in a whole new way. Cassie and Madie, two of the middle school youth, burst into laughter as they remember Jerry sucking green Jell-o through a straw. Recently, the middle school team began a practice of stopping by the fellowship hall after their biweekly meetings to greet and talk with the kids for a few minutes before the youth meetings begin.

For the high school youth, contact with the adults on the team began naturally. The high school team meeting would invariably be winding down as the earliest high school kids were showing up for their Sunday night youth meeting. One night the adults invited the youth to join their circle and pray with them. As the meeting ended and the adults traded their prayer cards with one another, the youth seemed intrigued that the adults were praying for them by name. In the weeks that followed, many of the kids continued to come early to join the adults in prayer. In time, Jen raised the ante. She suggested that the kids invite the team members to join them, every now and then, in their regular Sunday night meetings. Now, one Sunday every other month, the kids and adults meet together. They do the check-in, the prayer exercises, the games and discussions. The adults ask Jen not to turn it into a game night, but to give them an opportunity to talk deeply with the kids about issues that matter. So Jen makes sure there's a serious topic on the agenda, and splits them into small groups for face-to-face conversation.

A couple of years ago, Jen also brought adults into the confirmation process. The young people in the annual confirmation class are paired with adults who phone the young people each week, or meet them at the Dairy Queen, offering whatever help they can, letting the kids know they are being thought about and prayed for each day. At confirmation the adults introduce the youth to the congregation, and the youth are handed booklets containing letters written by their sponsoring adults, welcoming them to the church family.

Madie and Cassie, the two middle school kids I talk with, admit that it was uncomfortable at first to speak with adults they barely knew. But eventually, Cassie says, she found Nola easier to speak with than her parents. The youth appreciate the interest these adults take in them, particularly that they are being prayed for. "They're praying for us all the time," Madie says. "Sometimes in a soccer game I think,

I could really use some prayer right now, and then I realize Bryan is probably praying for me."

The high school kids seem a bit more comfortable forging adult-to-adult relationships with the team members. Jessica tells me: "I've gotten to know Marcia really well. I'm an artist and she's an artist. She's invited me over to her house a couple of times and looked at my stuff, and she's really supportive. She gives me advice on a lot of stuff. I really like talking to her." Kasey, who has a gift for speaking directly, says that having the adults at the meeting "can get kind of uncomfortable sometimes. The youth group know each other so well, we get really intimate; then the adults come, and it's different. But I like it now and then. It's nice to get a different perspective than we get from our typical melodramatic high school friends. The adults are more mature. Well, maybe not more mature in some cases—I don't know what that means—but they've been around longer than us, and we have a lot to learn from them." Mary Beth adds: "Last week they played kick-the-can with us, and showed us they were just kids, as goofy as we are. It was like their inner child coming out. They're kids at heart. When we're having a discussion, their views are almost the same as ours sometimes. They're a little more mature views, maybe more focused, and they understand more. But they're a lot like us, and it's so cool to be able to share. I think they learn new things from us just as much as we learn new things from them."

Jim is amazed that these kids want to be with the adults, and are willing to listen to the adults talk about their joys and sorrows. He thinks it's probably a healthy thing for kids to know that adult life is not very easy. He cries as he remembers hearing one of the kids say he liked having the adults involved in his life. "Something about that touches me very deeply," he says.

Jen says she always hoped these adults would become advocates for the kids to the congregation at large. But "there's something more intimate than advocacy going on here. I don't want to use the word *mentor*, although that's not far from the truth. I guess I'd rather use the word *friend* or *companion*." The adults are having conversations with the young people that they'd like to have with their own kids, and the kids are talking with the adults the way they'd never talk with their own parents. It's only beginning to gain momentum, but Jen believes an intergenerational community is growing at Westminster. And she thinks the kids are leading the way.

Perhaps the most prominent mark of the intergenerational community at Westminster is the honesty and vulnerability its members strive for in speaking with one another. In one joint meeting between adults and youth, an adult spoke about her father, who had just been diagnosed with cancer. Anne described how hard it was to be so far away from her dad during his illness. Later, one youth told Jen: "I feel honored that Anne trusted us enough to be honest." Jen also remembers when a sophomore, Nathaniel, gave a sermon on Youth Sunday. His parents had just separated, he was hurting, and he said so. "The adults just came out of there going, 'Man, there is something going on with these kids that they're willing to stand up in front of the congregation and bare their souls.' I think the adults sense that there is a depth to the kids, because of the spiritual exercises, that they're intrigued by and probably wish they had for themselves. The adults always seem touched by the kids' insistence that youth group is a safe place where they can be themselves. I think a lot of adults want a place like that."

In fact, more and more of Westminster's adults *do* have a place like that. Pastor John Pierce believes the church is showing greater interest in "spirituality" and is getting "more contemplative." He has always encouraged small groups to meet for nurture and fellowship. But over the last several years, these adult groups have begun using the Christ candle and check-in ritual to begin their meetings. Tom, one of the church elders, says: "This is a direct spin-off of what the young people do." Other new adult groups have formed around contemplative practices like morning prayer, *lectio divina*, and journaling. Jerry laughs as he describes the day the Mariners—a group of adult men—tried writing poetry prayerfully, as the youth group had done. "Adults have more inhibitions than the kids," he says.

John Pierce has encouraged the spread of contemplative practices throughout church life. He now begins "session" (business) meetings with a check-in. One elder says the personal disclosure and vulnerability have brought "a new sense of trust" among the elders; another has noticed the session meetings are "less businesslike and more spiritual." The pastor has also revised Sunday worship services at Westminster to include Taizé-style prayer choruses and longer periods of silence. (Some church members have complained that they have plenty of silence during the week and don't need more of it on Sunday.) John has instituted a second Youth Sunday each year because the congregation has reacted so enthusiastically. "Whenever it's announced that kids will lead worship, everybody's excited," John says. "It's not 60s-style stuff, with the kids trying to shock everyone. They just get up and talk about their spiritual journeys and the struggles of their faith."

Mike agrees that the kids have become the teachers at Westminster. "Everybody has been touched," he says. "Lots of the church people talk about it. We've never seen anything like this before. We're all out there in the pews, wiping our eyes when the kids are up front leading the service. For a lot of us, it's our favorite service. It's just our kids up there, talking from their hearts."

A SAFE, COMFORTABLE PLACE

Ron Taffel, author of *The Second Family: How Adolescent Power Is Challenging the American Family*, is well aware that teenagers can lead adults toward a deeper vulnerability and intimacy.[28] Today's youth, he writes, are "more honest, open, and willing to put their feelings on the line with their friends than adolescents once were." They have "richly textured" relationships and an astounding "ability to be vulnerable" with one another. "Because of what they've absorbed from the pop culture, not to mention the emphasis on communication skills in most schools...teenagers are beginning to learn how to speak the language of feelings." "In fact," he writes,

> Many of today's teenagers seem to be doing just about everything that advice books suggest to adults who want to deepen their intimacy. They make time for one another. On a daily basis, and from morning until night, they build and maintain their relationships. Rather than stockpile their feelings, they make attempts to say what's on their minds. They create rituals of initiation and belonging. Granted, they are just teenagers, so they don't have the benefit of years or the ability to look back and correct their course as an adult does. Still, these kids often exemplify what they need from us and, not so incidentally, what we're lacking in our own relationships.[29]

This does not mean today's adolescents travel a smooth road to adulthood. Taffel believes many teenagers are also angry, lonely, depressed, and anxious, caught in addictive and self-destructive cycles, and finding little or no grounding for a stable, healthy sense of self. Most significantly, he says, young people today have walled themselves into their own worlds, furnished by peer and pop culture, with little opportunity for honest relationships with adults who like and respect them.

[28] Ron Taffel with Melinda Blau (St. Martin's Press, 2001). Quotations are taken from pages 66, 58, 67-68, 72, 3, 18-19, 17, 12-13, 82, 40, 46, and 8, consecutively. For simplicity of expression, I will use Ron Taffel's name alone when referring to the book's authorship.

[29] I was surprised at the fairly sophisticated understanding of human personality and relationships that I found among even the middle school students at Westminster. Cassie and Madie mentioned to me that some of their friends at school are "rude." I asked whether they had any theories about why their friends are rude. Madie said: "Maybe because they haven't experienced anything that made them feel very good about themselves." Cassie added: "They could be just taking out their anger on other people, like maybe they have family issues." Madie said: "Sometimes people like to bring other people down just to make themselves feel better."

This isn't because our teenagers are particularly bad. It's because they're like the rest of us. Youth culture simply mirrors the wider culture in which we all live—"taken a giant step further with emblematic teenage flair." Adults are obsessed with image and possessions, and so are teenagers. Adults spend more time away from home, and so do teenagers. Adults have become egocentric, and so have teenagers. Adults relax by drinking or using drugs, obsess about their bodies, and live in a highly sexualized world—and so do teenagers. "In their most shocking and often frightening behavior...teenagers are telling us everything we need to know, not just about them, but about ourselves."

At the heart of the problem, Taffel believes, is the vast distance that has grown between teenagers and adults—particularly parents. Stay-at-home parents are rare in today's world. Family routines and rituals gradually slip away. Even when parents are present, they are not fully "present." Almost every child Taffel interviewed said something like "We don't spend time together in my family." They meant "undivided attention" time, not the kind of time when Mom is cooking, Dad is checking his e-mail, and the kids are playing computer games and watching videos in their bedrooms.

Feeling less connected with parents and siblings, and heavily shaped by the pop culture they imbibe from early childhood, kids begin to move away from their own families—often before they're out of elementary school. "They surround themselves instead with friends, forming a second, separate but equally important, [family] system. As kids become more and more attached to their friends and to the common interests they share, by early adolescence, it is a natural, easy step to divorce themselves not only from their first families but, often, from other significant adults as well." Parents know little or nothing about the daily texture of their kids' lives, partly because they "bury their heads in the sand" but also because of the unwritten code of silence that prevents teens from letting adults know what they and their friends are up to. The generations do not converse about anything that really matters.

Thus, the "second family" becomes the entire social nexus in which many teenagers live. The culture of the second family, shaped by pop culture icons and values, approves many behaviors that parents know to be unwholesome and self-destructive. But it also meets many legitimate teenage needs. It gives them a group of friends, a sense of security and support and belonging, shared interests and a shared "language," a sense that someone understands them and accepts them for who they really are.

What teens seek most in a second family, Taffel believes, is *comfort*. "Virtually everything kids do," he writes, "is motivated by the pursuit of comfort." The second family gives teens a safe, warm, easy, comfortable place to be, among friends who "don't criticize or correct but merely accept them for who they are." As one teenage boy put it, "I don't have to *do* anything. I don't have to be good at anything. There's no pressure." In other words, he can simply be himself.

In the check-in ritual and in my longer interviews with four of the high school kids at Westminster, I hear echoes of the same struggles and pains that plague the kids Taffel portrays in *The Second Family*. They feel "tired" or "exhausted." They're "busy all the time" or "falling behind." They have headaches and injured legs. They are bounced between angry parents. They are caught in difficult relationships. One youth mentions how complicated and fragile friendships are, how kids you thought were your friends stop being your friends, which makes it "easy to lose self-confidence." Another talks about her fears of being rejected and how angry she feels when she's being defined and dismissed by others. One teen tells me he spent his sophomore and junior years buried in despair over his parents' breakup, mostly hiding it, thinking life "pointless" and imagining suicide. Now that he has come through this, he's worried about what it's doing to his little sister. Often, the Westminster kids use the word *pressured* in describing how they feel, in the arenas of sports or drama or relationships or academics or home life. One says: "There are so many pressures everywhere you turn. Every single person in my life seems to want something different, including my parents."

As I listen, I notice a melancholy tone in their voices. Other tones coexist with it—mischief, levity, persistence. But when they get serious and quiet, the note of sadness is unmistakable. I wonder whether teens are perhaps a culture in mourning. The media barrage, social pressures, adult expectations, parental absence and family instability, personal trauma, and their own precocious awareness conspire to shove them rudely out from under the canopy of childhood before they are prepared to handle the requirements of adulthood. Innocence, safety, dependency have been torn violently from them. Their losses are profound. As with all humans, their losses engender shock and confusion, anger and sadness, and often enough, self-destructive or bizarre behavior. Why are we surprised? Why would comfort *not* be their highest value and prime objective? Is comfort not, quite often, the *only* thing one can offer to the mourner? Do we not *owe* a climate of comfort to those we love who are carrying an insupportable load of grief?

I ask the Westminster high school students why they spend Sunday nights in this youth group. Jessica answers: "Because it feels comfortable." It's uncanny how many others use the same word. And they use other words, many of them pointing in the same direction:

> It's somewhere I can just be myself and sort of release everything that's happened throughout the week.

> I feel a certain way here that I don't feel anywhere else.

It's relaxing. I feel calm here.

I feel supported here, and loved.

It's the opposite of how my life usually is. I'm surrounded by friends.

It gets me away from home and gets me a couple hours away from everything else so I can relax and not worry so much.

It's my outlet at the end of the week. I just sit down and breathe and go through what's happened that week and make sense of it.

I've really grown to like who I am here.

In the Sunday youth group, Westminster's young people are finding exactly what Taffel believes teens are seeking in the second family: "a place where they are known and feel comfortable." Nathaniel, a college student who came through the Westminster youth program, tells me he never felt judged or criticized at his youth group: "It was a place where you could be yourself." Mary Beth says: "In the youth group we can talk about mistakes and how to get through them. It's like no one judges you. If you screw up on a test, they're not going to say, 'Well, you're not cool anymore because you failed your class.' They're accepting and supportive. You can be human. You don't have to worry about being perfect." Kasey chimes in: "At school you're always hearing 'You're not doing this well enough, you're not doing that well enough.' There's all this pressure to be better. Here you can just be who you are. They're not pushing you to be anything but yourself."

DISCOVERING WHO WE ARE

"Being yourself" is no small achievement at any stage of life. Expectations and demands, from within and without, come at us relentlessly. During our teenage years, they come with particular intensity, destabilizing our fragile sense of identity, feeding our self-consciousness and self-doubt, making virtually every step we take clumsy and uncertain—or else, all too certain, as we try desperately to right our balance. It takes an extraordinarily safe environment to quiet these demanding and accusing voices so that we can begin listening to quieter, deeper voices and begin to know who and how we really are.

I did not feel this safety as a child. The love that my parents and other significant adults showed me, which they felt deeply, was tainted by wounds of their own difficult childhoods that were neither clearly understood by them nor genuinely healed. In their desire to be the best possible parents and mentors, they impressed upon me who I must be, how I must be. My father was a pastor in a succession of conservative evangelical churches, so my parents also felt pressure to demonstrate to their congregation that their child-rearing skills qualified them for continued pastoral ministry. In effect, I was handed a bill of particulars defining the behaviors, thoughts, and feelings of the perfect self. The list grew quite long, particularly after puberty, and with each passing year, my ability to measure up seemed more and more in doubt. Even as my desire to measure up diminished over time, my shame and self-accusation when I did not was unrelenting.

Because I was a child of the church, somewhere near the center of this nexus of fear and shame, expectation and accusation, lived God. This God had two faces: one warmly loving, the other coldly wrathful and punitive. I was expected to love the first face and fear the second. The two-faced God was so foundational in my youth that it was many years before I realized how emotionally incoherent and unbelievable a portrait this is.[30] This God presides over a vast religious empire that

---

[30] "There is no fear in love, but perfect love casts out fear; for fear has to do with punishment, and whoever fears has not reached perfection in love. We love because he first loved us" (1 John 4:18-19).

extends around the world and takes both Christian and non-Christian institutional forms. He also serves as the border patrol, regulating who's in and who's out. He wants you in, so he can shower his love on you. But you've got to come in legally and learn to be a good citizen. If you don't get in, for whatever reason (and here doctrinal explanations vary), there's some version of hell to pay. A God like this, the all-too-usual God of institutional religion, cannot provide the safety we need, at whatever age, to become fully ourselves.

Shaped by the expectations and demands of this God, the climate of my youth, and of my youth group, was inherently unsafe. We had a great deal of fun together. We found a modicum of comfort in one another's company, and we might have considered ourselves a "community," had the word been in vogue then. But it was not the sort of comfort or community that freed us to be fully present, without expectations or demands, or to tell one another the truth of our lives. It was not the sort of comfort or community that offered us the space to relax and accept our humanness. It was not the sort of comfort or community in which we learned truly to trust God or in which a genuine love for God grew deeper within us.

The pressure the Westminster kids often experience in school and at home, but not in the youth room on Sunday nights, was a pressure I felt most intensely at my weekly youth group meetings. I could never have said, with Kasey: "Here you can just be who you are. They're not pushing you to be anything but yourself." The God who presided over my youth group would not have permitted that.

I ask the high school kids to give me a word or phrase they associate with God. We go around the circle: "fun," "makes me happy," "love," "forgiving and loving," "comforting," "some sort of father figure," "loves you no matter what you do," "best friend," "unconditional love" (three times). One says: "He's a parent who knows you so well you're just forced to be open and honest with him, you can't be anything but yourself." Another elaborates on the "best friend" theme: "He's a best friend who you look up to because they're so amazing and before you say something to them they already know what you're going to say because you're so connected to them."

Mary Beth says: "God is someone that, no matter where you are or what you're doing, he'll be there to talk to you." When she has "stress attacks," Mary Beth finds a quiet corner and talks to God. "I know he'll be there to listen no matter what. He's like a friend who's always by your side. It's kind of neat. You don't have to go look for your best friend who is busy doing something else, you can just sit down and you know God will be listening to you."

Kasey says: "It's kind of a comfort thing. It's like, especially as a teenager, there are times when you feel really, really alone, and you're like, 'All my friends hate me and I'm gonna sit up in my room and sulk.' And then you think, 'There's somebody watching over me, somebody that will always listen and sometimes talk back.' It's just the comfort of knowing I'm never alone."

I ask the youth group kids whether there's any reason to be afraid of God. Matt answers immediately: "None whatsoever." Mary Beth doesn't think so, either: "God is one of the more comfortable things in my life. Not scary at all. Not like a supreme power who is so much higher than you and you can't approach." But Kasey admits that certain Bible stories that seem to portray a scary God do make her wonder: "It's like God has his bad days. He's a little irked sometimes." The other kids begin to admit that they're not entirely settled on this point. "Sometimes you do feel afraid, although there's no reason," Chris says. "You want to live up to God and you want to please him so much, you're afraid you can't do enough." Sonja says: "At first you worry that you're not going to be good enough, but then you learn that you cannot *not* be good enough." Heather says: "Sometimes you're afraid you'll make mistakes and he'll not forgive you. But in the end he will forgive you and he does love you, so there's no real reason to be afraid."

Mary Beth tries to explain the ambivalence she's hearing: "I can see why people would be afraid before they get to know God. He's this greater power you can't grasp easily because you can't see him. But once you get to know him there's no reason to be afraid of him, because he's this person that loves you no matter what you do even though it might be stupid. He doesn't care. He just wants you to grow."

Marcia, eighty years a Presbyterian, echoes the high school kids when she talks about God's character. "I think God is very loving. He loves me with all my warts. He's a forgiving God. I'm his beloved. That's the biggest thing. I do not see God as vindictive or punishing. I know it seems to be the case that if we mess up we somehow have to pay for it. But I don't think God's sitting up there on his throne saying, 'Whoops, she messed up, make her pay.' It's just not the way I see God."

Dawn joins the conversation at this point. "I was raised a fundamentalist," she says. She remembers the messages she heard in her childhood church: "Basically, you know, you're going to hell." She pauses. "Not that *we* were going to hell, or would be cast into fire and brimstone, but *somebody* was, and definitely there's a right and wrong and you better do right." She says it's been a "wonderful change to have a different view of God," to think about the possibility of heaven right here on earth, as if it's simply being in the presence of God, right now. "I don't think God rejects any of us. People may, but God doesn't."

When they wish to ground this belief in the biblical text, both the young people and the adults at Westminster point to the writing on the youth room wall: *You are my Beloved, in whom I take great delight.* There seems to be general agreement that these words say it all, and say it authoritatively, when it comes to understanding the character of God.[31] The adult team members, in particular, season their conversation with the words *beloved* and *belovedness*. Nola says: "The words *beloved* and *grace* were not words I had experienced a lot before this project began. But they've grown inside me. When I started hearing the kids talking about their belovedness, I thought: What a powerful thing, that this child who's 14 knows what I didn't know until just recently." Joann adds: "For me, the important phrase is "in whom I take delight." I never thought of myself as a person in whom God took delight. I saw myself as having too many wrong thoughts, making too many mistakes. I thought, other people, they have it right, but not me. I've got to somehow get to where they are, but I don't know how. I don't feel that any longer. We're all on the journey."

The words on the wall, of course, come from the biblical account of Jesus' baptism by John. As Matthew tells it, Jesus was stepping out of the river when "the heavens were opened" and he saw "the Spirit of God descending like a dove and alighting on him." And there was a voice from heaven, saying, "This is my beloved Son, with whom I am well pleased" (Matthew 3:16-17).[32]

I tell the adults I'm surprised how freely they assume that words intended for Jesus are also intended, by the Spirit of God, for them. Karen says: "I've been thinking about that. This was God talking to Jesus. In the past I would have wondered: Would he pass these words along to me? Now I'm perfectly comfortable that God is speaking to me." I ask Karen, partly in jest, whether doves alight on her. "Actually,

[31] Without the safety of a God who considers each human his beloved and welcomes all, just as they are, without drawing lines or enforcing boundaries, in this life or in the next, I do not believe such a community is possible. I have no quarrel at all with this safe, comforting, inclusive God. I believe it is the revelation of God in Jesus Christ. But it is not the only God represented in historic Presbyterianism, in the Christian tradition at large, or in common interpretations of the biblical text. I did not have time, during my visit, to adequately explore how the adults and young people at Westminster are working out the dissonances. Brief conversations on this topic lead me to believe the dissonances—particularly conflicts with historic Reformed doctrine—are mostly being ignored by lay people, who are much more comfortable thinking experientially than theologically about God.

[32] This familiar wording of Matthew 3:17 appears in the Revised Standard Version. The New Revised Standard Version reads, "This is my Son, the Beloved, with whom I am well pleased."

it seems like the dove descends on me very often, and in so many different ways. Now that I'm open to it."[33]

An intergenerational community is evolving at Westminster, a "second family" in which adults and young persons increasingly find themselves bumping into one another. If Taffel is right, this is a rarity among adolescents in America—a very healthy rarity. Somewhere near the center of this community—pervading it, indispensable to it—is the shared conviction that each of us can experience God's presence, and that this presence holds us in a very safe and comforting way.[34] In this presence, we can relax and reveal the truth of our lives to one another. We can listen with empathy and without "fixing," bearing each other's burdens. We can gently become more and more the persons we most truly are.[35]

In their surprising freedom to trust and to speak of these experiences, the young people of Westminster are leading the way toward fresh possibilities for being human and being Christian. And in their genuine enthusiasm for this same journey and their eagerness to learn from their young people, the adults of Westminster are experiencing new vitality in their own spiritual lives. And the adults are also

---

[33] When I raise this point with John Pierce, he seems at first to wish to preserve some sense in which Jesus' belovedness is different from our belovedness. But when I ask him whether that means God loves Jesus more than God loves us, he wavers: "That can't really be, can it?" Whatever the doctrinal fine points, John says, "It doesn't worry me that kids interpret this verse as referring to them at this point in their lives. They're encountering an awful lot that tells them they're not worth anything. I hope they'll find a way to stay grounded in their belovedness."

[34] Although God's presence seemed to be felt as a tangible reality by most of the young people I talked with, we did at one point discuss the inevitable experience, for most Christians at one time or another, of the absence of God. Several of them spoke eloquently of hard times when they "don't feel any presence" or when they find themselves "crying in a corner and where is God?" One said it this way: "I actually feel God's absence a lot. The last few years have been really rough, all this stuff happens and I'm just like, where's God in this, 'cause I'm told he's there and I'm told he loves me and he'll always be there for me, but then in the real world all this stuff is happening to me and I think about what people are telling me but I don't feel it. I try to think to myself that he's there and that he loves me and that it's all true, but I can't feel it, it's just talk." I admired her directness, and took it as a sign that she felt comfortable in this group. But I sensed that God's absence is not often talked about with the kids. I suspect such talk could be helpful, in part as a way to diminish the temptation to "fake it" when the presence of God is not being felt. When I ask Jen about this, she says: "We try not to define what God's presence looks like or feels like so that there isn't a right or wrong way. And when we do talk about what it might feel like, we say, "It just might not be working for you tonight, and that's okay." It occurred to me as I listened to the kids talk that it might be comforting for them to be informed of how often the experience of God's absence, or the "dark night of the soul," is reported in the Christian contemplative tradition. For an accessible, very brief description of this experience see Rowan Williams, *A Ray of Darkness* (Cowley Publications, 1995), pages 80-84.

[35] Included in the YMSP charter's description of "covenant community" is this sentence: "These groups offer prophetic witness to a way of life that is creatively resistant to the seductions of the market culture and the dullness that can inhabit Christian institutions." While I have not explored this aspect of covenant community, I hope it is evident that the practice of radical presence—to oneself, one another, and God—and the consequent freedom to become more truly oneself, are direct challenges to the image-driven strategies pursued both by the consumer culture, in its quest for profit, and institutional religion, too often in pursuit of a visible but inauthentic piety.

leading in their own way by helping their young people believe that growth toward honesty, vulnerability, and intimacy does not have to end when one takes up adult responsibilities. Becoming more truly oneself can be the challenge and the joy of a lifetime.

CALLED BY NAME

It's a Sunday night in mid-September. Jen and her advisors are leading the high school youth group in a "belovedness celebration."[36] They start, as usual, with a check-in and a prayer circle. Then Jen tells the kids she wants them to think with her about the difference between "talents" and "gifts." She suggests that talents have to do with skills, like kicking soccer balls and scoring well on standardized tests. Talents are inherently competitive and hierarchical—they create and reinforce divisions and inequalities between people, rewarding those who come out on top. Gifts, she says, are different. Things like kindness, listening, empathy, truth-telling, compassion, and gentleness are gifts. They help us connect, not compete, with one another. She asks the kids for examples of gifts, and writes them on a flip-chart. In a few minutes, they have a list of about 40.

Now they all head for "fellowship hall," which Jen and the advisors have strewn with balloons and bunting. In the middle of the room sits a cake on which the word BELOVED is written in large sugary letters. Each kid's name appears in the same sugary letters somewhere on the cake. Fastened to the walls are small posters, each with a picture of one of the youth and a Bible verse personalized for that kid: "Tomas, I have called you by name. You are mine. Love, God." Jen invites the kids, while eating their personalized pieces of cake, to circulate among the posters, writing on them affirmations of each other's gifts.

[36] At the time of this writing, Jen Butler was putting the finishing touches on her DMin. dissertation, titled *God's Beloved Children: Accompanying Adolescents from a Shame-Based to a Grace-Based Identity.* It elaborates a youth ministry curriculum that will be of inestimable help to churches that want to inaugurate a YMSP-like program for their young people. I recommend Jen as an advisor to any such program. Both she and John Pierce are unusually skilled in a style of leadership that exhibits a light touch because it has learned to trust both God and people.

They wander toward the church sanctuary. On the platform steps, Jen and the advisors have propped up the kids' journals, where they write or draw their responses to each week's prayer exercises. A copy of the poem "The Call," by Oriah Mountain Dreamer, sits near each journal, with a votive candle burning in front of it. One by one, Jen calls the kids forward. She hands each one the poster with affirmations of their gifts written across it. Another leader gives each youth a personalized note, handwritten by one of the adults of the church, assuring that young person that he or she is beloved.

Then Diane, one of the advisors, anoints each young person with oil. She draws the outline of a cross on each forehead, one by one. She looks into each face and addresses each by name.

"Hannah," she says, "*you* are God's beloved child."

Creating Space to Listen for God's Call: Discernment in Youth Ministry
by Kathleen A. Cahalan

Kathleen A. Cahalan is an associate professor of theology at Saint John's University School of Theology-Seminary in Collegeville, Minnesota. She earned her doctorate in practical theology from the University of Chicago Divinity School. She taught in the theology department at Rosary College, River Forest, Illinois, and served as the evaluation coordinator for the Religion Division of Lilly Endowment Inc. Cahalan is the author of *Projects That Matter: Successful Planning and Evaluation for Religious Organizations* (Alban Institute, 2003), and *Formed in the Image of Christ: The Sacramental-Moral Theology of Bernard Häring* (Liturgical Press, 2004).

A contemplative approach to youth ministry is guided by discernment. Just as Jesus prayed to know and follow God's desire (Luke 22:39-44), we also seek to discern and respond faithfully to the call of the Holy Spirit in our lives and ministry with youth. We practice and teach the disciplines of individual and group discernment so as to be fully available and responsive to the movement of God's grace in our covenant communities, allowing anxiety-driven youth ministry to become Spirit-led youth ministry. Companions of the project seek to learn and practice the spiritual disciplines of discernment as the basis for opening, listening, and responding to God's call in youth ministry.

—YMSP Charter, point 5

In the basement of an Episcopal church in downtown Richmond, Virginia, several groups of youth, divided by age, meet with adult mentors, on Sunday mornings and every other Sunday evening. As in many other churches, the number of youth involved is not overwhelming, and it's a challenge to recruit enough adult mentors each year. Yet the youth and adults are clearly committed to this time and place. Unlike many other congregations, St. Paul's Episcopal Church has honored its youth with space—a place to call their own. The youth and their adult mentors have a meeting place—a "lower" room in the church building. The space is not used for any other purpose, so there's no setup and takedown before and after the youth groups meet. It is not shared with children or with the church's outreach ministries. The space is for the youth and the youth have claimed it as their own.

The lower room actually consists of several rooms. There's a large gathering space with tables and chairs for meals, a game table, bulletin boards, and space for art and youth work; three sizeable rooms for the different age groups to meet, each with comfortable sofas, chairs, soft lighting, and, again, youth art work; and a fully equipped kitchen for cooking, storing, and serving food. There's also a chapel that the congregation uses for weekday services as well as a contemplative prayer service on Sunday evenings. The youth know this space: It is a home, a gathering place, a place for fun and conversation, a place where exploration takes place and discoveries are born. "This stuff is ours," Anna announces.

The lower rooms have also become a place of discernment. St. Paul's Church has given its youth a great gift—a time and place to listen to God's call.

1. RITUAL: ACKNOWLEDGING GOD'S PRESENCE IN OUR MIDST

Discernment is a word often associated with making decisions. Although discernment does involve decision making, it is more than that. Discernment is more like taking a journey than taking a vote. Like a pilgrimage to a distant land, discernment requires developing a plan, acquiring the proper gear, setting off for a destination, following a roadmap, sometimes getting lost, and arriving home safely. It involves listening, sorting, seeing, choosing, and acting. Discernment takes time; it cannot be forced or rushed. Some journeys of discernment are short, others are long; some are quick and easy, others are arduous and difficult.

At its weekly meetings, each of St. Paul's youth groups participates in a seven-step process known as the liturgy for discernment. The liturgy was developed by the Youth Ministry and Spirituality Project as a roadmap for Christians on their journey together. It outlines a meeting process that leaves space for groups to listen for God's voice through prayerful attention to God's Word and to the life of each group member. The liturgy is a form of prayer as well as a decision-making tool that enables groups to discern God's call in their ministry to one another and to the community. (The seven steps of the liturgy for discernment are outlined in appendix 5.)

The liturgy for discernment calls attention to the dynamics of the Spirit rather than the efficient productivity of the group. It has the feeling of a Quaker meeting interspersed with Ignatian discernment practices. A key to the liturgy for discernment is to leave aside all expectations that accompany a "normal" business meeting—agendas, goals, and deadlines. The liturgy for discernment invites an atmosphere of prayer in which emphasis is placed first on deepening relationships—with oneself, others, and the Spirit of God. Whatever work is accomplished, whatever activities are planned, they are the fruit of the community's discernment. The work done in group meetings follows and flows out of prayerful discernment, rather than preceding it.

Youth ministry teams who participate in the liturgy for discernment before their gatherings with youth have found that prayerful discernment allows people to clear away anger, frustration, and distractions that might otherwise keep them from being present to the youth. As the authors of *Grounded in God: Discernment for Group Deliberations* have pointed out:

> Groups that seek discernment when they have business to do and decisions to make often find that their meetings become more energized and productive. The priorities of the meeting shift. Those gathered grow in faith and in love for one another while addressing the issues at hand. When those present center in God and listen deeply, their varying needs and divergent views can move from discord to concord. Rather than entering into a contest with factions singing competing tunes, the group as a whole can discover a true harmony, satisfying for all."[37]

On a Sunday evening, Suzanne and Megan, mentors for grades 8 and 9 at St. Paul's, are seated in the room with seven youth. Simple elements like a lighted candle and soft background lights are gentle reminders that this is a special place and time. Also noticeable is what is not present. Unlike nearly every other space youth occupy at home or school or in public, here there are no computers, e-mail, cell

---

[37] Suzanne Farnham and others (Morehouse, 1996), 8.

phones, or MP3 players. There are few outside distractions. The space is peaceful and welcoming.

The ritual calls no attention to itself, as there is no precise beginning or ending. But everything about the space is different as the youth enter and begin their time together. Some youth bound into the room, full of energy and conversation; others come quietly, accompanied by a shy silence. The ritual begins as the group settles quietly and comfortably into the room.

Megan says the mentor's job is to create space for youth to share their lives with one another. "Our role is to help create space, rather than controlling what is going to happen, or coming up with some outcome. I see our role as protecting opportunities to allow people to say what they need to say. We try to honor each person."

The ritual that marks the beginning of the liturgy for discernment is simple and brief. It may be a song, a moment of silence, or the lighting of a candle. The purpose is to draw attention to the Spirit's presence. It announces to the group, "We are coming into an awareness of the presence of God." The ritual follows a similar pattern each week, so it becomes familiar enough to be repeated regardless of who is in attendance. The ritual does not need to be led by the same person each week. Rituals have a way of becoming known and recognized by the group without being defined; the group is able to lean up against a familiar ritual in times of confusion and pain. This first stage in the liturgy for discernment is marked by intentional action that gathers people in and breaks the usual rhythms and patterns of ordinary time. Sacred time has commenced, and the journey has begun.

2. RELATING: THE CHECK-IN

St. Paul's Episcopal Church, founded in 1843, stands at the center of downtown Richmond. The state government's offices are across the street, and the Medical College of Virginia is just a few blocks away. The church's mission, "Proclaiming Christ in the Heart of the City," is put into action through numerous outreach programs to its neighbors: During the day legislators, politicians, bankers, and business managers as well as persons who are homeless, jobless, and hungry visit the congregation for community, education, worship, and a meal.

Most of the 1,100 members of St. Paul's are white and affluent. Few church members live in the immediate neighborhood; most drive at least four miles to the church, and some commute from great distances on the weekends. In addition to its strong liturgical tradition and education programs, St. Paul's sponsors a Stephen Ministry, feeds the homeless, sponsors 12:05 p.m. daily prayer services for downtown workers, and hosts lunchtime forums with state legislators. Church members also serve the city through a mentoring program at a local elementary school and a prison ministry that includes a halfway house for recently incarcerated persons transitioning back to society. St. Paul's rector, Robert G. Hetherington, has served the congregation since 1984. His focus at St. Paul's has been building the laity for their ministries in the world—"in all the places where we live and work." St. Paul's employs 14 full-time staff and 12 part-time staff; 25 percent of the staff members have served time in prison at some point, though it is impossible to identify who they might be.

The Relating step of the liturgy for discernment constitutes a brief period when attention is turned to the members of the group. Each person is invited to "check in" by responding to a question. It may be broadly worded—such as "How are you?" or "What is happening for you today?" —or may have a more specific focus—such as "What does Advent mean to you?" or "How have you encountered forgiveness this week?" Each person speaks for two to three minutes sharing thoughts, ideas, feelings, or a story—anything to convey their answer to the question. The group listens quietly: No one asks questions, interrupts, comments, or offers a wisecrack. Silence is kept after each speaker.

The check-in requires attentiveness to each speaker's words, as well as to how the group listens and the moments of silence kept between different people's responses. Members of the group are invited to listen for the Spirit's promptings as they reflect on the question and then share what they have heard. Speaking before the group does not need to involve lots of words; it does bear the responsibility of choosing words carefully, speaking them clearly, and sharing words that can be heard and understood. Speaking that comes from deep listening helps the rest of the group hear and see the work of the Spirit. Speakers open possibilities for the group as it listens.

Listening requires a desire to hear and understand what is being said and to find God's Spirit in the midst of another's experience. Listening requires disciplined attention to one person, which means setting aside thoughts that can crowd into the mind. For example, when another person is speaking, listeners should not be formulating what they plan to say when it is their turn to speak. Listeners suspend evaluation and judgment. They turn their bodies, especially their eyes and ears, toward the person, and do not attend to distracting noises or events. By attending fully to each speaker, listeners say: "You are important to us, your life is valuable, and your experience is treasured."

Silence marks the time between the speakers. Since silence can be difficult for some people, group discernment can be aided by helping people gain skills for sitting in silence. The silence can be a time when listeners pray for the person who has spoken or allow what has been said to enter their own experience. Silence is the time to explore where God is present in what has been spoken and in one's own thoughts and feelings. For those who have been trained, silence can even be a time for no thoughts. Whatever takes place between people in silence, it is a time for creating greater interior space for the Spirit's dwelling.

According to St. Paul's youth minister, Steve Matthews, "The check-in is done in a very caring way so that it becomes our prayer. Our ideas of prayer have expanded so much through the liturgy for discernment. We have come to see that God shows up in other places and in people's stories—not just when we bow our heads to pray. The challenge is to accept what people have to share and not to try and come up with answers for them, but give them time to find the answers. Sometimes you don't have to say anything at all."

For the youth at St. Paul's, the check-in marks a time of "honesty, authenticity, and acceptance," according to Alex. "We are a group of friends outside of school that can offer a fresh perspective on life in a noncritical atmosphere. We like to talk about stuff, and we come here to experience acceptance for our beliefs about God."

3. RECEIVING: PRAYERFUL LISTENING TO THE SPIRIT

After the group attends quietly to each person's experience, it is ready to listen prayerfully to the Holy Spirit. Listening to the Spirit requires the same discipline as listening to one another: leaving aside distracting thoughts and giving our full attention to God. Discernment is the act of discovering and responding to God's inner voice of love in the unique circumstances of our individual lives and our life together as a church. It requires a discriminating ear to hear the call of the Spirit amid the many other voices that compete for our attention and response.

Yet listening for God is not the same as listening to one another. We don't literally see God or hear God's voice. And the primary ways we have to listen to God—prayer, worship, reading the Bible, and serving one another—are not always straightforward and clear. How do we listen? And what are we listening for? Can we really claim God is involved in the ordinary events of our lives, the transactions of a church meeting, or a 50-minute youth gathering? Do our decisions about what college to attend, what friends to spend time with, or what jobs to take really grab God's attention? Are the decisions of church business—where to go on a mission trip, whether to decrease support for a social ministry, what music to sing at the 11 a.m. service—really the kinds of decisions God wants to help us with? Are they part of "God's plan" and if so, how?

We may think there is a hidden blueprint from God that contains the right answers, if we could only find it. But discernment is not like looking up directions on Mapquest. In many ways, God has already given us our plan in the life of Jesus. Our call is to follow Jesus on the way of discipleship, and our discernments about individual choices take place within the broader discernment of Christian discipleship. In relationship to our choices, we can ask, "How will this choice or this decision help me remain faithful to the discipleship I have already been called to live?"

Discernment requires trust and patience. We may feel desperate to hear what God wants of us, but may not feel like we are receiving a clear signal. Discernment requires that we drop our agendas with God—or at least the agenda we secretly want God to communicate to us. Instead, we must be ready to wait in silence and faith, trusting that God's promises are true and trustworthy, that God's love will not abandon us, and that God's will for us is to live as faithful disciples (Luke 12:22-34). Frank Rogers writes, "God is present, hoping and urging, in the midst of all the situations of life. As Christians, we believe that God is passionately involved in human affairs and intimately invested in all our questioning. Moreover, we believe that God's involvement in our lives has purpose and direction. God is seeking to bring healing and wholeness and reconciliation, transforming this broken world into that New Creation where there will be no more sadness or injustice or pain. Our decisions and our search for guidance take place in the active presence of a God who intimately cares about our life situations and who invites us to participate in the divine activities of healing and transformation."[38]

In the liturgy for discernment, Receiving involves three movements of prayerful listening: (1) centering attention on the One who calls us to the work, rather than the work itself; (2) opening ourselves to the possibility of transformation in the silence; and (3) listening intently for the way God is inviting us to live and serve.

YMSP teaches two forms of contemplative prayer for use in the liturgy for discernment: *lectio divina* and the Ignatian awareness examen. *Lectio divina* is an ancient form of monastic prayer in which people listen to God's voice through repeated readings of a Scripture passage. In this process of "praying the Scriptures," participants give attention to those words that stand out for them as the Scripture is read, and in the silence that follows each reading. While *lectio divina* can follow several formats, YMSP recommends the fairly simple form of the exercise found in appendix 1 for use in the liturgy for discernment.[39]

Alternately, the receiving time may involve the group members engaging in the awareness examen, a prayer of discernment developed by St. Ignatius of Loyola. The purpose of this prayer is to trace God's presence and call in the concrete here-and-now details of everyday living. When used as part of the liturgy for discernment, the prayer invites the group to return to a previous meeting or activity and recall God's presence in that encounter. In a spirit of prayer, group members are asked to reflect on and then respond to two questions:

---

[38] "Discernment," Dorothy C. Bass, ed., *Practicing Our Faith* (Jossey-Bass, 1997), 106.

[39] For more on *lectio divina*, see M. Basil Pennington, *Lectio Divina: Renewing the Ancient Practice of Praying the Scriptures* (Crossroad, 1998).

For what moment am I most grateful?
For what moment am I least grateful?[40]

On the first Sunday of Advent, St. Paul's youth groups listen to the gospel reading from Luke 3:1-6. Announcing the ministry of John the Baptist, Luke quotes Isaiah:

> The voice of one crying out in the wilderness: "Prepare the way of the Lord, make his paths straight. Every valley shall be filled, and every mountain and hill shall be made low, and the crooked shall be made straight, and the rough ways made smooth; and all flesh shall see the salvation of God."

The juniors and seniors reflect on the passage in light of where they see God's path leading them beyond high school. The youth express their worries, fears, and excitement about the next stage of life before each of them. Andrew says, "I am living with the stress of what I'm going to do every day. I have no idea where I am going to college or what I am going to study." For Hannah the path of college and beyond seems clearer, but personal relationships are more difficult to figure out: "I'm mostly concerned about my friendships. I see what I have in common with my friends, but I also see what I don't have in common and how that affects our friendship." Rachel feels as though her future will be determined largely by her mother's multiple sclerosis: "I keep thinking about my life in 20 years. Will I take care of my mom when my dad can't? I could work for my dad in computers after high school, but what if I don't want to?" She struggles to find her true self in the midst of many conflicting images and ideals. "I'm frustrated with everyone labeling me when I don't even know who I am." Scott, a 34-year-old adult mentor, tells the group, "I'm constantly redefining what success is. I'm nearly 20 years older than you, but my definitions of success have altered in the past two years, and I'm not sure where that will lead me." Steve wants to enjoy life more:

[40] For more on the awareness examen, see Dennis Linn, Sheila Fabricant Linn, and Matthew Linn, *Sleeping with Bread: Holding What Gives You Life* (Paulist Press, 1995), pages 6-7. Other questions include: When did I give and receive the most love? When does it seem to you that the most love was given and received? When did I give and receive the least love? When does it seem to you that the least love was given and received? When did I feel most alive? When did it seem the group was most alive? When did I feel the most free? When did it seem there was the most freedom? When did I feel least free? When did it seem there was the least freedom?

"I'm not taking risks. I need to live a little edgier, less controlled, and more free."

The journey of every adolescent involves deep valleys where it is impossible to see the horizon, tall mountains that seem impossible to cross, and rough paths that make the walking difficult. The liturgy for discernment allows youth the chance to name the journey they are experiencing each Sunday morning. By listening to one another's journeys, they begin to see common elements: No one's path is easy, discovering God's plan is not automatic, and discipleship involves a community of pilgrims who can help one another face the tough choices that must be made.

4. RUMINATING: PRAYERFUL LISTENING TO THE OTHER

There are about 75 young people at St. Paul's Church, about 45 of whom are involved in the youth program. Modeled after the "Journey to Adulthood" program developed by St. Philip's Episcopal Church in Durham, North Carolina, the youth program at St Paul's is a spiritual formation process that honors the distinctive phases of adolescent development: Rite 13 is comprised of youth in grades 6 and 7; J2A, which includes confirmation, is for grades 8 and 9; and YAC (Young Adults in the Church) is for students in grades 10 through 12. Each group meets for an hour on Sunday mornings and every other Sunday evening. Sunday mornings follow a common rhythm that combines the liturgy for discernment with a discussion or activity based on the "Journey to Adulthood" curriculum.

Each group also participates in outreach programs. The J2A group embarks on an annual Urban Adventure to explore creative ministries in another city. In 2003 they traveled to San Francisco's St. Anthony mission; based on that experience, they are now discerning what kind of ministry to take up in Richmond. The YAC teens take a pilgrimage every other year to a holy site in the Christian tradition. For several years the group has also volunteered once a month at the Medical College of Virginia children's ward. The youth began this ministry after attending the congregation's community action fair and discerning that their serving together at one site over an extended period of time would be better than their serving individually at different sites. The group's monthly trip to the children's ward is the best attended event in St. Paul's youth ministry.

Each group is led by three adult mentors who have all made two-year commitments. They are the "front line" of St. Paul's youth ministry. In addition to meeting with youth, these adults meet twice a month for an hour and a half to engage in the liturgy for discernment. The youth minister, Steve Matthews, has been with the parish for eight years, a near record for longevity in youth ministry.

Historically, St. Paul's youth group looked like most other mainline Protestant youth ministries: Youth performed in the Christmas pageant, participated in outreach ministries to the homeless, attended weekend retreats, and enjoyed recreational outings. But in 1996 the vestry made the youth one of its top priorities: It hired Steve Matthews as its first full-time youth minister and adopted the "Journey to Adulthood" curriculum. Five years later, in 2001, the church began participating in the YMSP.

Upon coming to St. Paul's, Matthews found himself in a situation all too familiar to most youth pastors: He had a small core of adults dedicated to youth (though not nearly enough), numerous activities to manage (including the impossible task of recruiting youth for the Christmas pageant), and many important outreach and community service opportunities for youth. But something was missing, for both Steve and the youth program. "I sensed a largely unspoken longing for purpose and direction for the youth ministry. We have a fine curriculum, yet we are still thirsty for experiential faith. A new curriculum is not the answer and neither is more activity. Our youth are time-pressured and have expressed a desire to have time and space to simply 'be' with one another. We are a congregation of high achievers and the church's endowment encourages new dreams and visions. We speak prayers often and try to allow due process in the movement of the Spirit, yet I wonder if we are not short on listening."

Listening to one another is at the heart of the Ruminating stage of the liturgy for discernment. The group listens as its members share what they have noticed during the prayer time. If the group has prayed *lectio divina*, the leader might invite each person to share a word that came to him or her during the prayer. If the group has prayed the awareness examen, the leader may ask youth to share those moments for which they are most grateful, and those for which they are least grateful.

Such careful attentiveness takes time. When the group first began engaging in this process, Suzanne often felt concerned as a mentor that they would be unable to get the lesson covered: "I know the things we need to talk about, but now I don't worry about the lesson so much. The lesson is being a better listener. Sitting with these kids has helped me be a better listener. I'm on a journey, too."

Ruminating means listening to the fruits of the prayer in each person. It does not entail giving answers or telling people what to do. Mentors do not try to tell youth what decisions to make. By inviting the youth into discernment, and accompanying them along the way, mentors witness to the belief that each person will come to hear the Spirit's call if they stay on the path.

After listening to the Isaiah passage read twice, the J2A youth are invited to reflect quietly and then share a few words about the mountains and valleys they are experiencing. They are also invited to write some thoughts on a large piece of newsprint in the common room to share their insights and impressions with the wider youth community. Some kids don't say very much, and there are weeks when some people do not speak at all. What is happening when no words come forth? Megan, the J2A mentor, has sometimes expressed concerns about inviting kids into contemplative prayer: "How do we know anything is happening at all? Should we do something more? We are inviting kids into the castle of self-reflection through the back door, but this is less often the initial route. Is silence and contemplation an appropriate route for them? Is something really happening, or is this just blank time?"

Yet Megan has come to trust the silence as a place of possible discovery. She has grown more comfortable with offering the time and space to youth "to go back to these simple practices, to be still, and to sit somewhere and listen, to be quiet. I realize what a gift it is for these young people to just have some peace in a world that is so manic!"

5. REFLECTING: WHAT IS GOD'S CALL TO US?

In the liturgy for discernment, the Reflecting step is the pivotal point of the meeting. Throughout the previous four steps, which make up the first movement of the liturgy, the process has focused inward, centering on the group's connections with one another and with the Holy Spirit in their midst. Yet with the beginning of the second movement, the group shifts its focus to its central identity and calling: "Who are we?" and "What is God calling us to do?"

Reflecting invites the group members to take the insights, experiences, wisdom, and feelings that have emerged from the prayer and bring them into open conversation between members. The group seeks to answer the question, "Given all that we have heard and shared, what is God's call (or invitation) to us?" Discernment seeks to sort out all the information, feelings, and opinions in the group. It involves imagination, because it requires that all the possibilities be seen and named. And it also involves seeing what questions need to be asked, not just the answers.[41]

At the time of my visit, the YAC youth were planning a pilgrimage. They had decided earlier to travel to Turkey and retrace the journey of St. Paul, but their plans were disrupted because of the political situation in the Middle East. Now their discernment must start over—but there is not much time, since plans need to be made soon. Steve Matthews presents the group with several new options: a trip to Ireland to experience Celtic Christianity there, a visit to the Arizona desert to recreate something of early Christian desert monasticism, or the *El Camino de Compostela* (The Way of Saint James) in Spain. Turkey remains an option if the group will accept the chance that the trip could be canceled at the last minute. Steve has gathered materials for the group to read and offers information about each pilgrimage: the sites to see, the connections to the Christian story, the historical background, and something of what the days would be like.

Arizona is quickly thrown out by the group as too close to home. Turkey is longed for, but let go: Why risk not going at all? Why put the group in harm's way? The choice is between Ireland and Spain: Both are good choices, sound interesting and different, and are far away. Ireland sounds fun. Another youth group from St. Paul's took this trip and had a great experience. But Spain sounds different. Of all the options, it involves a true pilgrimage. *El Camino de Compostela* is the "way of the field of the stars" that begins in the Spanish Pyrenees near the French border and traverses 500 miles to Santiago. Pilgrims have walked the Way of St. James since the Middle Ages searching for companionship, reconciliation, and salvation. It is not an easy trip: mountains, desert, intense heat, and even snow mark the path of the pilgrim. The St. Paul's youth would take up the pilgrimage for 100 miles, about seven to ten days of walking. In the end they decide

---

[41] "Probing questions engage us in ways that help us to discover things for ourselves so that they become our own and bear authority for us. Answers provided by others seldom carry the same weight. Good questions can open us up to the creative flow of the Spirit. Well-framed questions can draw the entire group into a search for truth that enables its members to develop fuller insight together. Then answers and actions may follow more serviceably." *Grounded in God*, p. 19.

to take this rough and difficult journey because they believe it will be more rewarding. Walking with hundreds of other pilgrims from around the world sounds interesting, challenging, and life-changing. "It will force us to think about the group and not just ourselves," says Scott. "We will have to do it together." For Hannah, getting over her "unbelievable laziness" will be a challenge. Yet she is excited about the possibilities: "This will be real Christian community, because we can't just look out for ourselves. This could be a really amazing experience with each other and with God."

The group's discernment about their pilgrimage has included times of both consolation and desolation. It had taken them months to reach their original decision to go to Turkey, and Steve had traveled to Turkey to prepare for the group's trip. When world events closed off that option, the disappointment sapped the group's energy. Now, as they have discerned a new possibility, their tired and worn spirits have been renewed.

The group has not yet left for the trip, but the pilgrimage has begun. The months of discernment, the disappointments, and the starting over are all part of the pilgrimage itself. What are the signs that our choices are in line with God's calling? Anna, a 14-year-old St. Paul's youth, relates her process of discernment: "When I have to make a choice, I think about which way would make me feel like I'm doing the best thing. And I look at the consequences, even the worse possible thing for each choice. Which choice would make me feel the least bad? I test the water before diving in. I like to ask: 'What would help people the most?' I know the choice is right if my spirit is joyful. A choice that does not have integrity makes me feel bad afterward. You regret it. Sometimes I look to see what other people have chosen, and I realize I could have made a better choice."

Even when our choices seem clear, we cannot know entirely where they will lead. We never have certainty about how our choice will shape the rest of our lives. There is always some ambiguity and uncertainty. But discernments that are true callings are accompanied by a sense of peace, joy, and consolation. They will not lead us astray.

6. RESPONDING: TODAY'S BUSINESS

Even as the youth group is seeking direction for its summer pilgrimage, other discernment is happening everywhere at St. Paul's. Not every decision requires a careful process of discernment, but many do. Suzanne is wondering, "How do I know what people to serve?" The vestry is considering the direction for its prison ministry. Don, a young early retiree and confirmation sponsor, is trying to discern the next stage of his spiritual journey: "What is God calling me to do? I know what it is; it is just hard doing it. God is calling me to be mindful of God every hour and every minute and then to discern what God wants of me in that moment. But it's hard because my ego is in the way."

When the liturgy for discernment is used for church meetings—whether it be the junior high youth group or the board of trustees, the sixth step—Responding—is the time for business. Prayer does not stop, but continues in and around the discussion of other agenda items.

The vestry at St. Paul's is dealing with pressing financial concerns. Money is an age-old issue for most congregations—there is never enough. But for Virginia Episcopalians, these financial questions are particularly painful in the wake of the 1990s economic boom. For years, resources have been abundant and community ministries have thrived. But recent economic downturns have begun to raise questions about the financial viability of certain outreach ministries—particularly Spring Hill, the women's transitional house that is part of the church's prison ministry. Can this ministry be retained at its current rate of support or will some part of it need to be curtailed? The question is painful since everyone knows the prison ministry is necessary, worthwhile, and important. No one is arguing that the church should end its ministry at the women's prison. The call is clear, but the means to continue the ministry in its current form are not readily available, and it's hard to imagine how it might be done differently. If it is cut back, will it still be faithful service?

For the loyal advocates of the prison ministry, any reduction in support is a sign of failure by the church. Suzanne is torn by her call to "be with the people" and the need to run for vestry so she can be an advocate among church leaders to keep the prison ministry going. The ministry is vitally important to her personal calling as a member of St. Paul's. But the financial stewards of the congregation believe "business as usual" is an irresponsible choice because it affects the congregation's entire ministry, not just this one component. The Sunday bulletin contains the following prayer request for vestry members: "Help them to discern your direction for the future of this ministry."

Choices must be made—not every project, program, or initiative can be carried through in the way people might want. Such issues can paralyze a congregation: Personalities define the debate, people can become blinded by their own point of view, and a win-lose situation often emerges. There is often confusion and frustration. But in the face of difficult decisions, the liturgy for discernment can lead a congregation away from conflict and toward a shared vision of what it can do and how it can be done. This does not mean everyone will always agree, but it can mean that their disagreements won't destroy the community. In coming to choices together through discernment, the community can imagine beyond individual hopes and agendas to what the community is called to be and to do.

When used as a meeting format within churches, the liturgy for discernment aims at producing spiritual fruits, by drawing on shared leadership and a generous time for prayer. Teams of adults working in youth ministry can use the liturgy for discernment before or after meeting with the youth. This way of doing business may be quite frustrating for some: "Not enough is getting done." "Time is being wasted." "We aren't accomplishing anything." But the success of such an approach to meeting is not measured in terms of the number of items covered and decisions made, but rather in love, joy, peace, patience, kindness, generosity, faithfulness, gentleness, and self-control—the fruits of the Spirit (Galatians 5:22-26).

Rev. Bob says that the youth and youth ministry team are the "spiritual moles of St. Paul's" —referring to Thomas Merton's term for monastic communities that become concentrated places of prayer in the church. The youth ministry has become the place at St. Paul's where God is most intentionally invited into everything that is done. For Bob, "The youth ministry is the spiritual crux of St. Paul's that pushes stuff right upstairs. People are becoming more sensitive to the Spirit because of what is happening in the youth groups."

Could the congregation—and the vestry—conduct all its meetings using the liturgy for discernment? The authors of *Grounded in God* suggest the kind of mindset that would make this possible: "Envision the business meeting as worship. Think of the work of the meeting as an expression of our love for God. Then preparing for meetings becomes holy work, and developing an agenda becomes the planning of a liturgy."[42]

What lies on the path of discernment is usually...more discernment. Discernments exist within discernments and discernments raise the possibility of yet more discernment. Choices have consequences, and for youth—and all of us—it is often difficult to see far down the road of life and know what will happen as a result of our

---

[42] *Grounded in God*, 43.

choices. In the words of Alex, one of St. Paul's youth: "I don't have well-formed goals. It is all pretty hazy. I know what I'm doing now will affect my life 10 years down the road, but it is hard to see how."

The same is true for the vestry: a choice must be made for how best to support the prison ministry, as well as the rest of the congregation's ministries. It looks pretty hazy at times without knowing where each path will lead.

7. RETURNING: OFFERING OURSELVES TO GOD

At the end of their meeting, Megan and Suzanne invite the eighth and ninth-grade youth to form a circle. Hands are held, heads are bowed. A brief prayer is spoken. And with this step of Returning, the liturgy for discernment comes to a close for the day.

As the youth have become more active in the tools of discernment, they've begun to imagine new ways they can serve St. Paul's. Some youth are raising the possibility of their leading a worship service for the church. They are eager to share what is happening in their lives with the rest of the congregation. At St. Paul's "The mission of the church is not separated from the mission of the youth ministry," according to the pastor. "In fact, the youth ministry is playing a powerful role in shaping the mission of this church."

Just as pilgrimages have beginnings, they also have endings. Pilgrims come home, returning to familiar places, spaces, and people. If often takes the journey to a holy place far away for us to discover the holiness in one's own home, family, and church. When St. Paul's youth return from Spain, they may realize that the holiest place they know is St. Paul's, and the most sacred journey they make is the trek down to those lower rooms of the church in downtown Richmond each week. For the minister, Steve Matthews, "My hope is that the faith of our youth will deepen so that when they leave St. Paul's, they do so with a history of encountering God's activity and presence. I pray that they believe that God is real and that they are able to dialogue with themselves and one another about God's transforming work in their lives."

Discernment requires being rooted in a place and journeying to new places.

Discernment requires listening to other's stories and telling one's own.

Discernment requires seeing what is before our eyes and searching for the unknown.

Discernment means sorting and distinguishing all possibilities and setting some aside so others can become a reality.

Discernment requires time and patience.

Discernment requires faith, hope, and love.

Mission Projects, Prayer Retreats, or Bowling Nights: Practicing Authentic Action with Young People
by Frank Rogers Jr.

Frank Rogers is a professor of Religious Education and Youth Ministry at the Claremont School of Theology and the Director of the Narrative Pedagogies with Youth Project. He served as an advisor to the Youth Ministry and Spirituality Project throughout the length of the project.

A contemplative approach to youth ministry seeks to engage youth and adults in authentic actions that reflect God's mercy, justice, and peace. Just as Jesus came out of prayer and solitude to heal the sick, welcome the outcast, and celebrate with friends (Luke 4:18-19, John 12:1ff.), so we also seek to cooperate with the Holy Spirit in a way of life rooted in the Beatitudes that witnesses to Christ's love, passion, and joy. Communal practices of Sabbath, prayer, discernment, and accompaniment find their fulfillment in actions with youth that make visible the gifts of the Holy Spirit. Young people desire opportunities to participate in Christ's healing and liberating activity within the world. Companions of the project seek to support youth and adults in becoming instruments of God's grace who creatively reveal the reality of God's love and courageously resist the principalities and powers that oppress life.

—YMSP Charter, point 7

"Three days by yourself in the desert sounds way too intense—I don't care what the desert fathers did." Alicia was dead set against the prayer retreat her youth group was planning. The rest of the youth were equally disgruntled, albeit for different reasons.

"No TV, no music, no friends...No way! I'm not going. Besides, I hate camping."

"I'm sick of all these prayer practices that don't let you talk. If I have to sit in silence for one more minute, I'm going to scream!"

"This was the adults' idea from the beginning. Why don't *they* just do it?"

"I'm tired of all this spirituality stuff. Can't we just go bowling?"

"And if Emily is going, I'm staying home. I never wanted her in the youth group to begin with."

Of course, Emily was the sole enthusiast. "A vision quest in Utah? Cool! I *have* to try this."

The young people were venting about the year's focus for their youth group. Since the time the group regathered after summer break, the entire youth ministry program was planned around a weeklong trip scheduled for the following summer. The plan was to go to the deserts of Utah where the teens would stay at a mission for poverty-stricken Navajos, experience Native American culture and spirituality, then culminate the trip with a three-day vision quest involving absolute solitude, total silence, and no possessions beyond necessary survival gear, a Bible, and a journal. From day one, the youth grumbled. By November, they were ready to revolt. They griped through first-aid workshops and orienteering classes, they squirmed through prayer exercises and mini-immersions into solitude, they fussed through sessions on wilderness cooking and spiritual growth through journaling, and they zoned out during discussions of the spiritual ancestors who pioneered this approach to retreat and prayer. Several of the eight or ten youth simply stopped coming. Others sucked it up to be with their friends. But even they were a mere breath prayer away from torching the room full of candles. Where did all this come from anyway? Wasn't youth group supposed to be fun?

The adult leaders agonized over what to do. After they'd discovered for themselves the life-transforming power of spiritual retreat and the soul-renewing practice of contemplative prayer, the vision quest had seemed like such a great idea. They would introduce teens to spiritual practices throughout the year, gradually build up their tolerance for silence and solitude, and climax the program with three days of desert solitude for self-reflection and prayer. They could even teach the kids about the contemplative tradition within Christianity while also engaging them in a cross-cultural experience.

It had seemed like a great idea. But the youth's resistance was overwhelming. The last centering prayer session turned into a snoring contest. What was wrong with the way they were planning programmatic action for their kids? They vented their own frustrations in their planning meeting.

"I don't get it. I would have *loved* something like this when I was their age."

"Maybe we need to push past their resistance. They can't know yet how good this is going to be for them."

"I don't know. If we take them on one more reflection day in the wilderness, I'm afraid they'll stone us with their prayer journals."

"What would happen if we did just take them bowling?"

"Are you kidding? I'm not here just to entertain them. These practices can change their lives."

"But they hate them. And they aren't doing much good. Do you see the way they keep rolling their eyes whenever Emily speaks? What are we going to do about that?"

"I don't know but we can't just throw away our entire program. We've put too much into this."

"So what are we going to do?" They looked around at one another in frustration.

One adult finally summed it all up, "This contemplation and youth ministry stuff is a disaster."

What were they going to do? What kind of programmatic action authentically embodies God's invitation for this youth group? What actions would enable this youth group to "reflect God's mercy, justice, and peace...participate in Christ's healing and liberating activity in the world...and become instruments of God's grace who courageously resist the principalities and powers that oppress life, and creatively reveal the reality of God's love"?[43] As these adults were about to find out, it would involve a summer trip. But one unlike any they had ever imagined.

LOVING GOD AND LOVING THE WORLD

Lake Chelan Lutheran Church is a 171-member congregation located in rural Washington State. The surrounding foothills are lush with apple orchards, the community's primary source of revenue, while the majestic lake that stretches from the city's edge hosts an increasingly vibrant recreational tourist industry. The church has no paid youth minister so a group of adult volunteers, including the senior pastor, serves as the leadership team for the youth group. As participants in the Youth Ministry and Spirituality Project, these adults attended the project's weeklong spiritual retreats, where they were introduced to

---

[43] Youth Ministry and Spirituality Project Charter.

contemplative prayer exercises. They sat in silence, they practiced *lectio divina*, they walked in solitude, they chanted, journaled, and reflected on their experiences with directors, colleagues, and friends. Within this prayerful space, they reflected on the way of Jesus, and God's invitation of new life offered to themselves, their youth, and the wider world. To a person, they felt renewed, transformed even, as they soaked in the healing presence of the sacred like a warm wash in soothing springs.

The members of Lake Chelan's leadership team returned home renewed, energized, and eager to sustain this life-giving experience of God's Spirit. They created a covenant community, a group of people who committed themselves for one year to a liturgy of weekly prayer, sharing, and discernment. Through contemplative prayer practices, they dwelt in the presence of the Holy together, they shared deeply of their own personal journeys, and they supported one another in their daily walks. They also held their church's youth in prayer. Serving as the planning team for the youth group, this covenant community engaged in the practice of discernment. They reflected on the places within the youth group where God's Spirit either swelled with life or was stifled by blocks, and they listened for God's leading as they sought to encourage the youth in the direction of fullness of life, for all involved. In short they asked: *What actions could the youth group practice that would authentically nurture for the teens and the adults who companion them a deeper knowledge of God, a life of faithful vitality, and an embodied commitment to love and serve the world?*

The youth group at Lake Chelan Lutheran already had a significant history of engaging in meaningful action together that, even in its social justice orientation, had a decidedly contemplative spirit. Taking seriously Jesus' invitation to love not just God but the world as well, the Lake Chelan Church, for two years running, organized its youth group around spring-break mission projects. Both trips emerged out of a prayerful contemplative sensitivity both to the marginalized of our world and to their group's own cultural biases.

The first year they went to Nicaragua. They prepared for the trip for months—studying Nicaraguan culture, the social and economic challenges faced by the people, and the gospel values that inform authentic care for the poor and the marginalized. Excited by the adventure and emboldened by their Christ-like purpose, they arrived in Managua eager to serve the Nicaraguan people.

Their first three days in the Nicaraguan capital only solidified their concern for the poor. They saw firsthand the insidious web of social structures, bureaucratic processes, and cultural prejudice that conspired to bar the peasants from access to universities, opportunities in the business world, or voice in the government. By the time the youth were bused to the countryside for three days of living with peasants in their homes, their indignation was high and their sympathy deep as they burned to make a difference.

When they pulled into one struggling settlement, the teens were horrified to see a group of women, some pregnant, some elderly, hacking through hardened soil in the day's heat to dig trenches alongside withering coffee plants. Moved by their plight, the teens swarmed over and insisted that they relieve the women and dig the trenches themselves. The women, surprised at the youthful zeal of the *Norte Americanos*, stepped aside. Some of the teens were athletes strengthened by modern regimens of weight training; most were amply well-nourished on North American abundance; all were bolstered by the nobility of their Christian convictions and the invigorating rush when taking care of those in need. Within an hour they were ready to pass out. Exhausted by the labor and beaten down by the heat, they guzzled draughts of water, then napped in the afternoon shade. The peasant women smiled as they refilled the teen's buckets. Then they retrieved their tools, and dug throughout the rest of the day.

Their discussion that evening reflected upon the paternalism that permeates U.S. attitudes toward the poor, particularly within the church. A conversion of thinking took place among the teens. Their notions of poor and wealthy, service and empowerment, were turned upside down. They saw how taking care of another, however well intentioned, can mask arrogance and reinforce dependency. For the rest of the trip, the young people allowed themselves to be served by the vibrant Nicaraguan people, sharing the wealth of the Nicaraguans' culture and sense of community, their dreams for a better world, and their hopes fueled by festive faith and active organizing. The teens no longer tried to rescue the peasants. They simply asked how they might become their allies. They were learning about authentic action—action spurred by visions of justice and mutuality, chastened by the shadows that motivate us all, and energized by a commitment to birth power, not dependency. By maintaining hearts that were attentive, open, and vulnerable to the Nicaraguan people and their situation, the youth of Lake Chelan gained a new awareness of both the struggles of the poor and their own privilege.

The following spring the youth group went to North Carolina. In recent years, the small farming town of Lake Chelan, once almost exclusively Anglo, has witnessed a Hispanic influx. Large numbers of migrant laborers, finally released from restrictive immigration policies, have come to Lake Chelan to settle with their families. Though living side by side, the White and Hispanic communities are hardly integrated. The high school cafeteria is almost completely segregated—Anglo and Mexican teens dividing the space straight down the middle. Recognizing the racial tension in their own town, the adult leaders structured a year-long program for the youth exploring race relations and migratory flow patterns in the United States using the African American experience as a more accessible, albeit indirect, case study. The exploration culminated in a trip to Durham, North Carolina, where the teens stayed in African American homes, listened to the stories of Black ancestors fleeing slavery, and witnessed first-hand the continuing struggle to claim the elusive promises of work, equality, and a country you can call your home.

While there, the Anglo teens from Lake Chelan visited an African American man who had studied the intricacies of the Underground Railroad. He shared how this patchwork trail to freedom worked. Certain trees served as signposts. Slaves would find out about such places through coded lyrics in the spirituals they sang. Runaways would make for the markers, where they met up with other runaways, nourished themselves with food left by sympathizers, slept through daylight hours camouflaged under blankets in the branches, and read the signs laid out for them—crossed sticks at the trunk's base beckoning danger, parallel sticks a clear track for freedom. The teens were fascinated at the intricate route that promised a way free from the cesspools of slavery. The man told them that one such tree was but a couple of miles away. Would the teens like to see it? Of course.

The tree was a stately oak that stood out in the woods because of the breadth of its trunk and its low-lying web of branches. Standing at its base, their host showed the teens the knotholes where food was hidden, the branches that supported clandestine sleep, and the system of markers that pointed them to the next safe harbor on the long trail leading north. An untold number of frightened slaves had fled to this very spot for a few morsels of hope and a point in the right direction on their long march through the night. As they stood on ground both historic and sacred, the group settled into a reverent silence. For 20 minutes they sat, some with their backs against the tree, others a stone's throw away. The sun bathed the woods with a soft luminescence. Birds chirped from the branches overhead. The wind breezed up from the south and carried with it murmurs of memory. On its wings, echoes could almost be heard, whispers of the spirituals that coded the path to freedom. And borne by that unquenchable song, ghosts seemed to hover in their midst—runaways pausing from their frantic flight, abolitionists padding the tree with supplies, lynchmen scouring the woods for blood, unfortunates whose blood was found and let. The breeze carried them all, their murmurs mingling with the music. In homage to the tree that bound each one together, they lingered in the currents that breathed through both light and darkness. Then the breeze whisked them away, runaway and lynchman alike, to the distant lands of the North.

"Wasn't that amazing?" The kids debriefed the experience on the bus ride back to Durham. "That's right where it all happened. Wouldn't it be cool if there was a tree like that in Chelan?"

"Who says there can't be?" an adult said, launching a seed.

"What do you mean?"

"What about the people stopping at our town on their own flight toward freedom?"

"Like who?"

"Like any of us really. But what about the Mexicans? They're fleeing the slavery of poverty and following the dream of work up north. Where's the tree that will help them along their way?"

"So what are you saying—that we should start an Underground Railroad in Chelan?"

"I've heard worse ideas."

The teens played around with the image. As they did, they pondered authentic action. They held in their souls the experience of an oppressed people. Their willingness to be present to stories and experiences of African Americans on their trip had broadened their awareness, sensitivity, and understanding of racial prejudice and the suffering of others. They let themselves be moved by that people's pain and the dream that inflamed their quest for freedom. And they considered how God was inviting them to be agents of hope in the midst of slaveries still alive in the present day, right in their own community. They were practicing the way of Jesus.

"By the way," the adult leader asked as they pulled back into town. "Does anyone know a young lady named Emily?"

"The new girl at school?" a teen answered.

"Yeah. Her grandmother asked me if she could join our youth group."

"Over my dead body," Alicia declared. "If she's in, I'm out."

"Me, too," another teen joined in.

"I'm telling you," yet another concurred, "she's the most obnoxious person I've ever met."

Contemplation and authentic action: How do the members of a youth group hear and respond to God's invitation to follow the way of Jesus?

A CONTEMPLATIVE APPROACH TO BOWLING

Shortly after the North Carolina trip, Lake Chelan Lutheran was invited to participate in the Youth Ministry and Spirituality Project. The hope was that by intentionally learning and practicing contemplative forms of prayer and ministry, Lake Chelan might discover new and more effective ways of helping young people become present to God and others. After a transforming experience on their first YMSP retreat, the adult leaders experimented with crafting a contemplative approach to youth ministry. While exploring ways of incorporating prayer practices into youth meetings, they had the brainstorm of planning a vision quest for the youth.

The idea seemed perfect. The teens would be exposed to the transformative power of contemplative practice in ways that blended with the programmatic tradition to which they were already accustomed. The teens were used to a youth ministry program oriented around a yearly trip. Contextualizing the vision quest within an exposure to Navajo culture would continue the legacy of cross-cultural experience that had been so meaningful to the group in years past. Searching for resources within their community, the adult leaders found enormous support. Several enthusiastic church members volunteered to join the covenant community and help facilitate the event. One was a full-time contemplative, another was a person trained in wilderness survival skills, yet another was skilled in self-reflection exercises and group process. The vision came together. Personnel were in place. A curriculum was crafted.

There was only one problem. The kids hated it.

The leadership replaced the youth group's games and socializing with prayer meetings and teachings on contemplative prayer. So many adults were excited about the vision quest that there were more grownups than young people present at the youth meetings. So much time was spent in awareness exercises and processing feelings, youth group felt like group therapy. Across town, the glitzy megachurch organized water skiing and pizza parties for their youth program while the Lake Chelan teens were expected to sit through 30 minutes of excruciating silence in training for three days of solitary hell. And to make matters worse, Emily joined the youth group.

Emily had moved in with her grandparents because of fractured dynamics with her parents back home. She had the domineering brashness of a precocious child, and the porcupine instinct to come out stinging to avoid getting stung. She had opinions to the point of monopolizing conversations, she was an enthusiast for any group activity—be it praying, protesting, or playing pool. She was off-putting to the point where even the adults found it difficult to eat with her. She was a handful. But she was also hungry. Beneath the social blunders was a girl who longed to be loved. She ached to know God and a community that would hold her as one of their own.

Of course, Emily was the sole teen enthralled by the idea of a vision quest. Solitude was second nature to her. And she had a few questions to talk over with God. The other kids couldn't care less. The youth group had long since stopped being fun. If the adults wanted a vision quest, let them go on their own. Let them take Emily with them. As far as the youth were concerned, the adults could stay for three years. But the youth themselves weren't shadowing a desert for three minutes.

The adult leaders struggled with the direction of the youth group. Should they insist they knew what was best for the teens and plow ahead with the spiritual retreat? Perhaps they should emphasize the cross-cultural piece more, since that was so energizing on previous trips. Or maybe they should just throw it all in and head to the lanes and go bowling. What was happening within the youth group? What was God's invitation in the midst of these competing ideas? What action was authentic in the midst of such confusion? The adult leaders didn't have the slightest idea.

But they did have their weekly liturgy of discernment. In frustrating fits and starts, the adult covenant community struggled through the murky fog in three ways. First, they opened each meeting by dwelling in the presence of God through the practices of silence, *lectio divina*, and centering prayer. Those times of contemplation were like a steadfast tiller that keeps a ship steady through a storm. Second, they looked for and shared glimpses of where God's Spirit was swelling with life, hope, and joy within the youth group, as well as those places where that Spirit was blocked. Third, they explored their own attachments—the sometimes murky reasons why one feels so strongly pulled toward some directions and repelled by others.

The work was painstaking, the dynamics complicated. But gradually, some pieces came together. It became clear that the adults' persistence in pursuing the contemplative direction of the vision quest and the youth's resistance to that same path were creating a block to God's Spirit. Frustration and alienation abounded on all sides. So why were the adults so attached to this idea?

To their amazing credit, the adults engaged in the excruciating, soul-searching work of exploring their attachments. Within a spirit of prayer, feelings surfaced as they imagined the effects of abandoning the vision quest altogether. The feelings were quite diverse. One woman felt grief that she never had a chance to experience such an opportunity as a girl. Another leader felt sadness that she wouldn't be able to go on the vision quest herself. Someone else felt a violation to her sense of call as a contemplative—the whole reason she'd joined the covenant group in the first place was because of the commitment to teach the teens contemplative practices. Still another expressed anxiety because abandoning the trip felt like a threat to his determination to see every task he starts finished. Another felt anger that the male pastoral leadership would step in and control the youth group's direction.

While the adults' feelings were diverse, one thing was clear: Their attachment to the vision quest was not connected to an authentic desire within the young people for such an experience. With the exception of Emily, none of the kids seemed ripe for nor interested in such an intense contemplative experience. The youth's reception of the idea was unequivocal. They experienced it as burdensome and deadening, hardly life-giving and liberating. In light of all this, the decision seemed transparent. They would organize a personalized vision quest for Emily, and abandon the year-long program and trip for the rest of the group. Having made the decision, the adult leaders were down-right relieved—they were done forcing a foreign agenda upon young people who refused to go along quietly.

The decision to abandon the vision quest created a programmatic hole. If a cross-cultural retreat was not to be, then where was God leading this youth group? Recognizing that they were at risk of abandoning entirely any contemplative dimension to the youth program, the leaders let go of their prior agenda and simply looked for glimpses of energy and life among the young people. To their dismay, they recognized only one. Whether exhausted from weeks of "being spiritual" or out of a genuine love for having fun, the kids wanted to do nothing else but play. So play they did. The first youth meeting after the vision quest discernment, the adults took the kids bowling. The young people lit up at the news like death-row inmates granted a stay of execution. That evening, they strutted around in two-toned shoes, high-fived after nailing strikes, and chortled over sodas in the snack bar. The teens and adults had so much fun together they decided to do it again—with one twist. They would make dinner together at the church first, then stroll down to the bowling alley a couple of blocks away.

LEARNING TO LOVE ONE ANOTHER

So began Lake Chelan's bowling approach to youth ministry. Once in a while they took a break from the lanes to go rock climbing, try miniature golfing, or have a game night at the church. The adult leaders became quite creative in finding ways to hang out together with the youth, even inviting teens on family outings. Eventually, they even began a monthly candlelight prayer service, a time of contemplative space that deepened their sense of care for one another. But they always came back to bowling, laced with the frivolity of food and conversation.

Throughout their weekly discernment sessions, the adult covenant community continued to look for glimpses of God's Spirit. They found God in the laughter over burnt chili and the smiles the kids now wore when they came through the door. God was in Natalie's tears as she told an adult leader about her breakup with her boyfriend and in Alicia's matter-of-fact insistence on saying grace at the restaurant after a hike through the hills. God was in the way they continually high-fived one another after scaling a rock, sinking a putt, pulling out a Cliff Claven fact during a game of Trivial Pursuit. God was in the community that was forming, the sense of family developing as they spent time with one another. The teens were energized about being together. They took ownership for what they would do. They learned what it means to work together, to value one another, to see each other as Christ sees us all. In short, they learned to love one another.

That is, they learned to love everyone but Emily.

In spite of Emily's pit bull tenacity to be part of the group, the teens would not embrace her. They picked bowling teams without her and groaned at her gutter balls. They changed the topic when she talked and turned away when she asked a question. They ignored her answers during Trivial Pursuit and filled up the van's choice seats without her when they went away. During the weekly meal she would have sat by herself if not for the adults who sat down beside her. The other youth simply could not tolerate her.

Emily refused to let it get to her. But it got to the adults. Increasingly, each week's discernment became focused on the dynamics surrounding Emily. Week in and week out, planning for the group's activities got derailed as the adults agonized over the blatant cruelty Emily endured. They orchestrated various interventions: Adults modeled respect toward Emily; they talked with key youth privately about the way they rolled their eyes when Emily spoke; they nurtured empathy about the painful past Emily had lived through; they offered subtle reminders about Jesus' admonitions to love one another. But the teens' attitudes were too entrenched. As the end of the school year approached, it became a crisis.

That summer the Youth Ministry and Spirituality Project was hosting a weeklong retreat for youth from the participating churches. Four youth from Lake Chelan Lutheran could attend. The retreat promised to be a blast—a week in the San Francisco Bay Area with dozens of kids from all around the country. But which of Lake Chelan's youth would get to go? As soon as she heard about it, Emily just *knew* she had to be included. But the adults were faced with a dilemma. If they left it up to the kids to make a group discernment, the youth would either vote or manipulate a consensus to exclude Emily. On the other hand, if the adults simply decided which youth would go, they would not only rob the youth of any ownership in the process but would end up enflaming the hostility toward Emily. The adults prayed, agonized, and debated as they sought a way through.

Then they came up with a plan. They would discuss the trip with the youth, then invite each one into a process of individual discernment. All the young people were to go home and reflect prayerfully on whether or not they felt God was calling them to go on the trip. Anyone could feel so called. But there was one condition. The four going to the retreat were going as a community. Everyone who felt God was calling them to attend the trip was also required to make a commitment. They did not have to *like* everybody else going on the trip. But for the duration of the retreat, they did have to *love* them. The teens discerned. They came back a week later and discussed what such love would look like, they explored it in the Scriptures, they practiced it at the bowling alley, and they went home and discerned some more. In the end, God called four youth to attend the retreat. One was Emily.

Something was already thawing by the time the four traveled to the retreat. Emily roomed with Alicia, who had been one of the most demonstrative dissenters to Emily's presence in the youth group. On the first night, they had a conversation before falling asleep that was sparked when Alicia asked Emily about the picture of her parents Emily placed by her bedside. The next day the four youth and the one adult chaperone had to create a picture of the youth group's experiment with contemplative youth ministry. The teens laughed about the long-aborted vision quest and the decidedly unspiritual nature of their bowling alley youth group. Alicia and Emily stayed up late talking about cute guys and how lucky they were to have youth leaders who listened to them. As the week went on, they stayed up later, debriefing healing services, swapping their takes on the plenary talks, and giggling over the parlor games the various youth groups were introducing. And somewhere in the warp and woof of the week, through sharing a camera in San Francisco and laughing through karaoke, through making a collage of teenage seductions and a pilgrimage to the beach, through getting lost on the way to Golden Gate Park and holding hands in a community encircling a cross, threads of care and connection began to weave Alicia and Emily together, and Sam and Natalie as well. Over the course of the week, the tenuous strands of their budding kindness became knots, holding fast as the four were stitched together as friends. Having committed themselves to loving one another, they accidentally discovered they liked one another too.

When they returned home, their camaraderie was palpable. Emily was now part of the youth group's inner circle. Alicia, Sam, and Natalie made a place for her at the table. They shared stories of their week away. The others pumped them for details and anecdotes. The other youth listened when Emily spoke. Emily listened when they spoke. Together, they laughed and reminisced until the evening's draught of summer memories was drained to the fill of all.

Then they went bowling.

The teams were easy to pick. Alicia, Sam, Natalie, and Emily bowled as a foursome.

For the entire night, Emily did not land a single strike. But they high-fived her all the same.

AUTHENTIC ACTION

The Lake Chelan Lutheran Church experimented with implementing a contemplative approach to youth ministry. In doing so, they felt like total failures. The teens resisted imposed spiritual practices of prayer and retreat, and the adults, mired in frustration, scrapped their best attempt at a contemplative curriculum.

But a contemplative approach to youth ministry does not entail teaching youth to become contemplatives. It entails a leadership team committed to a contemplative process of its own that enables its members to see ways of crafting programmatic action that authentically participates with God in nurturing life and faith in young people. In this, the Lake Chelan leadership team was singularly successful in practicing a contemplative approach to ministry. Where others, enamored by their own creativity but blind to the cries of their youth, might have pushed their own agenda, these youth leaders let go of their own designs, listened deeply for the movements of God, and crafted actions that followed the pulse of their discernment. As such, they have much to teach us about the nature of authentic action.

First, authentic action depends upon and emerges from contemplation. Parker Palmer observes that the Christian spiritual tradition has often seen the active life and the contemplative life as in tension with each other.[44] An "ancient tug of war" has persisted, a battle that pulls action away from contemplative grounding and contemplation away from the mundanities of the material world. Such competition obscures a deeper truth: Action and contemplation depend upon

[44] Parker Palmer, *The Active Life: A Spirituality of Work, Creativity, and Caring* (Harper & Row, 1990).

each other to sustain a healthy spiritual dynamism. Action without contemplation becomes frenzied and fueled by personal shadow. Contemplation without action tends toward escapism and privatistic self-absorption. In truth, the Christian spiritual life entails a dynamic rhythm of contemplative connection with a sacred love and expressive actions of loving service.

Lake Chelan Lutheran demonstrates the transformative power of rooting action in contemplative practice. Often our actions emerge out of personal agenda; they are clouded by our shadows and conflicts, our wounds and prejudices. Desires to help Nicaraguan peasants can mask paternalism and a resistance to seeing both the pain and the beauty of those different from ourselves; desires to introduce young people to contemplative retreat can mask one's own unsatisfied longings and subtle resistances to seeing youth where they really are. Contemplative practice within a discerning community takes us to the deep center of divine presence where our shadows are exposed, our vision is cleared, and directions that promise life are revealed. Action that emerges from this center is freer from the shadows of personal agenda and more attuned to the movements of the Spirit.

Second, authentic action nurtures a humanity that is fully alive. As such, it enlivens the participants involved, rather than deadening or domesticating them. In a world of economic injustice where patterns of dependency are solidified in social and political structures, well-intentioned acts of charity can often disempower the marginalized and reinforce their domestication. The same holds true for young people. Authentic action empowers agency within youth, is responsive to the questions they bring, and energizes them to bring their gifts and passions into play as they participate in whatever programs are created. Young people who are building community and practicing authentic love while bowling are more filled with the Spirit than those fuming with indignation or smoldering in checked-out boredom through the most spiritually inspired prayer practice.

Third, authentic action is rooted in and contributes to Jesus' radical vision of the belovedness of all people. In the way of Jesus, *all* people are invited to the party, *all* people are welcomed at the table: Mexicans and Nicaraguans, Anglos and African Americans, the adolescents so popular there's always a seat for them at lunchtime and the ones so prickly they eat alone even at their own youth group. This vision of mutuality, celebration, justice, and universal inclusivity is the litmus test for all our programs and actions.

The authentic action that springs from a contemplative spirituality nurtures a sense that all are loved by God and helps create the conditions in which such love can flourish. To be sure, such action may involve radical acts of justice and the bridging of cross-cultural boundaries. At times, it may involve crafting opportunities for contemplative connection with the sacred love that holds us all. But play also is part of the kin-dom of God—especially play that embodies the inclusivity and celebration, the care and love Jesus embodied at the parties he hosted. God is present in the most mundane of activities, even bowling. And bowling, too, offers countless opportunities for the love of Christ to be experienced and lived out in our world. As such, bowling is as legitimate a part of a contemplative curriculum as mission projects and prayer retreats.

Emily discovered this to be true. Alicia, Sam, and Natalie did too. Maybe they didn't spend three nights of prayer in the wilderness. But their high-fives in the bowling alley sparkle with the Spirit's light. How much more authentic can action be?

section three

TESTIMONIES

Within the Youth Ministry and Spirituality Project we used a series of evaluation tools in order to document the experiences of youth ministers, church volunteers, pastors, and youth within the project. We visited and observed churches seeking to practice contemplative youth ministry, interviewed youth and adults, and asked youth ministers to journal their experiences. We held evaluation retreats in which church leaders could gather together and discuss their experiences. This section seeks to illustrate some of what we heard.

Chapter 9 features the gathered reflections of a number of youth ministers who participated in the project. This conversation was compiled from a series of on-site interviews, journal exercises, and evaluation retreats with the first group of youth ministers to participate in the project. The feedback and reflections of these youth pastors were edited together with my own responses to interview questions from project scholars and advisors. The chapter was then sent to the participating youth leaders, who edited and approved their responses. Chapter 10 presents the transcript of an interview I conducted with four youth in front of a live audience at a symposium on youth ministry and spirituality. Each of these youth participated in a church that was practicing contemplative youth ministry.

Learning to Listen to God: A Conversation with YMSP Youth Workers

In 2000, three years after the Youth Ministry and Spirituality Project began, we sought to capture the experience of the first group of youth pastors involved through a series of written evaluations and interviews. The conversation below was edited together from a number of separate interviews done with Mark Yaconelli and eight youth workers who participated in the project. Descriptions of the participants at the time of the interviews are as follows:

Jen Butler. Associate Pastor of Westminster Presbyterian in Eugene, Oregon. Westminster is a 300-member congregation in a university town. Jen's primary responsibility is youth ministry.

Tammy Clark. Director of Youth Ministries at First United Methodist in Valparaiso, Indiana. First UMC is a 1,200-member congregation in a university town one hour outside Chicago.

Robin Roybal. Volunteer Catechumen for St. Thomas Catholic Church in Abiquiu, New Mexico. St. Thomas is the mother church for five other Indo-Hispanic churches in the rural towns outside of Abiquiu. Robin is the mother of two teenagers and works full-time as a secretary with a local construction firm.

Chris Berthelsen. Director of Youth Ministry for Bethlehem Lutheran Church in Bayport, Minnesota. Bethlehem Lutheran is a congregation of 300 members in a small town that is struggling economically. After 20 years in youth and children's ministries, Chris was finishing up an M.Div. in a seminary affiliated with the Evangelical Lutheran Church of America. She has two elementary school-aged children.

Pam Chun. Sunday school teacher and youth volunteer at Judd Street United Church of Christ in Honolulu, Hawaii. Judd Street is a 300-member Chinese-American congregation. Pam works full-time as a secretary at an accounting firm in downtown Honolulu.

Doug Ladsen. Volunteer with the youth ministry at Saron United Church of Christ in Linton, Indiana, two hours south of Indianapolis. Saron is a 500-member church with strong German roots in a rural farming town. Doug is a lineman for a regional public utilities company. Doug is the father of two teenage children.

Steve Fawver. Full-time youth minister at Newberg Friends Church in Newberg, Oregon. Newberg Friends is an evangelical Quaker church with close to 1,000 members, located fifteen miles outside Portland. Steve has served Newberg Friends for more than 10 years.

Bob Eiselt. Volunteer with the youth ministry at Bethlehem Lutheran Church in Bayport, Minnesota. Bob is a financial manager at Trinity Lutheran Church in Stillwater, Minnesota. He has three teenage children.

Interviewer: Mark, let's start with you. What would you say is the purpose of the Youth Ministry and Spirituality Project?

Mark: The purpose of the project is to invite a shift in how congregations experience and engage in ministry with young people. We've been focused on helping people discover another way of "being" in youth ministry. This way of being involves a deeper awareness of and cooperation with the Holy Spirit. You might say that the primary purpose of the project has been spiritual transformation of people and congregations who minister with young people.

Interviewer: So this project really hasn't been focused on youth?

Mark: Actually, I think we're very focused on youth....but we have a different approach to "the problem" of youth ministry. You see, most people believe that the problems in youth ministry are the kids: "Why don't the kids come to worship?" "Why aren't young people reading the Bible?" And on and on. Our approach has been that the problem lies with the adults—they hold the power in the congregation and set the context in which ministry or church life takes place. The problem isn't that youth aren't receiving what the church offers, the problem is what the church is offering.

Interviewer: Which is...?

Mark: Well...first of all no one is quite sure of what they're offering. If you ask most pastors, they'll say they're offering a church family... in other words, membership. If you ask most parents, they'll say they offer a safe place where civic values are promoted. If you ask church elders, they'll say they're offering something that appeals to families and keeps memberships up. They're really isn't clarity about what churches are offering young people...and the kids sense this. Most adults don't know why they go to church or why churches exist...what their purpose is.

Interviewer: What do you think churches should be offering?

Mark: Well, we try to help churches realize that what most churches believe they're offering—church membership, civic values, and so on—is of no interest to youth, nor were these of interest to Jesus. So the project has tried to reconnect congregations to the one unique gift the church offers to people: spiritual living—more specifically, life within the Spirit of Jesus. Life that is in deep relationship with God, self, and others. Life in which the world is enchanted with God's Spirit. Life that is meaningful and hopeful.

Interviewer: How do you do this?

Mark: That has been the primary question in our work. How do you awaken congregations, youth ministers, etc. to the presence of God? Our approach has been similar to what my four-year-old tells me when we cross the street. Stop. Look. Listen. Then go. Most of what we've done with people is help them stop...slow down...sit in silence. Then look. Notice what's going on outside and inside you. Listen. Pay attention to how the Spirit is moving and the presence of others. And finally go. Move in response to what you notice, what you see, how the Holy Spirit is calling you to live and serve.

Often in youth ministry, everyone is sprinting everywhere without knowing where they're going or why they're running. The result is that a lot of people get flattened...mostly children and young people... but a lot of adults too.

Interviewer: Let's bring in some of the people who have participated in the project. What were your youth ministries like before you entered the project? Was it a lot of running without looking?

Chris: Yes...definitely. I was very busy and worked a lot of hours. Church was more of a business for me. God was *talked about*, but not *experienced*. I was very good at loving others and telling others of the love of God for them, but it was very hard for me to believe God's love was for me. I'd been doing youth ministry the same way for 20 years up until this project. I was Julie McCoy, the Cruise Director of *The Love Boat*—lots of fun activities, camps, retreats, mission projects. I kept up with what was current. I attended lots of conferences and workshops—always trying to keep up with what was cutting edge.

Robin: For me God was a duty. I prayed but it was just saying the Rosary or repeating prayers from memory or reading aloud a written prayer. God was so far from me. I had a lot of anger and would take it out on my daughters. My sense of self-worth was pretty low.

Jen: I don't think it was until I started the project that I realized that for the previous three years I'd been on the verge of burnout. I was isolated and leading all of the youth groups pretty much by myself. I had been at the church for only five years, but I think I was ready to quit.

Tammy: I'm like Jen. Before we entered into this project, I can remember sitting with my senior pastor, frustrated and burned out. I sat there wondering why God had called me to this place (I had only been there six months) and wondering how I would survive. By the time I started the project, I was bone dry, tired, and worn out.

Steve: I don't know if I was burned out before the project. It was more like I had this desire to do ministry in a way that was more transparent to the presence of Christ and I was frustrated because I didn't know how to make this happen. The project gave me the tools and space to make this a reality. Through the project I began to shift from an emphasis on busyness, movement, activity, teaching, to a place of listening, discernment, being, walking with people in their spiritual journey, noticing God's activity...There was a transformation for me, for the youth, for the ministry and our whole congregation.

Interviewer: Did you assume that many of the people coming into the project would be feeling burned out and tired?

Mark: Well, yes and no. I had experienced the isolation and burnout in my own youth ministry. But we had chosen these churches randomly...so I didn't know what we'd get. What's interesting is that, as Jen and Tammy mentioned, many of these people didn't know they were burned out or exhausted until they started the project. You see the first task of the project was to slow people down and help them locate themselves. In other words we wanted them to become aware of the lives they were living, the systems and structures in which they were doing youth ministry.

Interviewer: How did you do this?

Mark: Well, first we slowed them down. When they came to a training week we created a whole different culture. There was time and space. In other words the schedule wasn't packed with lectures and workshops. The whole event was structured to be more like a retreat at a monastery then a professional conference. There was morning prayer and evening prayer, long lunch breaks, silence, spiritual direction, small amounts of information and lecture, and lots of contemplative prayer exercises. By making space and time for people to rest, sit in silence, pray, talk in spiritual direction groups, people began to notice how tired they were, they could feel the inertia of their lives, their emotions could catch up to them, and they began to see more clearly how they were living and serving.

Secondly, at the very first gathering we began to describe and map out the current models and systems of youth ministry. We talked about how the youth ministry models in most churches tend to function around products, programs, and professional youth pastors—all of which are substitutes for direct relationships between the adult members of the congregation and their youth. We gave diagrams and other systemic tools to help people name and analyze their current ministry structures and how these structures impacted them. This naming of the "principalities and powers" along with the retreatlike culture of prayer and spaciousness allowed people to develop a greater awareness of the ministry models in their own congregations and the impact of these models on youth, their congregations, and themselves.

NOTICING GOD

Interviewer: So what changed as you moved toward a more contemplative approach? How was this project different from what you've done before?

Chris: It wasn't a "program." It was about a different attitude to life and ministry. It was about noticing God in all the experiences of ministry. Naming God in these experiences and nurturing our relationship with God.

Bob: For me the key was learning to listen to God. Through the silence, spiritual direction, and a focus on contemplative listening to others, I began to listen in a totally different way. I began to listen for God in others, to listen between the words, actions and experiences with others to hear how God was present. I began to realize I had to center myself in God so I could be present to God in all I do. I began to understand that only when I was centered in God was I able to turn outward to others. In fact it was only as I centered myself in God that I began to reach out to others. This not only affected my work in youth ministry but probably had the greatest impact on how I related to my own family, my own teenagers at home.

Robin: Like Bob I think maybe the greatest impact of the project was in my own relationship with my daughters and my own self-identity. I've learned through prayer that it's okay to be me, just as I am, mistakes and all. I've become more calm, relaxed, energetic, and truthful. My feelings of self-worth have increased. I take time now to reflect on the day and share it with my daughters. Prayer, I now realize, is more than repeating memorized writings...it is becoming aware of and in tune with the Lord—acknowledging his presence and not being afraid to express it openly and honestly.

Tammy: Each time I've come out to a YMSP retreat I've had an opportunity to be filled, to meet Jesus, to leave everything behind—to deal with my stuff. I've had a chance to discover who I am and whose I am.

I vividly remember sitting with my spiritual director at the first in-service. I had been so moved by an experience I had in chapel that morning. During our silent time I had this image of sitting knee-to-knee, toe-to-toe, with Christ under a beautiful tree. The sky was crystal clear, and there was a soft breeze. We weren't talking, just sitting. It was as if he knew everything inside my heart. And then he reached out and touched my head, rested his hand there. I felt his touch—it was palpable! I actually felt it! I have gone back to that place so many times. I've realized that the most important thing is that I am pursuing Christ—I need to be sitting with him, longing for him. It's not selfish to take Sabbath—it's necessary—a requirement! I've realized that nothing else in life could possibly line up right if I am not going to sit at Christ's feet.

Interviewer: This sounds very personally transformative. But what's going on here? Is the project simply a spiritual-renewal retreat for ministers?

Mark: As I said at the beginning, the focus of this project was inviting a transformation in how people experience and participate in ministry with youth. We call this a "re-Sourcing." We are shifting the current source of youth ministry from anxiety about teenagers, entertainment, and knee-jerk consumerism to an attentiveness to the presence of God within the congregation. In other words instead of the youth minister, the program, or the curriculum being the focal point of the ministry, we wanted people to be focused on the presence of God.

So the first task of the project was to help people see where their energy and attention was focused, to help them become aware of the destructive models of ministry they were engaged in. The second task was to help people redirect their attention to the dynamic presence of God within their own life and the life of their community and youth ministry. We call this "a contemplative approach" to ministry because the focus is on attending to God, developing a deepening awareness of God in the midst of the ministry, within the youth, within the life of those who engage in ministry.

It turns out that when you give people permission to attend to God, they feel renewed. It's almost like a conversion experience. Most people who work in youth ministry have a deep desire for God that they're never allowed to express or reveal. They're too busy doing the work of God. One of the primary responses we've had from people in the project is "Wow! You gave me permission to be a spiritual person, to seek God, to seek holiness, to reconnect with the sacred in my life."

Doug: Can I interject here? Before I started this project I had let my prayer life go for so long and built so many things into my life—even church things—that there was no evidence of God in my life. I kept looking for ways to create things with God instead of listening to what God wanted to create in me. I still lived under the work ethic of my parents: "Don't sit still! Don't sit around! Work hard! No daydreaming!" There was no time to shut down. I never allowed myself to be still. All I thought about was work and staying busy, and as a volunteer I brought this attitude to youth ministry. From my perspective what could be more important to youth ministry than helping the leaders learn to listen to God?

Pam: I spend much more time in prayer for our church and ministry since the project. I intentionally make more time for the Lord and my- self. I take hours to read and to pray for church school and for the young adults in our study class. I have become very protective of this time and space for prayer. I've slowed down, and I'm not always running from one place to the next trying to squeeze everything in.

Interviewer: So how does this take place? How do you help people "attend to God"?

Mark: We rely on the tested tools of the Christian spiritual life. Spirituality is about paying attention to experience, particularly our experience of the Holy. So we use tools that help people pay attention to their experience of God within their lives and ministry contexts. These tools come from the tradition, and many of them are Sabbath practices: time, silence, rest, and prayer. We also engaged people in regular spiritual direction, so that they have the experience of being heard and companioned in their discovery of the sacred within their experience. We also emphasize contemplative forms of prayer—prayer that is focused on being in the presence of God, resting in God, opening and becoming aware of God.

Interviewer: Aren't you really offering people a different image of God? Don't these practices contain a different experience and thus a different image of God than people normally experience in most mainline churches?

Mark: Yes, I think so. By continually engaging people in practices of presence and by continually asking people to notice the presence of the Holy within their ministry and personal life, I think we do invite people to experience God's nearness. What occurs for many people in our project is an awakening—a new awareness of the sacred dimension of life. As Chris mentioned earlier: Suddenly God is no longer distant. God is present, intimate to my everyday experience. God becomes superpersonal. Although people might believe this intellectually, I think we invite them to experience this—to encounter God within their life experience. This permission to "taste and see," to experience God in the midst of the chaos and drudgery of ministry, is a revelation.

Interviewer: Does this experience or understanding of God change how people approach ministry?

Mark: It changes everything. Suddenly, the isolation many of these ministers experience is shattered. This experience of "I'm not alone" or "God is really here" brings about new questions. It's no longer "What am I supposed to do to make this ministry happen?" Instead the focus shifts to "What is God up to?" "How can I stay close to what God is doing?" "How do I help?"

Tammy: I think I began to approach my tiredness and isolation in ministry differently. Through the project I realized I'm never alone. I still get dry and weary, but now I know to stick with it, and that those times will begin to bear fruit. Brother Lawrence says, "In times we feel furthest from Christ, we are actually closest to him." That brings great comfort. The project has helped me see that I've never been alone...in the midst of painful or wonderful times. The project has helped me be present to my life, seeing each day and each moment, giving me the tools to see and experience Christ now rather than having to look back in hindsight to find him. The YMSP has blessed me so much and helped me grow closer to Christ. Because of that I know I can help others be closer to him too.

Interviewer: Would you say that this is a healing process?

Mark: Actually, that's how our program manager characterized the project. She's often said, "This project is just about healing people." I think there is more to it than that, but healing may be the most central experience people have through our work. In fact, we hold a healing service at every event, and it's always well attended.

There is a healing that occurs in people's self-identity, as Robin expressed. They feel God's acceptance or the Spirit's solidarity with their struggle. They discover God's acceptance of their fear, mistrust, doubt, and pain. They also get honest about gifts that are being squashed, and all the other nasty tensions that are often swept under the carpet in churches. There is healing when this pain and tension is aired out in the presence of God and a community of faith.

There also is healing around their image of God. Most of these people serve a distant God with high expectations. As they're invited to pay attention to their experience, they notice a very different kind of God—a God who is close, who accepts them, who offers guidance and support. There is also healing in how they relate to this God. They discover ways of being with God that are more natural and authentic. They listen more. They rest in God. They express their true emotions. Their relationship with God becomes more multifaceted and pervasive.

Finally, there is healing in how they relate to other people. They begin to see others more as revelations of God and less as customers or competitors. Through contemplative listening, spiritual direction groups, and just lots of experiences of listening and praying with others, they begin to taste the first possibilities of real spiritual community. They begin to communicate how much they receive just by sharing the journey with others.

I would say that what happens to people in the project is that they no longer see themselves primarily as chaperones, or directors of ministry. They rediscover their identity as disciples, as people who fundamentally long to be in deep relationship with God and others. This is a healing process.

Interviewer: Do most of you agree with this project being a healing process of your self- and God-image?

Jen: I think so. The first thing people noticed when I began this project was that there was a shift in me, that I was different in some way. I don't think my image of God changed dramatically, but the depth of my faith had changed. People have even remarked in the last year that they can sense me speaking out of a new depth.

Chris: I think there has been healing, as Mark mentioned, simply in the way I approach life. I've learned to pay attention to God in silence, in music, in nature, in the lighting of a candle, in the Bible, and in ordinary, everyday happenings—a sunrise on the freeway, a baby crying on an airplane, in worship. One of the healings is that all of us in this project began to notice God for ourselves. We didn't just talk about God—God was an event, an experience, a moment suspended in time. God happened to us. For me this created a whole new sense of inner rest. My mantra from this project has been "just rest." This certainly has healed some of the anxiety I've carried into my ministry, my marriage, and my parenting.

This might be odd, but one sign of healing has been the way I've organized my office. I purged my office of unneeded books and just junk I had collected over the years. All these things made me anxious and just added clutter. I have begun to keep only those things with deep meaning for me—things that help create holy space. I've begun to do this in my home as well.

Robin: I like what Chris said about learning to pay attention to God for ourselves. Since the in-services I have a deeper desire to understand readings from the Bible. I am not depending on interpretation from the priest or others, but applying and interpreting the Scripture as it applies to me and the life God is calling me to lead. I've noticed that I've gone from praying only in church to praying wherever I go with a sense of pride. I'm able to talk to God without embarrassment. My daughters have noticed this and now remind me when we are in a restaurant that it is time to pray. Their initiative has been a rewarding gift...for them to say, "Yeah, Mom, let's pray!"

BEARING ONE ANOTHER'S BURDENS

Interviewer: I notice that the structure of this youth ministry approach is much more communal. Can you comment on that?

Mark: One way we sought to counter the isolation most youth ministers and kids experience in church was to encourage a youth ministry structure that is grounded in spiritual community. We were intentional about this from the very start. We always brought people to training events in twos and threes, so that even the training events were a communal experience. After spending the first week on contemplative prayer and attentiveness to God, we then asked congregations to call together a group of church members who would form an intentional spiritual community whose mission was to minister with youth. In other words the youth ministry was supposed to take place in the context of a spiritual community.

We saw this community as the "ritual elders"—the people who would accompany the young people on their journey in becoming adult Christians. This community would develop strong relationships, pray, discern, and serve together in youth ministry. The community was to represent the congregation, which meant it would need to have young and old, parents and single adults, and so on.

Interviewer: What was this shift to ministry in community like for those of you who participated in the project?

Jen: At first the most important aspect of the project was in helping me develop a community to help in the ministry. For years I was the only one who ministered with the youth. Now I have almost 20 adults who are committed to loving and praying for the kids, advisors, and leaders. Three years into the project these same 20 adults are still praying and loving these kids. I don't know of any other church that has that many volunteers and that kind of stability. It is what has allowed me to stay in the ministry at Westminster.

Tammy: This has also been maybe the most important impact of the project on First UMC. Three years ago, there were virtually no adults working with our youth. When the church hired me to do youth ministry, all the other adults left. Some would come occasionally but never regularly. They had all the classic signs of burnout.

Today, we have a good solid group of 18 youth volunteers/team members. The project has enabled our team of laity to be fed spiritually and to find what it is like to live in Christian community. No longer do they feel the weight of the programming on their shoulders, but an opportunity to walk alongside people of all ages in this Christian journey.

Interviewer: What are these groups like? How are they different from another church committee?

Doug: When I think of the people who minister on our team—Nancy, Jen, Kenny, and Frank—I feel like they're my brothers and sisters more than even my own blood. I have shared things with them that I haven't even told my wife. They bear my burdens with me without affecting my family life. The kids see our relationships, and I think it tells them more about the Christian life than what we're teaching them during lesson times.

Jen: I think the adults on our youth ministry teams have formed a very special and caring community that means the world to them—with folks they might otherwise have never known. The truth is that some of these folks I might not have known very well—but when we meet to pray and talk and work together for the young people, I feel a deep commitment to them, and I think it's mutual.

These groups really are about spiritual growth, not just doing church business. I've noticed lots of growth in our ministry teams. Our language about God has changed. There is no longer fear or distrust in our sharing and praying. Our prayers have lengthened. People mention how this group affects their work, families, and worship. The amazing thing is that no one wants off of these groups—now that's nothing like other church committees I've served on! I sometimes shake my head in wonder.

Interviewer: Why are these groups so different from other committees or ministry groups within the church?

Mark: First, we've asked churches to do a calling process that focuses on prayer and discernment. People are listening to whom God is calling to serve on these teams and are seeking to avoid the normal guilt and manipulation that goes into finding volunteers for youth ministry.

Second, the expectations for these groups are different. From the very start these people are asked to participate in a group that is going to build relationships, listen in prayer, pray for one another, and serve together. So people come with a different set of expectations than you might find in a normal church committee.

Often in the church we separate spiritual formation groups and business groups. In these youth ministry teams we've tried to combine both spiritual formation and service. These groups have all the elements that nurture spiritual life—prayer, service, and community. What else do you need in the church but opportunities to love God and serve others within a group of committed relationships?

Chris: For me this project has been a rediscovery of community. I've learned to no longer do youth ministry alone anymore. Before this I had always convinced myself it was easier to do things by myself— and to a certain extent, some of it is easier alone. However, the easier way or the quicker way is most definitely *not* the better way. In taking the very slow road of community and listening to each other's pain and joy, each person's story, we get to a safe place where each is valued and we can work together in mutual support, seeking out the unique gifts each person brings to the table. Our youth have truly resonated to this reality.

Interviewer: Were all of you able to form these communities of adults that serve in youth ministry?

Robin: No, this never really happened for us. For a time Father Donny began to gather a group of us working with youth in Sunday school. He would use the liturgy for discernment in meetings with us and with the lay leadership group of the church. But when he left, the new priest disbanded all of these groups. He decided he would teach all of the catechism classes and youth ministry groups. So we have been unable to meet.

Pam: I was never able to get one of these groups started at our church. There was so much I wanted to share with our church, but I don't think they were ready for it yet. I struggled a lot...trying to be patient but still wondering why they couldn't get it. I felt this project was such a gift! But whenever I went back to share the meeting process with our church and individuals, it seemed no one really wanted to hear what was said. It seemed people didn't get what we were sharing and were not willing to try it out. This included my pastor, who was resistant to contemplative prayer and never was willing to come to any of the training weeks and never asked about what we were learning or how we could implement it into the church. I was so moved by this project; I couldn't understand why they didn't get it! I felt very lonely in this process, but God let me know he was there with me as I struggled.

There were times our Sunday school advisors would let me teach them the contemplative processes we'd learned from the project. They would "graciously" let me lead them—but I never got the sense that they thought it was important. If I was not at the meeting, I know they would not do it on their own. Yet they were amazed when they saw the results of our time together.

What is interesting is that I have been invited to share the process of forming a spiritual community with many other groups outside of the church. I've shared it with a group of teachers who are advocates for a return to traditional Hawaiian language in the schools. Also, our denominational youth gatherings have used the discernment process. So I have found ways to try and create spiritual community outside of our church.

DISCERNING WHAT GOD IS ASKING OF US

Interviewer: What is the YMSP process that Pam refers to? I assume this is the process by which these ministry teams become spiritual communities rather than business committees?

Mark: Yes, that's right. The process that Pam and Robin are referring to is a way of running a meeting that we call the "liturgy for discernment." This liturgy is a seven-step process that each ministry team/community engages in each time they meet. We spent a lot of time teaching the church groups this meeting process. (For more on the liturgy for discernment, see chapter 7 and appendix 5.)

The process is designed to make space for what most people are looking for in church. There is time for relationships and sharing. There is time for prayer and spiritual growth. The business flows out of these relationships and prayer so the work feels more organic and meaningful, less disconnected. And the whole thing is done with others so there is community.

Interviewer: Why do you call it a "liturgy for discernment"?

Mark: One of the definitions of *liturgy* is "the work of the people." This is a liturgy in that it facilitates the work of the youth ministry team to serve young people. We use the word *discernment* because the process is designed to help the group locate themselves in relation to the Holy Spirit. Discernment first involves drawing close to God, locating yourself in God, and then seeing how the Spirit is drawing you to live or act. Through building relationships, prayer, and discussion, the ministry team is invited to discern how the Spirit is present with them and the ministry. They're better able to ensure that their actions and activities are rooted and grounded in the life of the Spirit, rather than their own anxiety or the compulsion of the culture.

Interviewer: Why is discernment so important to this model?

Mark: Most approaches to youth ministry never test the spirits to see what is driving their ministry. Is the Holy Spirit calling them to run the all-night pizza extravaganza? Or is this the spirit of the culture, the spirit of anxiety over the low numbers of kids in attendance, etc.? The question is: Why do we do what we do in youth ministry? What drives us? And where is God in all of this? If you are going to discern what the Holy Spirit is asking of you in your ministry, then you have to slow down. You have to pay attention to the kids, to your own experience. You have to listen to the kids and to the other volunteers. You have to pray. You have to listen in prayer. You have to talk, read Scripture, and pay attention to the fruits of your ministry. This takes all the attention off of you and places it on the activity of the Holy Spirit. What is God up to? What are we called to do? How do we stay faithful to that? This is what the liturgy invites, this is the kind of focus and conversation that the liturgy facilitates.

Interviewer: What about the rest of you? What has been your experience of this liturgy of discernment? Has it actually helped you discern what you do in your youth ministry?

Pam: The process has helped me share what was in my heart and helped me lead a group the way I've longed to lead them. I use this process with every group I work with. It has helped me create an environment that is comfortable, safe to share, builds community, and strengthens our listening to one another and our focus on God's Word for direction. As I shared, it has been difficult to get some of our church groups to use this process, but I have used it with a group of young people who are a leadership group for our conference. We call it our "ohana" or "family" time together. It has helped the group members get to know one another, and everyone always has something to share from the prayer.

Bob: I know for Chris and me it has been a really important time for prayer, and it has had a big effect in helping us be clear about what God is really asking of us.

Interviewer: Can you give me some examples?

Bob: Well, before we began the project we had a youth room with a pool table right in the middle of it. The room looked like a recreation room. As we began to pray and share together and discuss the question, "What is God's call for us?" we began to sense that we needed to create a youth space that was more sacred and less entertainment or recreational. We shared this with the kids and asked them to pray about it. We were totally surprised when they said they sensed the same thing. So together we dismantled the pool table and then had a month of meetings in which we talked about sacred space. We did Bible studies on Moses and the Holy Land and other kinds of lessons that referred to sacred space. Eventually one of the kids designed a big butterfly that we all painted on one of the walls. We even had a prayerful splatter paint night when we repainted the room.

Interviewer: Prayerful splatter paint night?

Bob: Yes. Actually it was quite moving. The kids were dressed in old clothes and we had tennis balls that we'd dip in paint and then hit them with rackets across the room. We'd splatter paint, then stop and sit in silence or listen as Scripture was read, then go back to painting. We had fun, but if you asked any of the kids they'd tell you it was also a very sacred time. And the point is that this all came out of our prayer and sharing. It was all a discernment of how God wanted us to alter the space where we did ministry.

Jen: We had a similar experience with space actually.

Interviewer: You did prayerful splatter paint night too?

Jen: Uh...no. The similarity I was referring to was in regard to getting a youth room. We didn't really have a youth room at first. As our team met and prayed, we began to sense that the youth needed a space of their own. The leadership of the church was totally against it at first, but our teams just kept listening and talking and praying. They kept going before the leadership and telling them we needed this room. There was no stopping these adults! I can't tell you what it meant to me to watch adults other than me advocating for the youth of the church. They were convinced this was what God was calling us to do. Well, I was as shocked as anyone when we actually got it. There was no doubt from any of us that this was led by the Spirit. From the second we began to paint it and move the furniture in, it has felt to me like sacred space. For almost three months, that feeling would overwhelm me every time I went in there.

Steve: The focus on discernment helped us move from a form of ministry that we had done forever to a totally new form of ministry with our kids. We had this program called "Bible Quizzing," which we'd done for six years. This is a conferencewide program that has had a big impact on many of our young people. This year I didn't feel like we had the energy to continue with this program. We began to focus on this in our youth team meetings. We brought it before God and began to discuss it. We all sensed God telling us to "Let it go..." Well, this was difficult to do. I had my pride involved. I also wondered what people would think. How would parents respond? What would the other youth workers in our conference think? But it seemed clear to let it go—so we did. We could have kept it going; we had enough parents and volunteers. But we really sensed Christ saying, "Let it go."

Later in the year we began to notice many kids asking questions about how to share their faith. Well, to make a long story short, our congregation began a 15-week outreach ministry called "Alpha" and invited our youth to participate. This seemed like a perfect program for our youth. The planning team decided the Alpha meetings should be held at 5 p.m. on Sunday nights. That was the exact time we would have had Bible Quizzing! I'm convinced that if we had not been discerning we would have had a major conflict in our ministry. As it was we were free to allow the youth to move into Alpha, and it has been a very significant experience for many of our youth. God moved, we responded, and he showed us after this movement why. It was a clear signal to me of why we need to be always discerning God's activity.

Chris: You know one of the biggest acts of discernment for Bob and me and the rest of our team was not directly connected to the youth group. As we began to listen in our meetings to what God was calling us to do in the youth ministry, we began to sense that the best way we could help our youth was to help the pastor and leadership of the church deepen their own spiritual lives. I think there was a way we sensed that the youth had grown past the adults! So on behalf of the youth ministry we discerned that God was calling us to help the senior pastor and the worship leaders get more centered and focused on God before Sunday morning worship.

So Bob began to invite our pastor and the worship leaders to gather in the pastor's study 15 minutes before worship. He would lock the door and then ask them to "check in." Just kind of a simple, "How ya doin'?" Then after they shared he would read the Scripture of the day and let them pray *lectio divina*. They would get a chance to share how God was present in the prayer. Then Bob would close with prayer and lead the group straight into the chapel to lead worship. Bob still does this every Sunday, and I believe it has helped our worship and our congregation be more centered on God, which we felt was the best thing we could do to help youth at our church.

ACCOMPANYING YOUTH ON THEIR JOURNEYS

Interviewer: So far much of our conversation has focused on the lives of adults. But what about the youth? Tell me what the project's perspective is on youth and how youth have been impacted.

Mark: Our perspective on the process of adolescence and the purpose of youth ministry is very traditional. Youth are in transition. They are moving from childhood to adulthood. In more traditional societies this passage lasts a week, a month, maybe a year. But in Western society we've created this long time of passage—eight, ten, maybe even fifteen years. Youth ministry is about accompanying young people through this period. It is about being in relationship with young people as they move from childhood to adulthood. In this passage the church invites young people into the sacred practices and teachings of the Christian community. We midwife young people into faithful adulthood.

Interviewer: So how is the relationship between adults and youth different in this approach than in another approach to youth discipleship?

Mark: Well, first of all there is a growing awareness among the adults that they are not finished yet as Christians. In other words, as they pray and share in their ministry teams they go through this process of becoming aware or awake to their own spiritual growth. They recognize their own questions and doubts. The faith becomes alive and growing, which, by the way, makes them more interesting to young people. This means that they no longer see themselves as the "experts" or "answer-people." They begin to realize that they are on the same journey with young people; they are still growing, still learning, still stretching. There is a spiritual mutuality, a recognition that we're in this together, which creates a deeper respect between the leaders and the youth. The adults have been on the road longer and have some wisdom from the road to offer. But the trip is still new, still mysterious, there is still lots to learn. I think this realization also makes them less "stressed out," as Robin shared.

The adults are engaged in the youth ministry as a part of their own spiritual formation. They come looking to be transformed by their relationships with youth. The expectation is that youth ministry is not only a place where youth are encountering God, it is also a context for the leaders' formation. This means they approach youth differently. The times with youth are opportunities of divine in-breaking, situations where the leaders expect to encounter the presence of God.

The ministry team really functions as the "ritual elders," or in Paul's language, the "stewards of the mysteries." They're tending the Spirit, they're keeping the sacred dimension of the Christian faith alive and available through their own prayer and relationship-building. They are tending their own Christian experience so they have something to model and pass on to the youth. They're practicing the "way of Jesus" so they can be guides and teachers.

From my interviews with youth, I'd say that the biggest impact they have experienced is that they feel connected to more adults, and that these adults seem alive and genuinely concerned and available for relationship.

Interviewer: So what does it mean to "accompany" these young people?

Mark: Accompaniment means you're committed to being in relationship with the young people. You're sharing the same road. Headed in the same direction. Sometimes that involves being a second pair of eyes and ears for the youth: I'm here for you to help you watch and listen, to help reflect who you are becoming and the ways in which the Spirit is becoming alive in you. In other words I'm doing what a good spiritual director does. I'm witnessing to your development as a person and helping you notice your gifts and where you seem most transparent to the presence of Jesus. It also involves serving as a guide: I'm going to invite you into the experiences, practices, and teachings that I've learned are most important for staying alive. I'm going to engage you in the Christian mysteries and then be available to you as you ask questions, share your experience, etc. But accompaniment also includes the expectation that *you* will grow. You realize you have much to learn. You expect to be transformed in the relationship, to be vulnerable to the ways in which the youth are ministering to you.

Interviewer: Can some of you describe what accompaniment looks like in your ministries?

Tammy: When I started the project, the youth had come to expect youth group to be fun, entertaining, and led solely by me. There was lots of turmoil as we began to get involved in the project. Accompaniment has meant more adults involved in the youth ministry—adults who feel called to this ministry and enjoy being with youth. It means we have given the youth permission to be involved in Sunday morning worship on a regular basis and have encouraged them to really own the service by playing music, reading Scripture, and sharing their encounters with Christ with the whole congregation. I think we've bridged the gap between adults and youth. The youth now welcome adults into their lives, and the adults welcome the youth.

An example of this is a recent crisis involving skateboarders. Lots of teen skateboarders skate on the church property. They love to "grind" their boards on the front church steps, and the cement began to crack and crumble from their skating. The church leadership decided to replace the steps and put up signs that outlaw skateboarding as well as put protective devices into the cement that will prevent the skaters from "grinding" on the steps. Some of our team members heard about the decision and went to the board meeting. They asked the board to reconsider and instead be grateful for the presence of the youth and find ways to build relationships with them. After a long period of prayer and discernment, the board decided not to put up the signs or the skateboard blocks and instead reach out to these youth.

A group of adults met with the skaters and basically told them about the church's decision. They invited the skaters to use any of the church facilities any time. They walked the youth through the building and showed them the bathrooms, kitchen, etc. They told the youth they were welcome to skate on the property. So we have the ugliest church steps in town—but we have all these kids who love to hang out and feel welcome at the church.

Doug: I know a powerful experience of accompaniment that involved one of our adult volunteers. I won't say his real name...I'll call him Dale. Dale has been a volunteer with the youth for three years and the kids just love him. He's a farmer, but in the past three years he's had nothing but bad luck. So bad he's had to get work as a janitor to make ends meet. To top it off, last year his wife left him. So he's had a very bad time. Well, one night last fall he was feeling so low he went to a bar and began drinking. Now this is really unusual for this fellow. But he was feeling pretty bad. He did a dumb thing and tried to drive home and, sure enough, he got pulled over by the cops and got a DUI.

Well, when the parents and church board heard about this, they wanted him immediately removed from the youth ministry and any contact with the youth. Our team went to the church board and asked them to let him meet with the kids one last time to at least say goodbye and explain himself. So Dale went before the kids and apologized, he basically opened up his heart and told them what he'd been through and that it was a dumb mistake and that his biggest regret was that he wasn't going to be able to work in the youth ministry. After he left the kids stayed and talked. They started talking about forgiveness: "Wasn't that what Jesus asked us to do?" and such. The kids went to the church board and asked to have Dale reinstated. They met with him and told him they forgave him for what happened and that they wanted him to continue to help lead the group. I'll tell you there were a lot of tears that night for all of us. And I'll also tell you that when kids have troubles, they go to Dale.

Jen: I notice that when our adults meet with the youth there is a real enthusiasm—the kids love the adults, and the adults love the kids. One sign of this is that the kids keep coming earlier and earlier to youth group. They see us adults in our team meeting, and they love to walk over to where we are praying and talking and just simply sit in. We have made photos of all our kids and written their names and prayer concerns on the back of the photos. The members of our ministry team carry these like trading cards. They carry them to work and home and pray for the kids all week. Then they trade them for different kids the following week. Well, we have one retired woman on our team who had been praying for these kids for three years even though she didn't attend the youth group and had never really met any of them. One morning she was asked to serve Communion on a Sunday when most of the youth were in the service. As the kids came forward she was overcome with emotion as she greeted by name the kids she had been praying for over the past three years.

One of the moments the kids still talk about is when Jim (a retired school administrator) crammed down through a trap door into a dark, small basement with some kids during a hide-and-seek game. They were down there 20 minutes. He impressed the socks off those kids.

Chris: I've noticed that anytime we gather with the youth the part of our time that they seem to value the most is the "check-in." They are quick to remind us if we forget, and the sharing continues to get more and more personal and intimate. They like hearing the adults as much as we like listening to them.

One night there was a low youth turnout, and I asked the kids if they felt intimidated by having more adults than youth. One senior boy said, "As long as you don't act like adults and just act like people it doesn't seem to matter what our ages are." I think the youth get this better than the adults! It seems harder for the adults to feel safe in their sharing. But we're getting there.

THE WAY OF JESUS

Interviewer: So if I were a young person attending one of these churches engaged in contemplative youth ministry, how would my experience be different than a church that had a different approach?

Mark: I guess there are three basic differences you would experience. First, you would encounter a youth ministry that has lots of adults. These adults would be a diverse group that represents the church. These adults would be authentically struggling with their faith in authentic relationships with youth. These adults would be (appropriately) transparent, exposing how they process their faith, not just their answers to Christianity's top 10 questions. You would also notice that these adults were consciously practicing the very faith they were trying to transmit—that they were in community with one another, praying together, and serving together.

Secondly, you would be invited into a mystical awareness of faith. All of our churches were trained in engaging youth in mystical forms of prayer, prayer exercises that invite young people to notice and name their experience of God. Almost all of our churches spend 5 to 45 minutes at each youth gathering in some form of contemplative or mystical prayer. This is a new development in youth ministry because it allows young people to be spiritually empowered—they are given permission to explore and name their experience of God in the midst of the community. They are allowed to participate in the mystical element of the faith. In this way Christianity is no longer limited to the intellect—reciting theological statements. Youth are invited into the primal Christian experiences that inspire all of our doctrines and theological musings.

Finally, you would encounter a youth ministry focused on spiritual practice. Young people would not only be learning the Bible and the teachings of their denomination but also practicing some of the disciplines of faith that encourage the same life-rhythms found in Jesus' life. So you may encounter churches in which kids practice regular periods of silence, journaling, biblical meditation, and regular prayer retreats, as well as service, regular attendance in worship, relationship-building with outsiders, and a deepening commitment to community. These practices encourage the rhythms of relationship in the life of Jesus—love of God, and love for others as you love yourself.

Interviewer: So no more fun and games?

Mark: No, you'll still find fun and games, curricula, dynamic youth leaders—all the "stuff" you find in other youth ministries—but the difference is that these are not the focal point, the forming center of the youth ministries. These churches are attentive to not only the message within their ministry but also the methods they are using and how these methods—fun and games or lecture and study—form and communicate the faith.

What we hope young people in these churches encounter is "the way of Jesus." By that we mean the rhythm or way of life Jesus was practicing—a way that involves mind, body, soul, and heart. This happens by being within a community of people who invite you to join them in practices that teach and encourage you to love God and love others as you love yourself. This is a move away from youth ministry as simply transmission of information, or youth ministry as entertainment. It's about learning a way to live in the world.

Interviewer: What about the rest of you? Are your youth encountering the "way of Jesus" as Mark has described it?

Steve: I realize that as a Quaker, I'm part of a tradition that has a rich heritage in mystical practices: open (or silent) worship, meetings for clearness, etc. But in the past our church hasn't been intentional in claiming these practices and inviting youth to experience them. Since being in the project we have made adjustments to help young people notice Christ's activity. I have been challenged and encouraged to make or create space for youth to encounter Christ. This has been amazing. I'm convinced that the heart of ministry needs to be creating space for youth and adults to "notice" God.

Our youth have also moved to a place of desire and deep calling to interact and be a part of the larger community at Newberg Friends. Here are some of the interactions I've noticed between adults and youth: For the first time since I've been at this church, youth and adults have participated in retreats together. Youth have been involved in long-range planning and visioning meetings. Youth are now helping to lead us in worship. We had a mission trip that was intergenerational—youth and adults as old as 70 worshipping, serving, eating, playing, and praying together. This has been an amazing opportunity to see the body function together. This has been important not only for the youth but also for the adults.

Interviewer: And all of this is a result of this new approach to ministry?

Steve: Well, I can't say all of this is happening as a direct result of YMSP—but isn't it interesting what is happening? I think maybe God is up to something, and the project has been an important piece of this working.

Jen: I think the changes in the kids are the hardest ones to track—at least when it comes to individuals. But there have been some significant changes in the tone of the whole youth group evenings. We have at least three "major" youth groups in our area with 150 or more kids. We often lose kids to these megagroups—which is always disappointing. But we know that our small group offers less fluff and more depth and intimacy. And indeed, several kids have returned to our group saying just that. Our groups like to check in each week. Making space for this kind of relational conversation has created a sense of community that is strong and encourages kids to interact. Even new kids feel they belong.

As Mark said, our youth encounter lots of adults who care about them and are struggling to live the Christian faith. From the beginning Mark talked about the lack of spiritual adults for our kids to bump into. Now we have at least 17 adults who would love it if the kids bumped into them, and I know these interactions will change our kids over time. I love knowing that there are people praying for each individual kid, and I think the kids love it too. I think contemplative youth ministry has helped us become more friendly and welcoming to young people. We now have a youth section in the sanctuary—this idea was generated by the youth themselves. There are now a few young faces at each service on Sunday. I hope this will continue to catch on so that sitting there during worship is always what we do.

In terms of the "mystical" element of the faith, our youth now expect to engage in spiritual exercises at each gathering. Their favorite is to decorate the sanctuary and then engage in worship, silence, or reflection. They also love journaling. We have challenged the kids in their faith and relationship with God, and the kids have risen to the challenge. I can see that many of them now work hard to keep a faith perspective on all aspects of their life.

Interviewer: What about the journey outward? Do you see more attempts to reach out beyond the youth group and church community?

Jen: Yes, I do. For example, our town recently cleared out all the homeless from the local city park. There were several families living in cars that now had no place to go. John, our senior pastor, and some of the adults on our youth ministry team worked with other churches to adopt these families. We had a family living in a trailer on our church parking lot. This family had teenagers, and immediately the youth invited them to come to the youth group. They felt so welcomed that when they moved into a place across town six months later, they wanted to continue in the group. So our adult leaders set up a rotation to ensure that these kids had a ride to youth group each week. To me this is a sign of welcoming the stranger.

Tammy: As I said earlier, most of our youth really didn't like the changes we began to make in the youth group at first. What were all these other adults doing here? Why all this biblical meditation in Sunday school? We liked just hanging out with our friends. Why was there all this focus on prayer? We'd always just played before. What were all these new "practices" about in confirmation? (Actually this question came mainly from parents.) And the list could really go on. Some of the kids really liked the changes—mainly the younger ones who didn't know any different. The older ones took some convincing....or should I say experiencing. We've been consistent about doing spiritual practices with kids, making space to encounter Christ. Some youth have got into it; others don't. But we keep doing them. We've also given kids permission to be involved in worship. Encouraging them to "own" worship and to share their experience of Christ in the service with the adults. We now introduce spiritual disciplines early on in the sixth grade. Our confirmation process is full of spiritual practices. Although we still play with the kids—the play now has a purpose and *lectio divina* continues to be the favorite practice they do.

We've come a long way and still have a long way to go. Do I think this project has helped our youth? Yes. It gave us direction and an excuse or reason to be more intentional about encountering Christ. It has given youth the bigger picture—helping them notice and participate in the adult community.

Chris: I think the most powerful aspect of the project has been giving young people the space and opportunity to notice God in their lives—what Mark called "the mystical experience of faith." Creating exercises where kids can notice God creates a sense of wonder: "Perhaps my daily experiences are connected to God?" Asking kids to notice their experience of God also creates freedom and eliminates pressure. Maybe you notice God, and maybe you don't. Finally, allowing kids to notice God creates opportunities for personal validation. It says, "I want to hear what you have to say about your experience." Each person is valued. Simply asking "What did you notice?" has caused senior high students, junior high students, Sunday school teachers and their students, congregational members, and me to "see God" in our ordinary days. When I've asked kids to tell me where they encounter God in worship, I've heard all kinds of wonderful responses: "When I lit the candles." "In the stained glass windows." "In my father's eyes during the sermon." "In the sharing of the peace." "In the sound of my own voice saying the Lord's Prayer."

Doug: Believe it or not the kids now thank us for the lessons and devotions. I mean really heartfelt thanks. They tell us they know this kind of opportunity to pray and share doesn't go on at all churches. Almost all of our high school youth use *lectio divina* on almost a daily basis. Our junior highers are still working on it. The kids journal at each gathering...mostly to write about their experiences of prayer. Our kids are praying more. One girl tells me each time she feels a breeze on her face it calls her to prayer. Some of our athletes have shared that they pray as they run. Many of the youth have asked us to help make regular space for prayer. I've noticed that the prayer concerns time at youth group now lasts longer than the one during Sunday morning worship. I wonder sometimes if the youth haven't passed the rest of the congregation spiritually. In fact our associate pastor is always scheming with the youth to have them help her introduce new ideas and practices into worship. It seems that if the pastor introduces them, the adults get upset; but when the youth do something new in worship, the adults are always supportive.

The youth really claim the church space and feel at home. We almost always have a basketball hoop or volleyball net up in the fellowship hall. The youth use this space to hang out, to have their after-game parties and weekend dances.

Interviewer: Again, I wonder if this project isn't presenting a different image of God than has been presented in traditional youth ministry strategies.

Mark: Yes, I think you see in all these stories a different face of God. I would say people experience a God of the Sabbath in this way of ministry. A God of rest and hospitality. A God of relationships and time. A God who is spacious and accepting. A God who is intimate, within our own experience. A God who offers a way of living, not just believing. A God who is approachable—a God we can experience and know. A God who is guiding and teaching, if we'll only listen.

THE ROCKS

Interviewer: So far the picture has been fairly positive. But there must be difficulties. What obstacles have you encountered in doing contemplative youth ministry?

Mark: Actually I usually tell people that this way of youth ministry is the most difficult way to disciple youth. What we invite people into is very simple—prayer, relationship, and service. But these simple, natural activities seem almost impossible in the present world.

Interviewer: Why is that?

Mark: Because such ministry is so countercultural. It requires time. Time to pray. Time for relationships with young people. Time for spiritual community. Nobody has time in our culture—especially for kids. This form of ministry also requires community. The ministry comes out of a community of adults—we don't do community well in North America. As these ministry teams spend time together, conflicts emerge, people don't like each other, there are power plays and heated disagreements. The culture says, "If it doesn't feel good, get out." So it's very hard to tell people, "No. Stay in those relationships. Christian community is not about liking one another...it's about a commitment to loving one another." That's difficult.

The other difficulty is that many pastors get threatened by lay people and youth ministers acting as their own religious interpreters. When you invite lay people into contemplative prayer and discernment, adults begin to identify their own experiences of God. This can be hard for some ministers to take. Youth are also allowed to do this kind of listening and speaking. This can be threatening—especially if the youth and youth ministry team are hearing something different than the leadership. Sometimes the youth group can engage in a way of living or spiritual disciplines that the adult congregation doesn't embrace. So there is tension.

Finally, this way of ministry requires a different kind of youth minister—someone who can facilitate relationships between adults and youth. Many times youth ministers are chosen because they can relate to kids, not adults, so they have difficulty sharing the ministry with adults. They prefer to do it all themselves.

Interviewer: Did the rest of you encounter these obstacles?

Chris: I think our senior pastor was threatened by this contemplative approach and threatened by me. He was always polite when we brought ideas, but he never embraced this way of ministry.

Pam: As I stated earlier my pastor never asked me about contemplative ministry or wanted to talk about it. At first he agreed to come out to one of the training weeks, but then he made excuses and never came out. He just didn't seem ready for this way of ministry.

Robin: Like I told the group our new priest disbanded our group and has taken on the youth ministry by himself. I realize now that I have to take what I've learned and first use it personally and with my daughters—and then look for ways to use it in our church.

Jen: I know our community was ripe for this way. People were looking for a way to grow spiritually; they were also very concerned for their youth...so this was a natural process for us. I also think it helped that our senior pastor, John, and I have a good relationship. John has always been an advocate for the youth and children and is a spiritual person—somewhat of a mystic—so he was very supportive.

Mark: Out of the 16 churches that began the project, only three or four churches really embraced this way of ministry. In most churches either pastors shut it down, the youth ministers never really shared the ministry with the rest of the congregation, or there was so much instability in the congregation it could never take root. Sometimes the project contributed to the instability. People would come to one of our retreats, get in touch with anger, depression, or frustration in their work in the church, and then leave the church.

Interviewer: So actually the project has been a disservice to many of the churches it worked with?

Mark: Well, maybe...yes, in the short run...in terms of the goals the church has set for itself. But in the long run I think it's more healthy for the whole church any time ministers or Christians grow in their awareness of God—even if this means some isolated local instability.

Interviewer: So what kind of soil is required in a church for this approach to take root?

Mark: You really need two things. First, you need a church that desires to be a spiritual community. And second, you need pastors who desire to be spiritual leaders. In other words you need a community of people who are seeking to grow in relationship with God and others. A place ripe for relationships. This is what kids are seeking—relationships with God, each other, and the adult community. If you don't have people interested in spiritual community, this will never take root. If you have pastors who are formed as CEOs and don't see themselves as spiritual leaders—people engaged in the spiritual arts of prayer, discernment, and study—this will eventually be squashed.

Interviewer: One final question: What about race and ethnicity? Is this whole "spirituality" movement really only about white, middle-class churches?

Mark: I don't think so. We've had Latino, African American, and Asian American communities participate in or observe the project, and they've said that much of what we're doing could be beneficial to their communities. The problem is more one of translation. There is another style and language in which one might approach this material that makes it more accessible to people of different cultures and ethnicities.

Interviewer: Did any of the racial-ethnic churches you worked with succeed in integrating this approach into their ministries?

Mark: No, not really. Although I don't know if race or ethnic identity was the reason that it failed. I do know that the people who participated from racial-ethnic congregations—including Robin and Pam here, as well as Gerald Arata from our Japanese-American congregation, and Sue Conner from Sojourner Truth, an African American congregation in the San Francisco area—they all felt the project offered important processes and tools for their ministries. As Pam mentioned, many of these people got resistance from their leadership; others from their community as a whole. I think that many of the racial-ethnic communities we've worked with aren't as disconnected from the Spirit or from each other as some of the white congregations. For example we're working with a Latino congregation in Los Angeles. Now there is a high value on community among Latinos, as well as a permission to directly experience God in prayer and church settings. So the project is not a revelation to these congregations as it might be to a white mainline congregation that has no prayer life and little sense of community.

Robin: As I mentioned, this project is not taking root in my church, and the current priest has shut it down. I come from a dry, hard land. The people who live in our community have been there since before this country was born. They have roots among the Native Americans and the early Spanish settlers. They are a hard and traditional people who don't change easily.

Almost all of them do some sort of gardening or farming. A good farmer always looks for possibilities in land that will produce a good harvest. But what is good soil? It takes a little more work to till and make ready barren land, but when done faithfully, that piece of land can be made good. It can produce a good harvest. So what about the rocks on a piece of soil? How can the farmer make this "good"? Well, are they big rocks or little rocks? Can they be moved by one person or do you need help from others? Then, move the rocks and use them for something else. Till the soil faithfully and make it good to harvest good crops. This is what I plan to do when I get home—starting with my own life and my own family. And that is what I would say to any church that feels like this is impossible. My hope is to be able to continue in this spiritual awakening and sharing it with others in my parish. My prayer has constantly been: *Lord, open my heart and eyes to your grace and love. Make me an instrument in your church by allowing me to share with others. Open the hearts of others, for surely they are my salvation.*

Seeking a Life of Love: A Conversation with YMSP Youth

In June 2004, 200 youth workers from across the country gathered at San Francisco Theological Seminary for a symposium on youth ministry and spirituality. Presentations were focused on the Youth Ministry and Spirituality Project's exploration of contemplative spirituality within church-based youth ministry programs. During one night of the conference Mark Yaconelli, Director of YMSP, interviewed four young people involved in the project in front of the gathering. They talked about worship, youth ministry, adult-teen relationships, and contemplative prayer. Descriptions of the four youth at the time of the interview are as follows:

Nate Spinney. Twenty-year-old from Eugene, Oregon. Nate grew up attending Westminster Presbyterian Church, a congregation that has spent seven years practicing contemplative youth ministry.

Amanda Frey. Fifteen-year-old from The Woodlands, Texas. Amanda attends The Woodlands Christian Church, a 400-member congregation outside Houston.

Lauren Dugard. Seventeen-year-old from Cleveland Heights, Ohio. Lauren attends Church of the Redeemer, a racially mixed United Methodist congregation in Cleveland Heights.

Nathaniel Reuter. Sixteen-year-old and attends Oakhurst Baptist Church, a racially mixed congregation in Decatur, Georgia.

Mark: From what you observe among your peers in school, and in your community, are young people interested in the spiritual life?

Amanda: Yes. I think they really do care and have an understanding and a sense of wanting to be on the spiritual path and getting where they're trying to go.

Lauren: For a lot of my friends and the youth I talk to, I think it is a very important aspect of their life. They might not know all of the Bible stories, but what seems to be important is belonging to a religion or having that community of a church and feeling the love, I guess, that comes with an understanding of Christianity and love of one another. And you can really see it. There's a difference in demeanor between those who have somewhere they can go and know they're loved and accepted, and those who kinda feel they've been turned away by different things. Or maybe they had a really bad church experience. So I guess young people really do yearn for a spiritual community. We have a lot of youth who come on their own. And that shows that, you know, it's their decision in their hearts.

Mark: How do churches help young people live the Christian life?

Seeking a Life of Love: A Conversation with YMSP Youth

Nathaniel: I guess kind of a perfect example of how this can play out is that one of the adults on the youth ministry team this past year is moving to France. She doesn't have a job there, and she doesn't have specific plans. It's just something she feels called to go and do. Seeing an adult with that kind of freedom, an adult that's alive and living is just beautiful and encourages my own spiritual journey. Another adult who volunteers in our youth ministry, Mary Sue, just got married at 35 and it's like, even though she's an adult, she's still living, she's still growing and falling in love and that's just inspiring—that life doesn't end with adolescence.

Mark: That *is* encouraging that we can be as old as 35 and still fall in love. You get about 29 and you basically think your life is over and it's time to find a retirement community in Florida. [Audience laughs.]

Nate: I guess it's the team of adults involved in the youth ministry program that has been most encouraging to me. There is one woman who really sticks out in my mind, her passion for caring for youth and her passion for the Spirit—just all of that combined—and when I see her I'm lifted spiritually. I'll be going along on my journey and then, one day I'll go to church and see this woman—her name is Marcia—and it's almost like she gets teary-eyed every time she sees me. She's just the happiest person I know. And it fills me up with such hope and happiness.

Mark: Both of you have mentioned adults who have been inspiring or encouraging to your Christian life. Could you say more about the kind of adults you find supportive in your own faith life?

Amanda: Well, you don't have to be an extrovert, but it is easier for youth if adults come and approach us in a nice way, like, "Hey, how are you doing? I've seen you around–what's your name?" And just be nice. And if we do something that's not quite right on the church grounds...just don't mention it to anybody. [Audience laughs.]

Nate: I want to add that the adults that really make the church experience a better experience for youth are the ones who really show an interest in who we are and take an interest in our lives—as well as the ones who are still interested and passionate about their own lives. Not only do they say, "Hey, how are things going with you?" They're willing to share their lives with us. Those are the people I really enjoy talking to when I go to church.

Nathaniel: That leads me into something I've heard adults in our program talk about: vulnerability. That's an enormous part of being able to relate one-on-one with somebody. And that's really what it comes down to. It's not one-on-ten or one-on-twenty or however big your youth group is. It's one-on-one—and that's really where you're going to get the connection made. You can't just have somebody reciting lines or reading a book or teaching you. You want someone who's learning with you and growing with you. That's how you learn that you're on a spiritual journey with somebody. They can't be at the end of the journey tugging on a rope trying to get you to come on—you know? They're right there with you. And you have to see that they're vulnerable and they're people, too. I'd have to say that I haven't seen a single adult enter our youth ministry and leave the exact same way they entered. I've never seen that. Everybody has changed. And that's just how it's got to be.

Mark: What do adults in the church do—one-on-one or in youth ministry—that impedes your life with God?

Nathaniel: [In a deep, formal voice] Friends, please open your Bibles to Luke... [Audience laughs.]

Amanda: I guess, like, babying us.

Mark: What do you mean?

Amanda: I mean, in youth group, we're teens. We're not kids. When we go somewhere we don't necessarily need you to hold our hands. We don't need chains connecting us to our partners. We can handle it. I mean, every other kid has a cell phone now. It's like, we need that trust, until we totally give you a reason not to trust. I guess I feel that, like, just trust us, you know, as individuals, like young adults instead of children. I don't know, I think there's a big difference between the two.

Nate: When you ask that question I think of the people I relate with right before we go into the worship service or right after the service. The adults who really get me are the ones who are like, "Hi, Nate, how's it going?" and then you start telling them and you realize they really have no interest. They ask it for the formality of the question but really don't care to listen. And I guess it's not only youth—I see them do it to my parents. This is not a great quality to have at church. Be involved in a conversation if you're going to get into one.

Nathaniel: I would say what's most irritating to me is people who are unwilling to allow the foundation of their theology to be questioned by anyone else. I guess I don't know any other way to say it. It just goes back to the idea of needing to be personable with somebody and needing that mutuality. When somebody refuses to be influenced by you, it's like, "Why are we communicating?" I mean, what's the point in this? If you're not going to learn from me, if you're not going to grow with me, then there's no point.

Mark. You seem to have a lot of energy around this issue.

Lauren: Yeah, along with what Nathaniel just said, I don't like when there's this barrier: "I'm older so I know more." I don't know—I guess in some cases, sometimes you really do need to listen. Like when an adult says, "I've been down this road, I can help you." But then sometimes, you know, you've got to test the waters for yourself. So I guess the mentality that "age brings wisdom" kind of needs to be thrown out the window when it comes to youth group members interacting with adults. And I have to say a lot of the adults in our church have been able to do that.

One of the things that really upsets me is when people are so set in their ways, like Nathaniel was saying, that they can't see another path and if they do see another path they think it's wrong. I guess I really think it's not our place to judge. Especially since a lot of us go to really diverse schools. And I don't think you can sit there and tell someone they aren't worthy of God's grace.

So I guess that's a real push-and-pull among the youth at my high school. When I try to invite them to church, they kinda say they don't want to come to an environment where people are going to tell them they're better than someone or they're worse off than someone. I guess they think that if they come in, they're going to be brainwashed in a certain way of being. I believe you kind of find your own way to Christ and there's no, like, specific way. It's about learning about each of the youth in your youth group and helping them move toward the same goal. And there's never a set path. Just because you might pray one way doesn't mean that you make everyone else fold their hands and get on their knees. I think that's really important, not only for adults but for every age. People need to understand that, when you're in a community, it's important to be accepting of different viewpoints.

Mark: Are there experiences within your church that used to drive you crazy that you now appreciate?

Nate: The sermons. I used to nestle up next to my mother and use that as the 15-minute nap time before it was time to go get cookies. I totally didn't appreciate it. If I did listen, I would just lose myself in all of the words the preacher was using. I would just stop paying attention—I'd have the little bag of crayons and stuff, and I'd just start drawing and coloring. And that always used to just turn me off. I would think, "Well, why did I sit through this just for a sermon I don't understand?" As I grew older I was able to be a little more patient and understand the words that the pastor was saying.

Nathaniel: I'd say that I've really learned to appreciate being part of the church community, a loving community. My parents always said, "We're going to keep you here whether you want to be here or not, because you need to be a part of this community." And, you know, that doesn't mean anything to a kid. But as I grew older and experienced different troubles and things going on in the world, stuff that kind of shakes you, I would wake up on Sunday morning and have to go to church and then I would realize, "Oh, you know, this is where I can go." I mean, I thank God that there was—and is—a community there. And that I'm still a part of it. And there's just nothing that's comparable to that.

Amanda: It used to drive me nuts when my youth director and my dad would go to these conferences on contemplative youth ministry and they'd come back and tell the group, "We need to sit around a candle for 15 minutes and be perfectly still and quiet." I was like, "What happened to dodgeball, you know?" [Audience laughs.] "There was nothing wrong with the marshmallow-and-spaghetti Bible lessons, you know? It was fine." But then our youth leader was like, "Okay, but still, close your eyes, relax" —and everybody's, like, making sure nobody else is looking at 'em: "Is everybody doing this or is it just me?"

But now, everybody relaxes and gets into a real comfortable setting, and it's much easier to pray with what's being said in the Scripture. So it's actually become really peaceful...sometimes *too* peaceful, you know? —after finals you're, like, zonked out. But even when you do that, you know, when you wake up, you're rejuvenated—you're like, "Okay, I'm good."

Mark: You're talking about a Wednesday night event at your church that's called "Sabbath" where you have silent prayer and personal sharing, is that right?

Amanda: Yeah.

Mark: What about others who have experienced contemplative prayer? People debate whether young people can really relate to silent forms of prayer. I know Nate, Lauren, and Nathaniel engaged in a lot of contemplative prayer at various YMSP youth events. And Amanda has regular experiences of *lectio divina* in her youth group. Could you comment on how you relate to these contemplative practices?

Nate: In terms of spiritual practices, there was something I heard when I came out to a youth retreat sponsored by the Youth Ministry and Spirituality Project. At that retreat the leader mentioned that the Spirit isn't going to tell you something every time you sit down to pray. I mean, you don't know when and how God is going to speak to you. You just kind of have to be patient for that. So I would do these practices in my youth group, and if it wasn't happening, it wasn't happening—and that was okay with me. For example, there were times in *lectio divina* when nothing jumped out at me. I would just, you know, kind of focus and use the time in silence.

I have done these practices and had moments where I walked away a completely new, spiritual person, and it really changed my life those few times. And I've learned to remember that it may not need to happen now, so let's not force it. And I'll just be patient.

Lauren: I think teens definitely have the capacity for silent prayer. They're very capable of it. Three other youth came with me in August [to a YMSP event on contemplative prayer] and we kind of just molded to it, very, very quickly. When we came I didn't know what to expect really, and I think one of the leaders said, "We're going to have three hours to take a spiritual walk, and please don't talk to your neighbors and don't let your mind wander." And I'm like, "Did he say hours?" [Audience laughs.]

I wasn't sure I could do it. I mean, teens nowadays are so busy and so stressed out, that it's kind of hard to imagine them ever sitting still and contemplating their lives, but it really does work. I mean, school was out, we were in summer, and we were able to just remove ourselves and pray or read or sometimes even sleep—whatever. It just came naturally—more naturally than we had ever thought. And I've taken it home. My mom knows that if I'm up at six in the morning and there's a little sticky note on my door that she shouldn't come in, it's because I'm sitting there trying to do those practices at home.

And I know my parents notice a difference in the way I act toward others. After I've had that time just to be silent and, I guess, be held by God, there's a difference in how I talk to others. My reaction time and what I get offended by is completely changed when I've taken that time to be within myself and then respond to other people. There's a quote I heard at the youth event from one of the spiritual directors from St. Seraphim. He said, "If you alone find God, thousands around you will be saved." And that's very true in centering prayer. I really believe it's about the way you treat others after you come inside yourself and see what's important and what's in your heart and how God's speaking to you. There's a complete difference.

Mark: But isn't contemplative prayer difficult, strange, or just plain boring?

Nathaniel: I don't know. I guess I'm a thinker. I process everything way too much. So sitting down and taking time to analyze what the heck is going on has just been a part of my life since the day I was born. Naming that as a form of prayer was what this project did for me. And that helped because teens always struggle with "How do we pray? What is prayer? I don't want to talk out loud. I don't want to ask for Christmas presents, you know?" [Audience laughs.] So naming what I was already doing—sitting prayerlike, in silence, and reflecting on life—really helped. If it's life giving, if it brings you back to God, and if it helps you be with yourself, then it's prayer. That's what it is.

Nate: I think a lot of teens, although they may deny it, will eventually appreciate silent prayer. It's a nice time to just be with yourself and God. If you don't like it at first then that may tell you that you don't like who you are. Sometimes it may be too painful, and you have to step away. That's just what you need to do. If you don't like yourself, if you don't want to stay at that state, you should try to fix that. And the being silent and just getting within yourself is very good. And for people like me—I talk too much and so it's nice sometimes to shut up. So the silent prayer has sort of matured me in a different way.

Mark: Let me get a little more general. What does it mean to be a Christian?

Nate: What kind of a question is that? Don't you know? [Audience laughs.]

Mark: Actually, most days I feel like I don't! I'm interested in your perspective on what it means to live a Christian life. What does it mean to live the way of Jesus?

Nathaniel: I would say it just means, for me, to live love. And taking that sense of unity and love and presence I've felt in prayer and retreat and taking it back home and living it out has been the most difficult challenge I've ever faced on my spiritual journey. And that's what I consider being a Christian. It is just to live love. If you live love, others around you will be affected by it—and that's just how I see it.

Lauren: I guess the underlying principle of Christianity for me would also be love. As you're walking down the street or as you look at someone you interact with every day, you try to see God. You can see God in others, trying to help you, trying to look at you and help you along your journey. I more readily see that in those who show love to everyone. Like Amanda said, they don't have to necessarily walk up to everyone and be extroverted and talk all the time, but you kind of just sense that love, and they can be someone you don't even know. Like even on the street, like sometimes their smile, I'll tell you, it can just brighten your day.

And sometimes if you see me and I'm walking and, like, we just exchange a glance—sometimes that really does, honestly, brighten my day, and I just feel that in my heart. I guess that's why I'm so open to people who don't necessarily believe the same things I do or follow the same doctrine I do. A person might not be a Christian, or might not be a United Methodist, you know, or someone might be of a different race—whatever—but you more readily see God in their eyes helping you and moving you along in your soul than in someone who screams at you from the Bible every day and tells you you're a horrible Christian because you've done this in your past or maybe because you're planning to do something in the future. [Audience laughs.]

Like Nathaniel said, I think the underlying principle in Christianity is really love. It's not necessarily about a certain interpretation of the Bible, you know? I was talking with a young lady today—well, I guess she's older than me. She's a youth director. She was saying how she was brought up in a conservative church and it's kind of hard for her to step away from that and see the underlying principles and not necessarily paying attention all the time to the words. And we got into a really great discussion about it. It was just great, it really lifted my day, because I love hearing other viewpoints—conservative, liberal, whatever—I just love talking to other people about not only Christianity but, you know, God working in your lives and loving others and living as Christ calls us to do.

Nathaniel: I know I've already spoken, but talking about the Christian life in this way reminds me of something. Last week I was in the deep South, and if you get far enough south you'll hit a region where everybody waves. We were in canoes and kayaks, floating down the river, and everybody waves. You pass somebody and you wave and, you know, you just say, "Hey, how you doing?" And I came back to Atlanta and I waved at somebody and they were like, "What the heck...?" [Audience laughs.]

Amanda: I think many people claim to be Christians and wear crosses around school and stuff, but you can definitely tell that this is not the kind of person that you want to be. This happens often in school. They have the Christian concert T-shirts or the crosses, they go to such-and-such church. But they'll act one way at church and they'll be all like, "I'm a great Christian and I'd never do anything bad," then they get at school and they totally ignore everybody else in their youth group and they're like, "I'm too cool to hang out with you" and "Who are you?" And, it's hard, cause it hurts that people you know and you've grown up with at church can just turn around and be so harsh and be like, "I'm not going to talk to you." And, like, you can't tell if someone is a Christian, but you can definitely tell when God is working in people's lives because they will smile on the streets. And you see that God is working in wonderful ways in other people's lives, and it just brings you to life. And you're like, "Wow, God does amazing things!"

Nate: I really like what everyone has said. However, I can't answer the question of what it means to live a Christian life without lying to you. I would not be able to give you a true answer. If I could, well, I would do it every day. I would be that Christian that I knew how to be—it would be that easy, wouldn't it? That's what, I think, a great part of life is—it's that day-to-day trying to figure out what I can do today to learn more about being a Christian, and what I can do to improve myself and live the life I think I'm supposed to live. I know what I think it means to be a Christian now, but will it change tomorrow?

Mark: Say something about your experience of worship. Most pastors and youth pastors are always under pressure to get young people into the worship service. Yet the most frequent comment I hear from young people is "worship services are boring."

Nate: I really don't like worship. I feel I'm at a point where I am very strong spiritually but almost zero religiously, as far as organized religion. I don't enjoy it. I get nothing out of it. I wish worship were just the children's time. When the pastor calls the children forward, you know it's never the same. It's the only time you'll see this transformation from the people in the church. People go from sitting back, sort of half-asleep, to sitting alert, leaning forward, trying to watch and hear what the kids are saying. That's what I think you need in church. You need that kind of attention. You want people to be involved and active and straining to hear what's said. That's the thing that happens during the children's time. It's fun and it's got that spirit there that everybody loves. And I guess that's the only thing I like.

Amanda: We have a contemporary service, and the music they play is more upbeat. So having just that change from boring old hymns once in a while is fun. And you'd be surprised at how many actual seniorly people enjoy the upbeat music, because some of the songs they play are hymns that have just been rejuvenated. So the older people are like, "What's this?" and then they're like, "I know that song! That's not how you play that, but this is kind of cool." I think most people would enjoy if you change the tempo once in a while and try to make it a little bit more upbeat, without changing too many other things.

Lauren: I serve as the youth representative on our staff-parish relations committee. And a while back they started to try and analyze our service. And we found that changing any one thing in the service is nearly impossible, because there's always going to be someone who enjoys the one thing you want to change or remove. And there's always going to be someone else who that's their pet peeve. At our church, everybody kind of finds their forte and is invited to share it in worship. You can play bells, you can sing, you can play flute. It's kind of like everybody's sharing their gifts together.

I find that, in terms of the worship service, the thing that really gets youth ignited is not only being involved, but seeing things switch up and sometimes being what they want and sometimes being what parents want and sometimes being what the elders want—and, of course, catering to the children. So, I guess, just seeing that the service tries to reach everybody, even if it's not always the youth at any specific time, is really my favorite thing.

Mark: Sometimes youth programs actually create greater distance between youth and adults. Do you feel like you are a part of your larger church community—and if so how is this maintained?

Amanda: We have a Sunday night program that ties together the youth program with one of the adult classes. It's one of the more fun adult classes, and both groups study the same subjects. Then once a month the youth group and this adult class have class together and try to integrate and learn from each other. And we really do learn from each other. It's much easier to stay connected if you have some scheduled activity with adults. If you try to integrate adults and youth during that four-to-six-year period when the youth are in middle school and high school, then it's much easier on the outside when they have to come back when they're college age.

Nate: Being a college kid, I think I can kind of answer that, as well. Having come up through the program, it was much easier to integrate [into the larger church] because the adults were so involved with the high school youth. So when I was out of there, and no longer a high school youth, they still accepted me for who I was, because they had watched me grow up and they were involved in my upbringing and they wanted to stay involved in my life after high school. They didn't, you know, violently shove me out.

Mark: How can pastors, youth directors, and other adults in the church build relationships with youth?

Nathaniel: I find that I'm receiving respect when the adults are listening. That's one of the best things adults can do to connect with youth, is not just talk all the time. Plus, I think it's a lot easier. You don't have to know what to say. You just have to know to sit there.

When somebody listens to you, it implies that they really care, that our opinions and thoughts and what we're saying matters. So that's how I feel like I'm being respected as a member of the congregation. Not just a member of the youth group, not just a teenager, not just an adolescent, but a member of the congregation. And I want to be given, and I want to give, the same amount of respect, and that's how it's done.

Mark: How do you help a young person realize the reality of God?

Amanda: Adults kind of have to show you, really. Like, they can tell you as much as they want, but they have to show you that in some way. I don't know how they do this, but in some form they show you that no matter what you do, even if you drop lasagna on the couch or anything, it'll be okay, like, "We'll get over it. The couch was ugly in the first place. One more stain won't kill it. Don't worry about it, because life goes on." It's just easier if they don't tell you, like, "Yeah, you're the beloved of God. Just believe it." It's easier when they show it to you. You can do stupid stuff, but they'll get over it and life goes on and you can tell that they love you, no matter what.

Nathaniel: Last August when we were here, we spent the entire week learning and thinking and praying about being the beloved of God. And then it came to the end of the week and we were all kind of thinking, "Wow, this world is a beautiful place!" You know, here's this community that can embrace one another, cry with one another, smile with one another, rejoice with one another—and for a moment

I got to thinking that this is how the world is. And toward the end of the week, I kind of started to think back about home and, you know, Iraq, and whatever else is going on in the world and I thought, "You know, as much as I want to think it, this isn't the case in the rest of the world." And that was hard.

So we were all in here having some service, I don't exactly remember what, and I stepped outside to take a breather, so people wouldn't see me cry—that's embarrassing for a teenage boy. [Audience laughs.] So while I was out there, Chris, my youth director, came out and just sat with me. And I was, you know, just grieving the fact that the world isn't in tip-top shape. It's not in the best condition. And he sat with me and I knew at that point that—well, I had known before—that I was the beloved. And for a few moments I was held in his arms and in the arms of God.

[At the close of these comments the audience responded with a standing ovation.]

Conclusion: Just Show Up

My friend Annie, who for 10 years has managed the Sunday school program at a struggling, interracial, Presbyterian church outside San Francisco, informally refers to her Christian education program as "Just Show Up." Again and again she encourages parents, kids, and teachers to "just show up" at church, promising that something good will come of it when they do.

The struggle my friend names in her "Just Show Up" campaign is that people, for the most part, don't show up. In North America, for a variety of reasons, it's becoming more and more difficult to find adults willing to be there for kids. In fact, I would argue that in the history of humankind, no group of young people has been as segregated, abandoned, and distanced from relationships with adults as this present generation of young people.[45]

In the Youth Ministry and Spirituality Project, we sought to take the "Just Show Up" approach even further. Not only did we seek to form youth ministries in which adults showed up physically, we also tried to create ministries in which adults were aware and present spiritually. We hoped to form youth ministers, pastors, and church volunteers who were willing to see and listen with patience and compassion to the hopes and struggles of young people. We hoped to inspire youth leaders to embody a more prayerful awareness—of youth, of themselves, and of the God beneath it all. We tried to teach youth workers to "just show up" to their ministries with trust and openness, with curiosity and an enlivening expectation that God would lead the way. We encouraged pastors, parents, and both volunteer and professional youth workers to show up—despite feeling inadequate, despite their uncertainty about whether the youth ministry was "working," despite failed teaching lessons and anxious church boards, despite

---

[45] These sentiments are also echoed in Christian Smith's *Soul Searching*, Patricia Hersch's *A Tribe Apart*, and Chap Clark's *Hurt*, as well as in the ongoing findings of the Search Institute.

jaded teenagers, anxious parents, and "ministry objectives" from church visioning committees. We encouraged youth leaders to "just show up." Show up and trust. Show up and wait in patient expectation. Trust that God is doing something. Trust that God is really working despite the failure and disappointment. Trust that your desire to share the life of God and your love and presence will be enough.

FACING THE OBSTACLES

After 10 years of researching contemplative youth ministry, I think it's important to admit that contemplative youth ministry is probably the most difficult approach to youth ministry a church could undertake. In the distracted and fractured culture in which children and youth are being raised, it is becoming increasingly hard to find adults who have the time and willingness to be present to God and young people. It's much easier to give kids a video, a handout, or an activity than it is to provide them with spiritually alive, open-hearted adults. It's much easier to ask adults to bring cookies, drive a van, or chaperone a game night than it is to invite adults to sit still and listen deeply to God and young people.

Despite the many youth leaders and youth who expressed a sense of transformation through contemplative prayer and presence, it's important to name the ways in which churches struggled and often faltered in their attempt to practice contemplative youth ministry.

Time. As we've stated, this approach to youth discipleship is based in deepening relationships with God and young people. And relationships take time. It takes time to pray, time to discern, time to be with young people. This seems to be the primary obstacle in engaging in this form of ministry. The most common difficulty we heard within partner congregations was that youth, parents, and congregations were suffering from a shortage of time. Without a regular commitment of time, it was difficult for church leaders to help young people establish Christian mentoring relationships or develop consistent spiritual practices. This is why the first grounding principle of the Youth Ministry and Spirituality Project is "Sabbath." As long as congregations perceive a scarcity of time, this approach to ministry will be challenging if not impossible.

Churches Formed By a Business Culture. Despite the enthusiasm expressed by both pastors and youth leaders for this contemplative approach, ministers frequently reported tremendous resistance to grounding congregational systems in prayer and discernment. Youth leaders and pastors described congregational cultures as "possessed" by a "business mentality" focused on efficiency and productivity. Often youth ministers expressed a sense of powerlessness amid congregations acclimated to a certain speed and efficiency in which relationships were reduced to business transactions. Pastors and youth leaders spoke of the frustration, resistance, and even anger they encountered when they asked church members to slow down and spend time in prayer and relationship. Contemplative prayer was seen as "inefficient" and "unproductive." When youth workers and pastors invited church members to stop and pay attention to their lives with God and their relationships with others, people sometimes became agitated and frustrated, often seeing contemplative prayer and presence as frivolous. Sometimes this resulted in increasing the separation between the youth ministry and the adult congregation. Jeremy from Christ Lutheran Church in Valparaiso, Indiana, explains:

> It was really hard to incorporate this contemplative approach into the life of the whole congregation. It's a common conversation now in youth ministry to talk about not isolating the youth but incorporating them into the overall life of the congregation, and we found ourselves at times doing exactly the opposite. As we were trying to incorporate this into our ministry, at times we found it was really isolating our

youth, because the way decisions are made in our congregation, the way we worship, and the way we use time with one another was so businesslike and different than the way we were doing youth ministry—and our youth were very aware of this difference. And so this approach really did, over the course of a few years, isolate them in a way, which I wish would not have happened.

I would say the shift that took place in the youth ministry was a good thing. I don't think it was unhealthy. I'm sad that the youth ministry is isolated from the overall life of the congregation; but I think for the adults who participate in the youth ministry, their eyes are opened enough to see what is happening. They know there is life there and are now starting to say, "Maybe this is a model for the rest of the church." And it might be another 4, 5, or 10 years before that really happens, but it's starting.

The resistance to contemplative prayer and presence as a basis of ministry was particularly apparent in denominational offices. Denominational leaders often reported great resistance, some even risking their jobs, as they tried to introduce contemplative processes within staff meetings. We were continually struck by the secularization of denominational and congregational systems. It was surprising to find that most churches relied on secular business consultants or work models developed within the marketplace that focus primarily on material outcomes. It was disheartening to listen to pastors and youth leaders talk about the difficulties they faced in creating ministries that highly valued prayer and spiritual discernment.

Stressed and Harried Families. Contemplative youth ministry is based on the assumption that what youth need most are relationships with significant adults who are spiritually alive and willing to accompany them on their journeys in faith. Even if a ministry is successful in providing "living" adults, what does it mean when young people have no support at home for slowing down? In interview after interview we found that young people are under constant pressure by their parents (and the surrounding culture) to achieve, produce, and perform. How do we communicate that Sabbath and prayer are not just practices for youth group but a whole way of life that must begin at home? What does it mean when youth who attend our formation events rate an afternoon of solitude, rest, and silence as the highlight of the week—surpassing karaoke nights, beach trips, and hanging out with friends? When asked to explain this rating, the young people reported they'd never experienced such a long block of time unaccompanied by expectations to accomplish something. Clearly there is a way in which a contemplative approach to youth ministry needs to include parents and families; without their support, young people can be painfully caught between two cultures.

Lack of Understanding of Spiritual Practices. One primary reason some pastors and church leaders resisted contemplative youth ministry was rooted in a lack of understanding about how contemplative prayer, silence, solitude, and mystical experience is grounded in Christian tradition, theology, and practice. This was especially true in Protestant churches where we encountered pastors who were resistant to contemplative youth ministry because it seemed to challenge a Christian tradition that relied on more "word-based" practices such as preaching and teaching.

When the Lilly Endowment awarded us a grant in 1997 to establish the Youth Ministry and Spirituality Project, Program Manager Chris Coble remarked something to the effect of, "I hope this doesn't culminate in a book titled *101 Spiritual Practices for Kids*." It has always been the intent of the project to avoid the promotion of spiritual practices disconnected from Christian tradition, theological understanding, and congregational life. However, Christian publishers capitalizing on the spirituality trend have now begun to produce books that promote spiritual practices disconnected from any historical or theological roots. Icons, prayer beads, and labyrinths are now commonly found in youth rooms across the country. Unfortunately, there is often little understanding of how these sacred objects and practices relate to a congregation's doctrines, theology, and tradition. We have tried to address this through development of a charter and theology that undergirds contemplative ministry. Yet there persists a great ignorance surrounding spiritual practices now commonplace within North American youth ministry. (See appendix 7: "Spirituality and Youth Ministry: What Are We Doing?)

It's Hard to Pay Attention. In a culture in which multitasking is encouraged and rewarded, contemplative presence is increasingly rare. It's hard to pay attention to God and others when there are so many interesting activities, ideas, and experiences readily available at the push of a button. It's becoming increasingly difficult to invite youth and adults to "come away to a deserted place for a while" without phones, musical devices, computers, the Internet, and video games. It's tough to invite adults and youth to slow down when the speed of life has increased. (We work an average of 163 hours a year more today than in 1969, adding up to an extra month of work annually.)[46] It's difficult to pay attention when, as David Whyte comments, we live within a culture in which "The hurried child becomes the pressured student, and finally the harassed manager...The process is begun very young and can be so in our bones...that the inability to pay real attention to our world may be difficult to recognize."[47]

It's difficult to pay attention when there is great suffering and pain in the world. It's much easier to stay distracted and busy when slowing down often means confronting our pain, experiencing feelings of helplessness, or acknowledging the ways in which we are hurting ourselves, our children, and our world. Who wants to slow down and notice a world that is increasingly becoming what former President Jimmy Carter recently labeled "a culture of death"? Who wants

[46] Sylvia Ann Hewlett and Cornel West, *War on Parents* (Houghton Mifflin, 1998), 48.
[47] David Whyte, *The Heart Aroused: Poetry and the Preservation of Soul in Corporate America* (Doubleday, 1994), 23.

to slow down and recognize the pain and violence so many youth are forced to live with? Who wants to pray and become vulnerable to bleeding and brokenness within so many families? Who can really stand to look and see the devastation occurring in our natural world? Who wants to be aware of the ways in which our faith, our churches, and our ministries seem so inadequate at inviting any real change or hope within people? It's difficult to be present. It's difficult to see and hear.

It's also difficult to be vulnerable and aware. And yet, as biblical scholar Walter Brueggemann reminds us, our central task in ministry is making people aware. We trust the truth, we trust the stories of faith passed down from generation to generation, and most of all we trust God. We trust God that our sins, our brokenness, our fears, and our mediocre attempts at loving are not the last word. We trust that God is on a mission of love and that love, like Jesus, always comes vulnerable, undefended in weakness and trust. Can we believe that our weakness and helplessness make us more available to God's love and presence?

In *God Laughs and Plays*, author and conservationist David James Duncan relates an interview he did with Gerri Haynes, a nurse who heads a group called Washington Physicians for Social Responsibility.[48] Gerri began organizing physicians and medical personnel to travel and care for the dying in Iraq after the first U.S. invasion of Iraq in 1992. In what is referred to as the Gulf War, the U.S. military targeted and destroyed the primary water treatment plants within Baghdad and many of the larger metropolitan areas. The result from the loss of clean water and the ensuing embargo was that by 1999, UNICEF reported 500,000 children had died. Gerri Haynes raised money, staff, and supplies for three missions of mercy to Iraq. What she found as a result of U.S. military action was shocking: "Children we saw everywhere had the distended bellies of the chronically malnourished. Twelve-year-olds looked like eight-year-olds...An already

---

[48] The Triad Institute, 2006.

burdened person can hardly bear (such) news. Most Americans are kindhearted. The plain sight of suffering and dying children would inspire almost any of them to realign their lives, change their work, their habits, their thinking, anything, if they saw they were contributing to thousands of children's demise. It's very, very hard to hear this kind of thing."

In May 2002, even though she had been diagnosed with breast cancer, Gerri organized a fourth mission of mercy to Iraq. Her daughter tried to persuade her to stay home but finally, after Gerri's insistence, she simply offered her mother this piece of advice: "If you do go, be completely present, wherever you go." Duncan relates the following:

> These words returned to Gerri in May 2002, in an Iraqi hospital virtually bereft of medicine and hope. While her group moved from bed to bed, Gerri approached a woman sitting next to her dying child. Gerri speaks no Arabic. The woman spoke no English. Trying to be "present" anyway, Gerri looked at the child, then at the mother, and placed her right hand over her own heart.
>
> The Iraqi mother placed her right hand over her own heart.
>
> Gerri's eyes and the mother's eyes simultaneously filled with tears.
>
> The hospital was crowded. Gerri's visitation time was short. She started to move to the next bed, but then remembered her daughter's words: "completely present." She and the mother were already crying, their hands over their hearts. There was nothing Gerri could do, despite her medical training, for the child. "How much more present," she wondered, "is it possible to be?"

She stepped forward anyway. With no plan but vague allegiance to the commandment, "Be completely present," the nurse without medicine stepped toward the bed of the dying child and inconsolable mother. She then put both of her hands out, palms up.

The Iraqi mother fell into her arms.

"If only this experience were unique!" Gerri told me. "But I can't tell you, any longer, how many mothers I've now held in this same way."

Contemplative youth ministry is an invitation to be completely present—knowing that we will fail, knowing that it is impossible to be fully aware and present to God and others, knowing we have no medicine, no quick fix, and yet, knowing there is no other way. The true way of relationship, the true way of faith is to again and again return our eyes and ears to the presence of the Beloved, to return our eyes and ears to the presence of the other person. It's in this willingness to open our hands, this willingness to look and see, this openness to receive the pain and suffering and joy and struggle of others that God is known.

IT IS THE SPIRIT THAT GIVES LIFE

The spiritual disciplines the Youth Ministry and Spirituality Project has emphasized— disciplines like prayer, silence, solitude, spiritual direction, and contemplative listening—are desperately needed within a culture that seems to be losing its ability to attend to the depths of life. These disciplines seem necessary if we're to ever bridge the growing chasm between teenager and adult. But anyone engaged in the struggle to communicate the freedom and peace of Jesus is also deeply aware that contemplative prayer and awareness can only be the beginning of the reformation so desperately needed within youth ministry (and the church at large).

The young people we serve today must be prepared to face a host of troubles that are both devastating and deeply entrenched within humanity. Indeed, it will take a great deal of cooperation, persistence, trust, creativity, sacrifice, and humor if the human being is to continue to carry the image of God into the next centuries. The long disregard and destruction of water, soil, and air, along with other species; the knee-jerk reliance on violence as a way to solve problems; the absence of real encounters between the privileged and the growing number of suffering and powerless people; the fascination with technologies that carry the potential and power to destroy; the unwillingness to face the shadow-side of North American life—the arrogance, isolation, fear, and violence that the rest of the world finds so frightening—all of these threaten our survival, much less our capacity to bear the freedom of Jesus Christ.

The young people who carry the gospel to the coming generations will be the young people who have souls. They will be people of prayer, people who know how to be renewed by the spring of God's love. They will be people of hope and humor, people humble enough (and crazy enough) to follow the voice of Jesus. They will be people who are not afraid to look and see and respond to suffering. They will be people who know how to feel—people who grieve, dance with joy, and speak out when they're angry. They will be people who enjoy the company of strangers. They will be people willing to sit and listen to those whose speech, dress, food, and even prayer are different. They will be people who crave truth, even hard truths—people who have the capacity to look at their own shadow, their own faults and participation in evil.

These young souls will be people living within the Spirit of Jesus. Like Jesus, they will embody a sense of trust, freedom, and well-being, even in the midst of fear, passivity, and increasing cynicism.

The Youth Ministry and Spirituality Project was an experiment— an attempt to counter the isolation, hyperactivity, and emphasis on efficiency that plagues ministries with youth. It was a project that sought to resurrect the contemplative aspect of the Christian faith as an intervention to heal the more destructive aspects of the way youth ministry is often practiced within a North American context.

What we learned within the project was in some ways quite basic: When youth leaders practice the presence of God within their ministries, lives are changed. When youth ministries pray and attend to God, there is greater patience, generosity, kindness, self-discipline, hope, joy, and love, as well as other fruits of the Spirit. Sometimes the transformations we witnessed were limited to youth leaders, or youth; other times they spread to families, church staffs, and entire congregations. But the overwhelming discovery was in many ways something that has always been known by followers of Jesus: "It is the spirit that gives life" (John 6:63).

Perhaps the most unanticipated, encouraging, and even heart-breaking discovery was the deep longing for life in the Spirit. It was revealed in the number of youth leaders longing to listen for God; the many youth surprised and delighted to have their souls addressed; the pastors and church elders yearning for someone to give them permission to attend to their own experiences of God. The great secret we uncovered within our work was that youth leaders and youth have souls, and despite the conventional wisdom, these leaders and youth don't need Christian rock bands, or amusement parks, or clever curricula. The secret we discovered is that what they need and desire is God.

Appendix 1

Lectio Divina

Lectio divina is Latin for "holy reading" and comes out of the Benedictine monastic tradition. This prayer can be described as experiencing God through Scripture. It's a classical form of prayer designed to draw a person gently into the depths of her or his heart in order to meet God. For centuries *lectio divina* has introduced Christians to the practice of contemplation.

Lectio divina invites us into contemplative prayer by way of meditating on a particular biblical text. Before entering into the prayer, it's helpful to recognize that there are many ways in which we "read." We scan the newspaper for information. We study a book to increase our knowledge or hone our critical faculties. We become absorbed in a good novel. When we engage in *lectio divina*, we are not seeking to read the Bible for knowledge or instruction (although both of those may come) nor are we seeking the escape of a good story. Instead, we come to the words of the Bible seeking to be with God. We come to Scripture as if it were a meeting place, a secret rendezvous where we hope to spend some time with the One who loves us.

The steps of this prayer might seem arbitrary and complicated at first. But as you engage in the prayer, you'll find the process is quite natural. (You may even notice you've practiced a similar form of prayer or Bible reading on your own.) The steps are as follows:

Preparation. Begin by finding a passage of Scripture to pray with. You can choose a passage based on a lectionary or daily devotional, or simply by selecting a passage on your own. Make sure the Scripture is not too long. Next find a quiet place where you won't be distracted or interrupted—a place where you feel safe and comfortable opening up to God. Often it's helpful to light a candle or set out a sacred object, something beautiful that quiets your spirit and reminds you of God's nearness.

Silence. Once you've found a place to pray, take a moment merely to rest, relaxing into God's presence. With each breath become aware of God's love for you. Say a simple prayer offering yourself to God and welcoming whatever the Holy Spirit has for you.

Reading. Read the passage once to get oriented to the text. Then read it slowly a second time, and a third, listening for a word or phrase that seems to shimmer or stand out in bold—a word that seems to address you. It may be a word that draws your attention through either attraction or repulsion.

Meditation. Once a word or phrase has been given, repeat it to yourself, allowing the rest of the text to fall away. As you prayerfully repeat it, different thoughts, feelings, and images may arise. Allow this word to touch all that arises—thoughts, hopes, memories, images, and feelings. What do you notice? What is being offered?

Oration. Let yourself express prayers of petition or gratitude as they arise. Your meditation on the word may uncover a place of pain or regret. Pray about it to God. You may notice a person or situation that needs prayer. Pray that to God, too. Honestly express your deepest thoughts, feelings, and desires in dialogue with God. Pray yourself empty.

Contemplation. Finally, allow yourself simply to rest in God, like a child resting in her mother's lap. Lay down all of the insights, words, and images you've encountered and simply dwell in the presence of God. Sink into God beneath all your thoughts and feelings.

Appendix 2
Centering Prayer

Although the term *centering prayer* and its particular format came into being only within the past forty years, the prayer is a summary of various silent prayer practices that can be traced back to the very beginnings of Christianity.[49] This form of prayer trusts the direct and immediate availability of God, the "indwelling Christ," who is nearer than our own heartbeat.

Centering prayer is a simplified form of contemplative prayer. We may think of prayer as thoughts or feelings about God expressed in words. But this is only one expression of prayer. Contemplative prayer is the full opening of mind and heart, soul and body—our whole being—to the Spirit of God, the ultimate mystery, utterly beyond thoughts, words, images, and emotions. We open our awareness to the God who is dwelling within us— closer than breathing, closer than thinking, closer than choosing, closer than consciousness itself.

Centering prayer is not meant to replace other kinds of prayer; it simply puts other kinds of prayer into a new and fuller perspective. Within the silence of centering prayer, we consent to the power of God's presence and unconditional love working within us.

THE GUIDELINES [50]

1. Sit comfortably in a space where you can open yourself to God. Have a set time to pray—20 minutes or so is good for starters. You may want to light a candle to help remind you of God's nearness.

2. Before you begin the prayer, choose a sacred word as the symbol of your intention to be with God. This word expresses your desire to

---

[49] Forms of centering or silent prayer can be found in the writings of the early Desert Fathers and Mothers, Julian of Norwich, John of the Cross, and other mystical theologians, and are most clearly articulated in the anonymously written 14th-century devotional, *The Cloud of Unknowing*. One of the modern "founders" of centering prayer, M. Basil Pennington, sees centering prayer as a direct outgrowth of *lectio divina*. For more on the history and tradition of centering prayer see "The Christian Contemplative Tradition and Centering Prayer," *Centering Prayer in Daily Life and Ministry*, Gustav Reininger, ed.

[50] These guidelines are modified from Thomas Keating's description of the method of centering prayer found in many of his writings including *Open Mind, Open Heart* and *Centering Prayer in Daily Life and Ministry*.

be in God's presence and yield to the movement of the Holy Spirit. Ask the Holy Spirit to reveal a word that is suitable for you. Examples include *Jesus, Lord, Abba, Love, Mercy, Stillness, Faith, Trust, Shalom,* and *Amen.* Once you've selected a word, stick with it. Occasionally people get caught up worrying whether their word feels right for them, wondering about the various meanings of their word, comparing their word to other words, or wondering if some other word might be more "spiritual" and produce "better" results. Don't take your word so seriously. It's simply a reminder of your desire to be with God. What's significant in this prayer is your intention (to be with God), not your particular word.

3. Before you pray, close your eyes and settle yourself. Allow a spirit of rest and hospitality to come over your body. Welcome God into this time. Briefly and silently introduce your sacred word as the symbol of your consent to God's presence and action within and around you. Thomas Keating suggests introducing the sacred word "inwardly and as gently as laying a feather on a piece of cotton."

4. As you pray, you will become aware of thoughts, memories, commentaries, and images. When you notice your mind wandering, gently return to the sacred word. Thoughts are a normal part of centering prayer; yet by quietly returning to the sacred word, minimal effort is used to bring attention back to God.

5. At the end of the prayer period, remain in silence with your eyes closed for a minute or two. You may want to close with the "Our Father" (Lord's Prayer) or some other formal prayer as a way of drawing the prayer to a close.

Appendix 3

The Awareness Examen: A Prayer of Discernment

The awareness examen helps us trace God's presence and call in the details of everyday living. The examen was part of a series of spiritual practices Ignatius of Loyola discovered through his own spiritual conversion. *The Spiritual Exercises* of Ignatius became the founding formational experience for the Jesuits and are used widely today by all walks of Christians for spiritual growth and discernment.[51] Of all the practices and exercises he employed in the Jesuit community, Ignatius felt the examen was the most essential.

Over my 10 years of consulting with churches across the country, I've found the examen to be a powerful practice for helping youth workers, parents, and congregations become more aware of the Holy Spirit and more present to young people. The examen invites us to spend time looking back over our encounters with young people, noting when we were most open and loving toward God and youth, and when we were "forgetful" or closed to God's love. Just as you might lie in bed at night considering the experiences of your day, this prayer asks you to review a particular encounter with young people and prayerfully ask two questions:

For what moment am I most grateful?
For what moment am I least grateful? [52]

These two questions, prayerfully invited, help us identify moments of *consolation* and *desolation*. *Consolation* is a classical term used over the centuries by praying Christians to identify moments when we are more open to God, ourselves, and others. These are moments of connection, moments when we feel more alive, more transparent to God, and more loving toward other people. *Desolation* refers to the opposite experience—disconnection, depletion, alienation, a sense of being blocked to the presence of God, others, or ourselves. By paying attention to these two types of moments in our

---

[51] *The Spiritual Exercises* were written for retreat leaders and spiritual directors who had experienced the 30-day retreat. It is not recommended reading without first experiencing the exercises with a knowledgeable retreat leader.

[52] Dennis Linns, Sheila Fabricant Linns, and Matthew Linns, *Sleeping with Bread*, (Paulist Press, 1995). These two questions come from the Linns' simple description of the awareness examen and its application to daily life. The alternate questions at the end of this section are also drawn from or based on the Linns' exploration of the examen.

lives, we become more aware of the revelatory nature of our experience. Sometimes we notice patterns or occasions when we are in the flow of God's love; other times we see moments when we seem to be caught up in our own wounds and blindness.

After an activity or encounter with young people, I've found it helpful to look back and remember all the moments of gratitude, moments when I was open and receptive to God. Then I recall the moments of least gratitude, moments when I was blocked in some way to the presence of God and young people. Over time, as I've reflected on these consolations and desolations, I've found that I have become better attuned to the movement of the Holy Spirit in my ministry and better able to be my true self with kids.

Take a moment now to set aside your reading and experience the prayer of examen. Find a place where you can pray without interruption. Light a candle to focus your attention and remind yourself of God's presence. Then spend a few moments in silence, allowing yourself to become aware of God's presence and care for you. When you're ready, ask the Holy Spirit to accompany you as you review your last encounter with young people. It might be a formal activity like Sunday school or youth group, or an informal interaction with youth in your family or community. As you recall your experience, let the following question arise: For what moment am I most grateful? Allow little things to emerge: a smile, a greeting, a kind word, sunlight in the room, an engaging conversation. Stay with whatever moment God seems to give you. Don't force anything—just be open and let the moment arise that seems to hold the most gratitude.

Let all else fall away as you spend a few moments holding this experience of gratitude. What did the experience feel like? What were you like? What were the youth like? What might God be seeking to teach you through this experience? You might want to journal some of these insights.

Now go back over your experience with youth and ask: For what moment am I least grateful? Again allow God to bring your attention to whatever moment seemed most filled with desolation. Take a few minutes to prayerfully journal what you've noticed. Or, as Ignatius might have you do, share these insights with Jesus and see what emerges.

Other possible questions to use within this prayer:

When did I give and receive the most love? (or, When does it seem that the most love was given and received?)

When did I give and receive the least love (or, When does it seem that the least love was given and received?)

When did I feel most alive? (When did it seem the group was most alive? etc.)

When did I feel least alive? (When did the group seem least alive? etc.)

When did I feel most free? (When did it seem there was the most freedom?)

When did I feel least free? (When did it seem there was the least freedom?)

Note: The questions can be modified to refer to oneself, "you," "the group," "the meeting," etc.

Appendix 4
Guidelines for Leading a Prayer Exercise with Youth

The following suggestions for leading a prayer exercise with youth developed and evolved out of the work of the Youth Ministry and Spirituality Project. Youth leaders in the project found these guidelines to be helpful reminders as they designed prayer exercises for their young people.

Hospitality

Before you begin, dedicate your efforts to God and trust that God will work through the exercise. Remind yourself that the prayer is not about you; it's about God.

Have a set order and time for the exercise. Have all materials ready and available. Think through how the exercise will take place. Create a welcoming space for the prayer to take place. Pay attention to the senses—is there beauty? Does the space help draw attention to God's presence?

Invitation

Describe the whole exercise to the youth in simple terms. Make sure everyone understands how the exercise will proceed. Try to maintain an "experimental" tone during the invitation to prayer. Say something to the effect of, "We're going to try an experiment in prayer. It may or may not be the way in which you pray. You might feel a little strange or uncomfortable with the silence, but I want to ask you to give it a try to see what happens. God can surprise us sometimes and show up in ways we don't normally expect."

Sometimes it's helpful to talk about the different ways we're in relationship with other people: We talk, we listen, we do things together, and sometimes we're just together, without words. Try to help youth see that the prayer is similar to listening or just being with a friend without speaking.

Be sure to acknowledge difficulties. Point out what may not work. Make sure kids understand there is no "right" way to experience the exercise. I often say something like, "Sometimes when we pray it's difficult to focus—our minds are moving too fast, we're tired, or maybe this just isn't the best way for us to pray. That's okay. Don't get stressed if you're having a hard time with this exercise. Just simply say within yourself, 'God, I want to be with you right now,' and let everything else fall away."

Allow the group to get physically comfortable before you start.

Prayer

Lead group members in a centering exercise as you begin the prayer. Darken the room and light a candle to help them focus their attention. Have them pay attention to their breath, relax their bodies, and turn their attention toward God. You may prefer to have the group sing a simple chorus to help prepare their hearts for prayer.

Invite the youth to dedicate time to God. Remind them that their desire to be with God is what's most important in prayer. Then simply allow the group to spend some time in prayer. Make sure you pray along with the youth. Trust that God is at work—try to ease up on monitoring the kids. If there are youth who become disruptive, speak the truth in love. Call them back to prayer using an economy of words. In silence we often worry that nothing is "happening." Remember that silence is God's first language—try to let go of worries about whether the exercise is "working."

At the end of the prayer time, invite youth to offer thanks to God for whatever occurred during prayer. Have an appropriate closing for the prayer (maybe the Lord's Prayer or a simple song) and then make the transition back to the group.

Testimony

Sometimes at the close of the prayer it might be appropriate to invite the youth to express their prayer experience through some physical act or ritual: lighting a candle, placing a rock before a cross, etc. Other times it might be important to have kids spend time journaling their experiences. Even after journaling it's helpful to invite youth to speak their experiences in the larger group. It's good for kids to hear the variety of experiences within prayer. This also gives the leaders a chance to answer questions and respond to theological or spiritual issues that arise.

If you give kids a chance to talk about their experiences, make sure you respond with open hearted, nonjudgmental remarks. You don't know what God is doing within these young people, so be open. If you're concerned about a young person's prayer experience, follow up with him or her privately. Let kids know this exercise may not work for everyone—it's just an exercise; it's not God. Allow people to talk about "flat" experiences as well: "I fell asleep." "I couldn't focus." "I had no sense that God was present in this prayer." Such experiences are common for both youth and adults.

Let kids know that every prayer experience, whether enlightening or flat, is part of trying to be in relationship with God and is common among Christians throughout history. Remind them again that their desire to be with God is what's most important and pleasing to God.

Appendix 5
The Liturgy for Discernment

The liturgy for discernment is a process for group meetings. The word *liturgy* comes from the Greek word *leitourgia*, which means "the work of the people." In the Christian tradition this word has usually referred to worship but can also be understood more broadly as the way in which we gather in the presence of God. Discernment is the process of listening for the voice of God. The "liturgy for discernment" is a communal practice that invites us to deeper cooperation with the Spirit in the midst of the work of ministry.

This liturgy was originally designed for people engaged in youth ministry, but it can be used whenever Christians gather to do the work of God. The liturgy changes the tone and spirit in which the "business" of ministry is done. The liturgy invites an atmosphere of prayer and listening rather than efficiency and productivity. In typical church board or committee meetings emphasis is often placed on accomplishing tasks. In this process emphasis is placed on deepening relationships—with oneself, others, and the Spirit of God.

The liturgy for discernment has two basic movements. In the first half of the meeting, the process moves "inward," centering the group in relationships. Through ritual, conversation, listening, and prayer, the group members are reconnected with their own hearts, with each other, and with the Spirit of God among them. These relationships are then focused around the call, or central identity of the group. This is the pivot point of the meeting, when the group's attention moves outward, reflecting on its collective sense of identity and God's call ("Who are we and how is God calling us?") Business items are then responded to within this deeper awareness of self, other, God, and communal call (or group purpose). As a group practices this way of doing ministry, the group begins to operate less and less as a business committee and more and more as a spiritual community—lives are shared, relationships are built, spirits are formed, and gifts are exercised. Below is a step-by-step description of the movements within this process:

Ritual. As people gather to meet there is an opening ritual. This should be a simple activity that draws the group's attention to the presence of God. It could be a song, a moment of silence, or the lighting of a candle. The ritual consecrates the meeting, changing the context from ordinary time and space to sacred time and space. The ritual announces to the group, "We are coming into an awareness of the presence of God." Avoid pastoral prayers or other rituals that rely on the gifts of only one person. The ritual should be repeatable no matter who is in attendance. The ritual should last no longer than a couple of minutes.

Relating. This is a time for building relationships within the community. Each member of the group is asked, "How are you?" and is given one or two minutes to check in. (That may not seem like much time, but when real listening is present, people tend to be more mindful of their words, making it possible to share a lot in a brief amount of time.) This is a time of deep listening, of attending to one another. Jesus says there are only two things required of Christians, to love God and to love one another as we love ourselves (Mark 12:28-34). In this time we love others through our eyes and ears. We listen without interrupting or commenting. We leave silence after each speaker to honor what has been said. The hope is that in the midst of silence and careful listening the speaker is able to hear herself, and thus is able to speak from a deeper place. At times you may want to change the check-in question to something like, "How is your faith being nurtured in this ministry?" or "How is your family life?"

This time is valuable because it allows people to drop whatever baggage they may be carrying (joys or anxieties). The sharing helps create more space within them to pray and focus on the work of the group.

Receiving. After listening to one another, we turn our attention more fully to God. This is a time of prayerful listening—full attentiveness to the Spirit of God within and among us. The prayer makes room for these three movements:

1. Centering: Our attention shifts from the particulars of the agenda to the One who calls us to this work. We remember who we are and *whose* we are.

2. Transformation: In the silence we become available to God. A new word is given, wounds are tended, and renewal takes place.

3. Call: We get in touch with the Spirit's longing within us, our calling, and the unique way in which God has invited us to live and serve.

Either the *lectio divina* or the awareness examen can be used in this time of receiving. I have found it most effective to alternate the group's use of these two forms of prayer.

When the group uses *lectio divina*, a short passage of Scripture is selected for the prayer time. The passage can be chosen from the lectionary, the curriculum being used with the youth group, or selected specifically for the meeting. One person should explain the process of *lectio divina* to the group—*being sure to tell the group how long the silence will last.* After a brief time of silent prayer, the leader slowly reads the passage aloud two times, urging each individual to listen for a word or phrase that jumps out. The group then observes five to ten minutes of silence before the leader invites the team members to draw their attention back to the group. (For more on *lectio divina*, see appendix 1 or Thelma Hall's *Too Deep for Words* [Paulist Press, 1988].)

When using the awareness examen, the leader should begin by explaining the prayer to the group members and informing them how long the silences will last. The group is then invited to a time of silence. The leader then says, "Ask God to go with you over our last gathering with young people [or whatever other activity is the primary focus of the group] and consider the following question: *For what moment am I most grateful?*" After another few minutes of silence and contemplation, the leader then says, "As you're ready, ask God to go back with you over our last gathering with youth and consider, *For what moment am I least grateful?*" Allow a few more minutes of silence before inviting those gathered to draw their attention back to the group. (For more on the awareness examen, see appendix 3 or *Sleeping with Bread* by Dennis Linn, Sheila Fabricant Linn, and Matthew Linn [Paulist Press, 1995].)

Ruminating. In this movement the group takes time to listen to what each person noticed during the prayer time. If the group has prayed *lectio divina*, the leader might say something like, "I'd like to invite you to share the word that came to you in the prayer as well as any other insights." If the group does the awareness examen, the leader might say something like, "I'd like to invite each of us to share what came to us in the prayer, one moment where we were most grateful and one moment where we were least grateful." Allow each person to speak without interruption. This should be a time of deep listening to how God is speaking to the group.

Reflecting. We then take time to reflect on our call. In this movement we are moving out from our individual sharing to focus on our group identity and group purpose. Someone asks the following question to the group: "Given all that we've heard and shared, what is God's call to us?" (Some groups replace "call" with "invitation.") The group has an open conversation, allowing silence after each speaker. This is a moment for the group to remember its call and reflect on new words or insights that have come out of the prayer. This should take anywhere from five to ten minutes.

Responding. The group then begins to address the business items on the agenda. As the group moves into the business, it is important that the leader remind the group to continue to be aware of the prayer and sharing that has occurred.

Returning. At the end of the meeting the group shares a closing prayer, returning its attention to the Spirit of God. Prayers of gratitude, intercession, and blessing may be offered.

YMSP Reading List

The charter of the Youth Ministry and Spirituality Project (see chapter 4) is a compilation of the seven grounding elements of contemplative youth ministry. Here are our top reading recommendations for each of these elements. For a more extensive bibliography, log onto the project Web site at **www.ymsp.org.**

Sabbath

Sabbath: Restoring the Sacred Rhythm of Rest by Wayne Muller. This book will touch your own longing for space, time, and balance. While the book is inter-religious, Muller is a UCC pastor who relies heavily on the Jewish and Christian practices of Sabbath. The text is readable and filled with testimonies and simple practices from ordinary people who are struggling to slow down amid a speed-driven culture. For something that is more solidly grounded in the Christian tradition, try *Sabbath Time* by Tilden Edwards.

Prayer

The Awakened Heart by Gerald May. This is a beautiful and accessible guide to contemplative prayer (in the tradition of Brother Lawrence). May knows how to talk about the heart with its desires and deceptions. I've given this book to many non-Christian friends. Anthony Bloom's *Beginning to Pray* is a simple but powerful book on prayer in the midst of God's absence. For something with more variety, try Daniel Wolpert's *Creating a Life with God*. Wolpert gives a variety of prayer practices that incorporate body, Scripture, imagination, and silence.

Covenant Community

Community and Growth by Jean Vanier. This is a classic book on Christian community. Vanier is the founder of L'Arche communities for the mentally handicapped and their helpers. His work features beautiful, meditative, and practical reflections on the nature of Christian community. *Life Together* by Dietrich Bonhoeffer is another classic. This little book is based on the community life practiced in secret by Bonhoeffer and many of his seminary students in Germany during the rise of the Nazi party. This book is theological, practical, and inspiring.

Accompaniment

How To Talk So Kids Will Listen & Listen So Kids Will Talk by Adele Faber and Elaine Mazlish. One of the best practical books on accompanying youth, children, and anyone else who happens to be in the room. This book is a classic and one of my top three books for parents. You will discover new skills in speaking and communicating with kids that will deepen your relationships with them and free them to be themselves. Excellent cartoons and exercises will help you develop better skills to listen and respond in even the most difficult situations with young people. *Contemplative Youth Ministry: Practicing the Presence of Jesus* by Mark Yaconelli seeks to orient youth ministers to an attitude of spiritual companionship with youth.

Discernment

Listening Hearts: Discerning Call in Community and *Grounded in God: Discernment for Group Deliberations* by Suzanne Farnham, Joseph Gill, R. Taylor McLean, and Susan Ward. These two little books are simple, practical, and meditative works on the practice of discernment in Christian communities. These are foundational books for our understanding of the role of discernment in ministry. Another great book is *Sleeping with Bread* by Matthew, Dennis, and Sheila Linn. The Linns describe the practice and power of the awareness examen as the primary prayer used for discernment within contemplative youth ministries.

Hospitality

Black and White Styles of Youth Ministry by William Myers. This classic study on "white" and "black" styles of youth ministry sheds light on the ways in which youth can be excluded or included within the life of the church. Myers' description of the "kinship" model of youth ministry common within most African American congregations provides a model of welcoming youth into the life of a congregation.

Authentic Action

The Active Life by Parker Palmer. This book reveals the powerful connection between contemplation and action. Palmer describes the spirituality of action, contending that our creativity, spontaneity, work, and efforts to care are just as nurturing and necessary to spiritual living as prayer and solitude. Another favorite is *Way to Live: Christian Practices for Teens*, edited by Dorothy Bass and Don Richter. This book is written for a youth audience but is just as powerful for adults. It is a series of meditations by teens and adults on how Christians live the way of Jesus—from how we care for our bodies to how we resist oppression.

Appendix 7
Spirituality and Youth Ministry:
What Are We Doing? by Mark Yaconelli

[Reprinted from the November/December 2004 issue of *Youthworker Journal*]

It was clear the couple was in distress. For weeks they'd left urgent messages asking for an appointment. "We have a situation that has arisen in our youth ministry, and we need to talk to someone." They took a day off from work, drove five hours to the seminary, and after thanking me profusely for the meeting, sat holding hands as they told me their story. They were happily married. They'd raised four kids. They'd spent over 25 years doing youth ministry in the Presbyterian Church. They were tired of the same "fun and games" programs. They went on a spiritual formation retreat at a youth ministry conference and had been inspired to develop a new method of youth ministry.

"We decided to create more of a 'spirituality kind of youth ministry.' We designed a prayer room and started a contemplative worship service for youth with candles and chants from the monastery in Taizé, France." They continued to attend spiritual retreats and learned various prayer styles and spiritual exercises. "We just felt so nurtured that we started sharing these new spiritual practices with our youth. The youth loved the new ministry approach, and so did we."

Then came time for the church's annual youth-led worship service. "The kids were excited to share all this cool stuff we were doing in youth group. So when we led the Sunday service we had candles everywhere and this beautiful icon of Jesus displayed on the Communion table. We led the congregation in Christian chants, and instead of a spoken sermon, one of our students led a silent meditation and then invited the congregation to walk a labyrinth we purchased from a youth ministry catalog. People loved it."

They paused and looked at one another. Here was the problem: "After the service the senior pastor asked us into his office. He wasn't mad or anything, but he just looked at us and said that what we had led wasn't a Presbyterian worship service. He told us he wasn't sure it was even Protestant. He then explained that Protestants don't use images of God and that it's really not considered worship in the Protestant tradition if there isn't preaching. He then asked if we knew a biblical justification for the labyrinth. We really couldn't respond."

They paused and stared at me for a moment. Then the wife spoke up: "Can you please tell us what we're doing?"

The Rise of Spirituality

Ten years ago I began work at San Francisco Theological Seminary exploring the integration of youth ministry and Christian spirituality. At that time *spirituality* was a common word within the culture but was still mostly absent from the field of youth ministry. If you look at youth ministry catalogs from the early '90s you won't find books on prayer or spiritual practices or products promising to nurture kids' souls. Nor would you find youth events promising to help kids "experience" Jesus. Ten years ago you would've been hard pressed to find a labyrinth or even a candle in a youth room.

In 1996, when I began leading spiritual retreats for youth leaders, I spent most teaching sessions answering questions regarding whether or not "spirituality" was satanic. I even had a Christian radio broadcaster call me for an interview concerning whether or not there was even such a thing as "Christian spirituality." She was certain spirituality was something invented by the New Age movement. In 1997, when I offered to lead a workshop titled "Contemplative Youth Ministry" at a national youth ministry gathering, I was told the title needed to be changed because either people wouldn't understand it or would think it was Buddhist. Taizé music, *lectio divina*, and spiritual direction were all viewed with suspicion and regarded as a return to ancient pagan practices.

We've come a long way, baby. Now youth ministry conferences and catalogs offer labyrinth kits, scented prayer candles, and journals with orthodox icons on the cover and quotes from classics (usually dead people) like Hildegard of Bingen. Now the heading above the youth ministry section in my recent copy of a popular Christian publishing catalog announces, "Help Youth Contemplate!" Now you can't spend more than 10 minutes at a youth ministry conference without someone saying, "Well, my spiritual director told me..."

Despite the rise and popularity of spirituality within youth ministry the question brought to me by the concerned youth ministry couple still persists: "What are we doing?"

What Is Spirituality?

In *The Upper Room Dictionary of Christian Spiritual Formation*, pastor and author Keith Beasley-Topliffe writes, "Every generation must discover for itself that experience of God and a living relationship with God are more important in our lives than knowledge about God." The current spirituality movement is engaged in this exploration of what it means to live the Good News in communion with Jesus. Many of us grew up within a Christian culture that preached a "personal relationship with Jesus," yet focused on beliefs (doctrinal correctness and defending one's faith), morality (regarding sex, drugs, and rock 'n' roll) and emotionality (praise music and charismatic speakers), with little or no space given for actually experiencing the reality of our relationship with Christ.

The revived interest in spirituality is motivated by a desire to experience God (with all of the consolation, desolation, and ambiguity) as a necessary aspect of Christian living. It's a recovery of the mystical dimension of the Christian life. Although it may appear to be a recent phenomenon, there's nothing new about spirituality. Christians have always been concerned with spiritual living—living within the Spirit of Jesus. Its popularity in recent years, however, comes largely in reaction to 19th-century forms of Christian faith that deemphasized the experiential or mystical aspects of the Christian life. Spiritual retreats, spiritual directors, prayer practices, and the use of labyrinths emerged from primal yearnings for intimacy with God and solidarity with other human beings.

Spirituality seeks to remind us of the nearness of God, our relatedness to Christ, and the inspiration (in-Spiriting) of the Holy Spirit—all of which empower us for acts of mercy, justice, and peace in the world. It concerns the way we organize our lives in light of our desire for God and our commitment to share Christ's compassion for others. It encompasses how we eat, play, socialize, consume, and spend our time. It's the heart of Christian discipleship.

Discerning Spirits

For those of us in youth ministry who are tired of frumpy old "religion" with its pews, hymnals, committees, and denominational meetings, spirituality can feel like a more faithful alternative. After all, spirituality is about being with God, living in communion with Jesus, and participating in the works of the Holy Spirit. But is spirituality a "higher," uncontaminated means to God? Does the integration of spirituality into youth ministry—with its scented candles, prayer practices, and emphasis on "being" with God—result in kids who are closer to Jesus and his way of love? Are all things labeled "spirituality" really of God? To put it more crassly, what's the difference between our candle lit youth rooms and the Pottery Barn showroom?

Perhaps now that youth ministers are beginning to embrace this notion of spirituality, the next step is to discern what kind of spirituality we have. The Scriptures tell us there are many spirits at work in the world. As spirituality becomes more prevalent in youth ministry, we must learn to "test the spirits" and distinguish between the spirituality of the marketplace culture and the spirituality of Jesus. The vital question brought to me by the youth ministry couple ("What are we doing?") needs to be asked more frequently by youth ministers, pastors, and Christian marketers. As I watch the rise in spirituality books, practices, and events, it's apparent there's an uncritical acceptance by many of all things "spiritual" without the awareness that "spirituality" is just as vulnerable to the spirit of mammon as it is to the Spirit of Jesus. Here are three distinctions (there are many more) that may be helpful to those of us in youth ministry who seek a deeper awareness and integration of Christian spirituality.

Relationship versus Self-Reliance

The spirituality of Jesus is demonstrated by a life lived in loving relationship. It's the active desire to love God and others as we love ourselves. There are two aspects of this relationship.

The first, most commonly associated with spirituality, concerns our relationship with God. Christian spirituality requires living in a way that seeks greater awareness of and receptivity to God's love and empowerment. It's life lived in greater openness to Christ's offer of friendship (John 15:14-15).

Many of us engaged in Christian spirituality recognize the deep hunger among Christians to experience God. This hunger is what has prompted the increase in spiritual retreats and events designed to help young people and adults encounter God. These spiritual encounters can be wonderfully inspiring and healing; yet the spirituality of Jesus seeks a more constant relationship with God.

A spirituality of relationship means attending to our lives with God even when our experiences in prayer and spiritual activity are dry. In youth ministry this means we need to engage young people in consistent practices of attending to God within a community of faith so that students can feel the boredom and agitation that's part of life with God as well as the moments of deep spiritual enlightenment. In this way young people can recognize that relationship with God requires the same consistency needed in any real, ongoing relationship.

The second aspect of a spirituality of relationship concerns our interactions with others. This is often ignored in discussions about spirituality. However, just as Jesus was never satisfied to remain on mountaintops and places of retreat, so we, as friends of Jesus, seek greater awareness of and connection to all of God's creatures— the Palestinian immigrant and the suburban developer. Christian spirituality seeks an increasing intimacy with God and others. In fact, Scripture often suggests that unless we're seeking to share the suffering of others, our prayer lives will become illusory and self-centered.

In contrast, the spirituality of the marketplace is a spirituality of self-reliance. This is the "pull-yourself-up-by-your-own-bootstraps" spirituality—the way of life represented by the scribes and Pharisees. This is a utilitarian spirituality that trusts that the spiritual life comes from our own hard work and study. In the secular culture this is epitomized by the infomercial hosted by the sculpted and serene yoga instructor who is obviously a spiritual master because he's in such good physical shape and is flexible enough to clean his ear with his pinky toe.

Those of us attracted to this image of spirituality thrive on words like *discipline* and *practice*. We're inspired by stories of saints who fasted, slept in caves, and crawled on broken shale to chapel. This is macho spirituality, a spirituality of perfection. If we're not careful, we may begin to notice that our interest in spirituality, our engagement in spiritual direction, our spiritual books, and our prayer lives are more about proving our spiritual worthiness than learning to live in greater vulnerability with God and the people and situations we encounter in daily life.

Poverty versus Possessiveness

The spirituality of Jesus is a spirituality of poverty. It's life lived with a growing acceptance that we are finite, broken, and in need of love. It's living into the reality that there's no possession or experience that can satisfy our longing for God. A spirituality of poverty means trusting that our naked desire for God is enough.

The spirituality of Jesus doesn't rely on possessions or accomplishments or even spiritual experiences, but is a spirituality of repentance, a life that continually turns to God for guidance and care. It's a life that seeks simplicity and sacrifice in order to release all that might stand between ourselves and God, ourselves and the suffering of others. Every spiritual exercise, retreat, or discipline is an exercise in repentance, a letting go of all that we cling to in order to be open and available to God. This is the "downward mobility" of Jesus that Henri Nouwen described. It's living the way of the cross, an increasing willingness to be emptied of everything that impedes our love for God and our solidarity with other people (Philippians 2).

In contrast, the spirituality of the marketplace is a spirituality of possessiveness. It's a spirituality of accumulation that asserts the belief that human beings increase their worth through material goods. In North America, where we express who we are by what we buy, it's easy to believe that being spiritual means consuming spiritual products. Meditative CDs, books by ancient saints, cruciform jewelry, and aromatherapy candles all seek to communicate to ourselves and others that we are, indeed, spiritual. What we may not realize, however, is that our sacred purchases expose the influence of the market culture and its spirituality of consumption.

Marketplace spirituality asserts that our truest identity is that of consumer, and that buying and accumulating is how God is mediated and faith expressed. Perhaps the best example of this is the use of labyrinths in youth ministry. A labyrinth can be a powerful tool in helping young people deepen their awareness and experience of God, yet the increase in youth groups devoting funds to possess and promote their individual labyrinths can sometimes feed the same hollow appetite for materialism that the market economy depends upon. Sadly, spiritual stuff is profitable, so Christian businesses, sometimes innocently, continue to promote the conviction that buying spiritual products brings us closer to God.

Engagement versus Escape

The spirituality of Jesus takes place in the ordinary, not the otherworldly. While lecturing at Regent College, author and pastor Eugene Peterson was asked to define Christian spirituality. He replied, "Spirituality is going to the mailbox to get your mail." I like this definition. I believe Peterson was trying to communicate that spirituality isn't concerned solely with prayer and blissful experiences. Spirituality is about how we live our daily lives: how we pick up the mail, eat dinner, and tuck our children in at night. In this way Christian spirituality is more concerned with the mundane than the mysterious.

This means that if we want to grow in faith, we need to pay less attention to our religious accomplishments and more attention to our home lives. Our kitchens, our children's schools, grocery stores, and church parking lots are where Christian spirituality takes place as much as or more than at the retreat center. This reality means that the spiritual life is often filled with anxiety (the student who gets lost on a night hike), agitation (a young person who continually disrupts Sunday school), and discomfort (the homeless people who sleep near the church), as much as peace, healing, and comfort.

In contrast, the spirituality of the marketplace is a spirituality of escape. It's a spirituality of bliss. In this image, Christian spirituality is reduced to a tonic for the anxieties of modern living. This is "spatuality." Feeling tired and stressed out? Getting snippy with the kids?

It's time for a spirituality retreat. Solitary strolls by the ocean, quiet nights in prayer, and meditative massage all promise an escape from the drudgery of ordinary Christian living. In this image, spirituality is limited to spiritual things—prayer, worship, and solitude with God. Cleaning house, administrative paperwork, and van rides appear to be lesser activities, distractions from the spiritual life God intended.

This form of spirituality ignores the fact that Jesus spent most of his life fully engaged in very ordinary circumstances (eating, walking, sleeping, conversing). In many ways his witness of God's love is most powerful in these ordinary activities. A spirituality of engagement means that we seek to be open and present to God in all areas of life, not just those designated as "spiritual."

Spirituality in Youth Ministry

Spirituality is a needed corrective within youth ministry. How can we share God's love if we don't take regular time to let God love and empower us? How can young people trust our words about God if they're not given the time and space to encounter God? Silence, prayer exercises, candles, and labyrinths can be helpful to young people and adults in noticing God's presence within and among us. Yet, our spiritual exercises and experiences can be distracting and deceptive if they're not grounded in the spirituality of Jesus. As adults responsible for the spiritual formation of young people, we must discern the spirits within our spirituality programs.

If we trust that Christian spirituality is about relationships rather than self-reliance, then perhaps we need to spend as much time nurturing friendships and increasing the diversity of people within our youth programs as we do in prayer. If we believe Christian spirituality is about poverty rather than possessiveness, then we can repent from forms of youth ministry that rely on mystical props and exotic outings and trust more in the presence of God. If we believe Christian spirituality is about engagement rather than escape, hopefully we can have confidence that the ordinary tasks within our ministries will be enough to convey the gospel.

St. Francis once said, "Preach the gospel, and if necessary, use words." Perhaps God's love is best expressed in how we greet kids, how we drive the church van, how we spend our money, and how we are in friendships and interactions with parents. Spirituality is much more than how we pray; it's about the life from which we pray.

What are we doing? We're doing the same thing we do in all our endeavors in youth ministry—we're trying to help kids follow in the way of Jesus. The hope of youth ministry isn't that young people will become more spiritual—it's that young people will become more open and available to the presence of Jesus and his ways of compassion.

What we need to ask within our spiritual, conventional, or postmodern ministries is whether we're helping young people and adults grow more committed in their relationships with God and others. Is the spiritual life we're promoting consistent with the life of Jesus? Are the fruits of the spiritual exercises and practices we offer young people in harmony with the fruits of the Spirit that Paul outlines (Galatians 5)? Is there greater generosity, kindness, patience, love, joy, and self-discipline as a result of these experiences? These are the questions we need to consider in order to help discern what we, as youth ministers, are doing to accompany young people on the way of Jesus.

Contemplative Youth Ministry is a more organic approach to youth ministry, allowing you to create meaningful silence, foster covenant communities, engage students in contemplatice activities, and maximize spontaneity—and to help your students recognize the presence of Jesus in their everyday lives.

Contemplative Youth Ministry
Practicing the Presence of Jesus

Mark Yaconelli

RETAIL $21.99
ISBN 0-310-26777-3